Zulu Shaman

Credo at ceremonial rock used for fertility magic

Zulu Shaman
DREAMS, PROPHECIES, AND MYSTERIES

Vusamazulu Credo Mutwa

EDITED BY STEPHEN LARSEN
FOREWORD BY LUISAH TEISH

Destiny Books
Rochester, Vermont

Destiny Books
One Park Street
Rochester, Vermont 05767
www.InnerTraditions.com

Destiny Books is a division of Inner Traditions International

Originally published in 1996 by Station Hill, an imprint of The Institute for Publishing Arts, under the title *Song of the Stars*

Library of Congress Cataloging-in-Publication Data

Mutwa, Credo Vusa'mazulu, 1921-
  [Song of the stars]
  Zulu shaman : dreams, prophecies, and mysteries / Vusamazulu Credo
Mutwa ; edited by Stephen Larsen ; foreword by Luisah Teish.
    p. cm.
Originally published: Song of the stars. Barrytown, NY: Station Hill, 1996.
Includes bibliographical references and index.
  ISBN 978-0-89281-129-8
  1. Zulu (African people)—Medicine. 2. Zulu (African
people)—Religion. 3. Shamans—South Africa—KwaZulu-Natal. I. Larsen,
Stephen. II. Title.
  DT1768.Z95M829 2003
  398.2'089'963986—dc22
                                        2003016055

Printed and bound in the United States

20 19 18 17 16 15 14 13

Text design and layout by Susan Quasha and Vicki Hickman
Photographs on pages ii, xii, xxx, xxxii, 76, 120, 125, 127, 172, 194, 199 by Boris Said and Derek Shirley

Contents

Key to Petroglyphs

Abundance

Bird of Light Eating
Serpent of Darkness

Cause of Parting

Children of Star

Come

Goddess of Creation
Mother Source

Immortal

In

Jackal

Peacemaker

Tomorrow

Unity of People - Love

We

Foreword

I am an incredibly fortunate person to have lived long enough and well enough to see a great desire of mine fulfilled. Years ago I was very thirsty for some spiritual knowledge of traditional Africa. I went to a library and had to sit in a locked room to read Credo Mutwa's *Indaba, My Children*. (The book was originally published only in South Africa and was very rare.) The more I read, the more I longed to learn about South Africa and its folklore — and specifically about this amazing man, Mutwa.

So here I am, twenty-odd years later, writing the preface for his first publication in America. It's a miniature of the fulfillment of the wish so many of us felt for so long for the liberation of South Africa. For me as a black person the whole issue of South Africa was something that one prayed about and worked for, feeling helpless but trying to contribute something. But I was afraid I might die without ever seeing any progress of peace here, without even being able to go there safely. And I wondered, would I live a long life and die without any real knowledge about South Africa that was not polluted by some anthropologist's opinion?

But the publication of this book is an event for me beyond the political — it represents a spiritual liberation and a kind of homecoming; and it is a manifestation of the miraculous in my life. Here is authentic material from an elder, a wise man, a medicine man of the Zulu culture! It is a very great gift that bespeaks a great time of change and transformation! Now we who seek spiritually for our roots can turn our faces and learn from South Africa. Now the medicine, the history, the folklore — the great contributions of that part of the world can be given freely, no longer having to be snatched and twisted from its people, but given freely.

There is a wisdom rising to the surface, and for me this rising begins with Mandela and Mutwa. Now I and so many of us will be able to hear the words of our Southern Cradle elders. We will be able to compare stories, process these concepts and ideas, and begin to get a sense of the whole picture. This is a move toward wholeness — our being able to talk to this man and being able to hear these stories. It makes me whole just to be able to hold this book in my hands and know that I have someting that is grounded in a particular person who functions in his community, who has a genuine spiritual base behind him — not the pickings and choosings of someone who pulled together an anthology with misinterpretations of his story.

There is a medicine for the soul in here. Credo Mutwa talks about the most amazing things in a voice that seems so very very commonplace — about our relationships to each other, to the natural world, to what some people call the supernatural, and to beings from other places among the stars — without fear, and without pretense. One feels his wonderful humanity and the genius of his people in these stories.

As I look at the folklore, because this is my love, there is so much in Mutwa's lore that is related to what I know of West African folklore and much of what I know of Caribbean and African-American folklore. The kinship is very very clear. Here we have the Tree of Life and the Great Mother. Here we have ugliness and beauty, gods and goddesses; the wonders and terrors of their lives light up our sky with color and constitute one of the great blessings of the African view on life. Here we have flood and rain and great desert, cold and scorching sun. Here we have tricksters — Kintu very much resembling Alegba and Anasi and Ejopa and all the other tricksters that one finds in African folklore. Some of the names — *Odu*, or *Nommo* — are the same, with similar or slightly different meanings, depending upon where they are found in Africa. This speaks strongly in favor of the Southern Cradle theory of civilization — that the civilizations of Africa did not drift down from the north but evolved from the south and spread out across the world. This is confirmation of that.

The person who holds this book in her or his hand may find the names of deities they never heard before — especially additions to the growing list of goddesses. This can help us to fill out our picture of the feminine face of God, and reveal how people view the dialogue of the feminine principle and the masculine dynamic in nature. Here we have the ripe Great Mother and lustful Tree of Life. Here we have the principle of raw evil worming its way into the world at the very beginning.

I like the idea of filling out and complementing Mandela's political journey with Mutwa's mythology. Putting the two together gives us a more whole, complete picture of South Africa: the secular-political and the magical-mythological. I have sat with storytellers in Australia and heard the stories of the Orishas told with different names — same ideas, same feeling, very similar results. Again I hear the stories of great ancestors, of powerful deities, of natural force at play — only the names are different. This similarity is a real testimony to that which is common in human experience, and it really should help to ensure our humanity in each other's presence.

I am awestruck by the miracle of the existence of this book. I hope that it will land in the hands of many Black Americans, but also native Africans, and Asians and Europeans as well. I want to see men and women pick this book up and read the tales, investigate the culture, and draw the parallels — then more understanding might begin to flow. I am grateful to destiny that Father Mutwa has lived long enough to give me this gift and that I have lived long enough to receive it. Because, as he says, when we dream, we have to get out of bed and walk toward the dream.

Being able to have this book in my hand is the dream come true of a teenage girl, locked in a room in a library, searching for her roots. It's incredible. You know, for all the talking I do to people in lectures about how the creative spirit manifests, I am still stunned when it really does. I ask for Father Mutwa's permission to tell his stories and he says, "Thank you." Traditionally I'm supposed to beg and be put through changes for permission to do that, you see. But he said it gladdened his heart to know that I would tell his stories — and I will do it as far as my wings can take me. I am looking forward to telling these tales everywhere.

LUISAH TEISH
AUTHOR OF *JAMBALAYA* AND
CARNIVAL OF THE SPIRIT

Acknowledgments

This book has been through its own initiatory death and rebirth since it was first conceived in 1989. Many people have lent their time and support to its final becoming. Thanks are due first and foremost to the Ringing Rocks Foundation for helping a dream come true for many of us: seeing Credo Mutwa relocated to a safe place where he may teach for the rest of his days the wonderful lore that he holds, living surrounded by his loved ones and students.

Special thanks to my shaman-brother, Dr. Bradford Keeney, a white medicine-man who hovers between the daylight worlds of university discourse and literature, and the shadow realm from which dreams, healing and creativity emerge. Without his mediation and his magic this book could not have come to fruition. Thanks also to George and Susan Quasha for believing in the project, and to Charles Stein for his skillful work in editing and shaping. Dr. John Mack recently served as an emissary and (terrestrial) angel to Credo.

Susan Phipps Cochran generously allowed us to use transcripts from audio portions of tapes to which she owns the rights as the starting point for some chapters. Babara Zucker Johnson typed almost inaudible discourses on tape with strange Zulu words. Luisah Teish lent her wonderful warmth and encouragement to the process when it seemed to languish, and helped to convince me of the value of Credo's legacy for African-Americans. Two of Credo's American "children," Luis Mangual and Kykosa Kanjangu, gave encouragement all along, along with Debra Denker, a sister in Credo's spiritual family. Gary Sinclair should be acknowledged for his unflagging loyalty to Credo; and Lesley Ann Tintinger, for her efforts to organize Credo's literary legacy. John Eppard gave high-spirited benefit concerts and helped with fundraising when things seemed at their lowest. Timothy White donated space in *The Shaman's Drum* for requests for help with the Credo Project and published my biographical article on Credo in 1994. John Brockman and Katinka Matson have been very patient with what at times must have seemed like a quixotic project, arranging all publishing contracts.

Boris Said, trickster and international entrepreneur, set many of these wheels in motion; and Drs. Stan Grof and Cecil Burney arranged the first magical occasion in Japan, on which I met Credo. Dr. Stanley Krippner, mentor and friend, has lent his biographical sketch of Credo and supported the value of this work.

Last but by no means least, my son, Merlin, has kept a wonderful sense of connection with Credo and the value of his legacy, and my wife, Robin, has been her usual supportive and loving self, listening to strange and marvelous Zulu tales far into the night.

STEPHEN LARSEN
EDITOR

Stephen Larsen, Ph.D., is a mythologist, shamanic scholar, and writer, who has worked with Credo Mutwa since 1989 recording, organizing, and editing the material for this book. He is author of *The Shaman's Doorway, The Mythic Imagination,* and *Joseph Campbell: A Fire in the Mind.* He and his wife, Robin Larsen, are the founding directors of Center for Symbolic Studies in New Paltz, New York.

Credo in his workman's clothes and with an Eagle-Headed Shaman's Staff

Editor's Introduction

Ultimately I saw that the lore of my people was destined to die with those of us who knew it, and that it would then die forever. I felt I gradually recognized that by breaking my oath — something originally made to protect the sacred lore in times that were very different from these times — I was doing something for my own people, preserving the eternal wisdom that had been carried on for centuries; and also doing something for mankind as a whole. For there are people of many lands and many races who should share in this wisdom and learn the wonder of these stories — they existed for the good of our people, but also now for all people. This realization helped me to overcome my fear.

My first meeting with Credo Mutwa was under most unusual circumstances. It was during the 1985 International Transpersonal Association Conference in Kyoto, Japan. Several hundred psychologists, therapists, writers, and creative artists from around the world came to look deeper into the mysteries of life — and death — with people such as thanatologist Elisabeth Kübler-Ross, philosopher William Irwin Thompson, psychedelic researcher and founder of the ITA Dr. Stanislav Grof and his wife Christina, Governor Jerry Brown, and astronaut Rusty Schweikart. One of the goals of the conference was to bring together diverse spiritual traditions, as well as modern researchers; so the presenters included not only the expected Zen Masters and Shinto priests, but a Parsee mage, a South American bishop, and the Zulu shaman.

It would be an understatement to say that Vusamazulu Credo Mutwa was consipicuous in the midst of Japanese decorum. The setting was a modern conference center built on the design of the traditional Shinto temple, situated in the northern section of Kyoto. The center was surrounded by a lake and beautiful gardens and had its own formal tea-house. Many of the opening presentations naturally focused on the exquisitely elaborated Japanese rituals of *Cha no yu*, tea ceremony, the ghostly *Noh* drama, and *Ikebana*, flower arranging. But here, amidst these aesthetic austerities, wrapped in a traditional Zulu robe of scarlet, with magnificent bronze ornaments bedecking his three-hundred and fifty pound frame, was the man named so intriguingly in our conference program: Vusamazulu Credo Mutwa. In the (abundant) flesh, the Mutwa sparkled with mirth and warmth, laughter bubbling ceaselessly and spontaneously from himself and the little group of colorfully attired women around him. They included his wife Cecelia, and several of the *Sangoma* women, his students and friends, clairvoyants and healers for the Zulu people.

"I have enjoyed seeing how the Japanese people venerate their mountains," Mutwa said, opening his plenary address. "That is because I have a kinship with them. People have mistaken me for a mountain!" The sedate audience, especially the Japanese, roared with laughter. He was, he told us in his elegant English, "just an ordinary man, a poor man, from a distant land," who brought us his own experience of life, for what it was worth. There seemed an instantaneous warming toward the mountainous man who could laugh at himself in public, and who had flown ten-thousand miles to share both the wisdom and the suffering of his ancient race.

With a vast and kindly sense of ceremony, perhaps honed by years of diplomacy among the dozens of different African tribal groups, Mutwa praised the ancient culture of his hosts; opening common ground by saying that he had already discovered dozens of words in common between Japanese and Zulu — being an inveterate comparative linguist. The correspondences were found to be rather astonishing (the Japanese *katana*: sword; from the Kasai of Zaire, *katanga*: sword). His explanation was that we are one human family, in both our origins and our destiny. Somehow Credo Mutwa invited us, nay, drew us irresistably, into a collective vision of ourselves as points of light on an enormous web of evolution, a planetary family, indeed. But then again, he urged, the planet was itself but a point in an intelligible web of relationship starting within each human breast and extending out into the immensity of the universe. And though this Earth and humanity are indeed in great peril at this time, our possibility for healing is as great as that for destruction. There is a longing in this Earth, isolated in a self-imposed exile, to rejoin the larger universe — to participate once again in the Song of the Stars.

The more that Credo Mutwa talked, the more we became aware that indeed this was no ordinary man who stood in our midst. His jollity and unpretentiousness concealed a massive erudition and a sparkling, engaging wit. Verily, the Mutwa seemed to be what the Japanese call, "a living national treasure."

He bears the title of *Sangoma*, a shaman or healer, and *High Sanusi*, clairvoyant and lore-master, a word he believed to be related through the Indo-European language matrix to the Sanskrit *sannyasin*, holy wandering mendicant.[1] Like the yogi, he claimed, the sanusi was an "uplifter of his people," one who had a foot in the yonder realm and could act as a conduit for spiritual realities. Sanusis or sangomas are sometimes pejoratively called "witch doctors," but this is misleading. Neither of these roles involves sorcery or the wielding of magic to attain ordinary human objectives. The sanusi, he told us, is a person who strives ceaselessly to be ethical in everything he does, for the fate of the tribe or nation may depend upon his discernment. He is accountable both to the natural and the supernatural realms, and ultimately to the entire pattern of the universe.

For many of us it was a marvel simply to witness an immense black man do metaphysical ballet. In a spellbinding way, Mutwa held the international audience of several hundred rapt with the breadth of his knowledge, his wisdom and his humor. Unlike some of the native English speakers, he also was able to modulate and slow his presentation for simultaneous translators.

Then something strange happened. A Japanese interviewer from the press inquired about the meaning of the burnished bronze ornaments worn by the Mutwa. "Do you really want to know?" the wizard asked, puckishly.

"*Hai.*" (Yes.)

"Well sir, you see, in Africa we have a tradition that there are extra-terrestrial intelligences watching this Earth. Do you not have reports in Japan of what are called 'Flying Saucers,' like they do in The United States, the Soviet Union, and Europe?"

(A somewhat shocked silence before a tentative, "Yes?")

"We have had them in Africa for many years. We call them *abahambi abavutayo*, the 'fiery visitors.' They figure in our mythologies and the origins of our culture. But these ritual ornaments are intended so that when one of these vehicles comes to Earth, and extraterrestrial beings, who wish to establish contact with humanity, emerge, they will know the right person to talk to!"

The response brought down the house, with cries of astonishment in five or six languages mingling with the laughter. Was this a joke? But Mutwa went on quite seriously, saying that according to the mythology of his people, the origins of humanity are tied in with the stars. The idea of extraterrestrial visitation is congenial to many Africans, because they have been hearing tales of the stars since childhood. Indeed, for the Zulu legends (some of which are related herein), the progenitors of humanity began on another world, travelled all the way to another solar system, (that of the star Sirius, so prominent in Dogon mythology), before finally ending up on this Earth.

The following day Credo Mutwa spontaneously instituted a ritual that would continue for the week-long conference. At lunch break, beneath a carefully dwarfed tree on a little peninsula in the nearby lake, the eloquent mountain arranged himself among his sangoma women, and began to tell traditional African stories for whoever came to hear — soon a crowd. His fund of tales seemed inexhaustible, full of wisdom and full of laughter. In the first hour, Mutwa had established himself as a master storyteller as well as a sit-down comic of extraordinary dimension. The following day I urged my wife, who loves storytelling, to abandon her explorations around Kyoto and come to the luncheon storytelling. We both felt, comparing notes afterwards, that we had just been listening to one of the finest storytellers in the world.

My friendship with Mutwa began then, and continued through the completion of this book. Our working conferences were largely conducted by transatlantic phone in what we referred to as our "dial a witch doctor service" (at the time this book was written Mutwa was residing at the art village he created in Bophutatswana, South Africa, and was reachable there by telephone and post). The work on the book project also involved tape transcripts and correspondence. Susan Phipps Cochran allowed us to make transcripts from a filmed interview made with Credo in the 1980s to which she owns the rights. The film transcripts helped to elicit further commentary from Credo about current political events in the world, and some of his prophecies about the future, and formed the basis for several of the later chapters of this book.

In this book, the reader will find many of the dimensions of Credo Mutwa's lore explored — from the story of how he became a sangoma, to the sangoma's lore of the human soul and how healing is conceived of by sangomas and *inyangas*, another category of shaman. We move to a sampling of his vast knowledge of African folklore, first through creation myths, with a focus on those of the goddesses, to stories of that scurrilous trickster, Kintu, his outwitting of cannibal giants, and his theft of fire — a worldwide mythological motif. As we begin to discover how interlaced Zulu mythology is with lore of the stars, tales of the extraterrestrial origins of humanity and the lore of the "fiery visitors" to this Earth from outer space are brought in, including stories of Credo's own "close encounters" of several kinds. We conclude with some of his human wisdom in relation to such things as dreams, the family, the commonalities of wisdom and language traditions throughout the world, and some prophecies concerning the future of humanity. In this way, *Song of the Stars* is less a book about a particular topic in African folklore, and more a condensation of the multidimensional human wisdom of one living lineage-holder and healer, a true son of Africa, and a "living national treasure" indeed. For more specific treatments of Zulu mythology, the reader is referred to Credo's other published works discussed in the next section.

In order that Credo's voice be given the fullest authenticity, I have tried, wherever possible, to render the vividly spoken word into prose with minimal editorial alteration. I have not tried to make his ideas conform with other systematic exegeses of African mythology. The stories are true to his telling; however, I have tried to render the mythological names and terms he uses in a manner consistent with his own system of transliteration of words from Zulu and other African languages into English. Nor have I sat in judgement on the veracity of his tales — including those which may seem to have supernatural or even "science fiction" elements — leaving these almost verbatim for the reader's own judgement. Having had no experiences with extraterrestrials, nor previous familiarity with UFO literature, I thought I should do some reading in order to annotate chapter 6 of this book in a useful way. I was subsequently surprised to find how extensive this wing of the "twilight zone" is. Some of the correspondences between the African and Euro-American accounts of "close encounters" and "alien abductions" seemed quite spooky, but I have adduced only a few of the more outstanding comparisons in the notes. The real specialist in this genre will find, I am sure, all kinds of interesting parallelisms in this heretofore unpublished material.

Wherever Mutwa's mythic tales seemed to invite comparison with African or other world mythological themes, I have placed this material in notes so as not to interrupt the flow of the narrative. Interested readers may choose to follow the notes separately as a kind of running comparative mythology commentary. Such comparisons seem to me to be quite fertile from the viewpoint of Archetypal Psychology, and speak to a waxing number of enthusiasts beyond psychology: anthropologists, folklorists, and storytellers who are open to a transpersonal interpretation of such materials as these found herein. Ever so slowly, it seems, we are learning a new—or very old art — the interpretation of the mythological materials found in traditional societies — but from the viewpoint of their own reality system, not ours.

Credo Mutwa's vision has been of a world united in peace and harmony across cultural boundaries, and this book is a messenger toward that end. The traditional lore of the Zulu nation continues to be in peril, even with the recent favorable turn of political and social events in South Africa, and the seeming end of apartheid. Even as many Native American elders and teachers, such as the Sioux Black Elk (who, when the poet John Neihardt arrived to record his words, said, "What's kept you so long, let's get started!")[2] and the Dogon Ogotomelli, who disclosed many important tribal secrets (including the mysterious Dogon star-lore) to Marcel Griaule during the earlier part of this century,[3] have felt compelled to break their vows of secrecy, so too Credo Mutwa has seen the tragic possibility that the lore of his people would be lost forever, and hence decided to open his knowledge to the planetary community. It seems truly sad that these luminous revelations from traditional societies emerge only through the nova-flare of cultural death and dismemberment. But this momentous background adds additional poignancy to the facts of Credo Mutwa's life and to the revelations of his stories and teachings. He himself is most eager for his words to reach receptive minds and hearts in America as well as South Africa, and hopefully throughout the English-speaking world.

The reader may find some small duplication of details between the biographical sketch I provide in this editor's introduction and the autobiographical material in chapter 1, "The Way of the Witch Doctor." There has been no biographical study of Credo in print, and while there is autobiographical material laced throughout his own books, this relatively short essay is an effort to give the reader a flavor not only of who this remarkable man is, but some sense of the shape of his life and the magnitude of his accomplishments, seen from an outside perspective. (His own modesty sometimes renders this impossible from an autobiographical point of view.) I am indebted to Dr. Stanley Krippner for sharing with me an earlier biographical essay he had done on Credo, which helped with details. The essay in chapter 1 is Credo telling his own story — but entirely from the viewpoint of becoming a sangoma.

Royalties from sales of this book go to Mutwa, and thus to his family and the community of healers and artists that work with him. Thus, both in the buying and in the reading of this book, you the reader help to close a circuit both economic and spiritual, whereby resources flow back from us — the beneficiaries of the ancient wisdom he has been so gracious as to share with us — to its living source.

Living mythology has been described by Joseph Campbell as an inexhaustible source of wisdom for those able to open themselves to its "instructive wonder." Years after having studied with Campbell, my appreciation has deepened for his approach. Once we have learned the deep structure beneath the languages, their grammar and syntax become increasingly accessible and intelligible. It is "one shape-shifting, yet marvellously constant story," as Campbell put it in *The Hero With a Thousand Faces*. This approach is clearly congruent with Credo Mutwa's own outlook.[4]

"Our wise men hid their wisdom in what seem like children's stories," Mutwa told me, "to protect it." The art of the storyteller contains many levels of knowledge, but the deepest speak of what has been called "the perennial philosophy." Was there not a time in which, as writer Roderick Macleish phrases it, "things were less well-known, but better understood"? There is something timeless in the predicaments of humanity, and something timeless in the wisdom that must address them. And perhaps mythological wisdom must be packaged as if for children, because we are still child-like as a species.

With Credo Mutwa, the boundaries of reality do indeed inter-penetrate: the personal and the spiritual, angels and aliens, tribal history and the song of the stars. Yet Mutwa feels our vision must enlarge to embrace each paradoxical new mystery of life as it is disclosed. Ultimately, the universe, like the human soul, he tells us in the following pages, contains its own history and contradictions within it. Yet we must never doubt for a moment the importance of our own participation in its evolution.

Biography: The Making of a Sangoma

Vusamazulu Credo Mutwa was born in the Natal area of South Africa on July 21, 1921. His very name is a composite of his cultures of origin. "Vusamazulu" is a Zulu honorific, meaning, "Awakener of the Zulus," and came through his initiation as a sangoma. But the name, "Credo," was given to him by his father, a Christian. It is from the Latin: "I believe." "Mutwa" is Zulu for "little bushman." "Vusamazulu Credo Mutwa," then, may be rendered: "Great Awakener, I Believe (in) the Little Bushman."

As a babe, Credo was baptized into the Roman Catholic Church, his father having held the position of "catechism instructor." His mother Numabunu, however, was the daughter of the shaman-warrior Ziko Shezi, who had survived the awful battle of Ulundi, which ended the Zulu Wars. Shezi was a sangoma, and custodian of Zulu relics. The split in religion was to prove decisive for his parents' relationship, and they never formally married, separating soon after Mutwa was born. Fortunately, Mutwa received early training from his grandfather, and in a way that would later be memorable for him, the child would carry his grandfather's medicine bags full of sacred objects to ceremonies.[5]

Credo Mutwa from an early time showed a proclivity for art, especially sculpture, and would sit on the *koppie*, or little hill above his kraal, and make sculptures of the cattle. One day a terrifying but funny adventure befell him. He writes:

Ruling our district at this time was a very colourful chief, Manzolwandle, the son of Cetshwayo, who was famous for his tremendous appetite and girth; and I decided to make a clay portrait of this great chief....

It was not long before my work attracted the attention of some of the locals who climbed the koppie to admire the work. The crowd attracted two elders, who obviously had no appreciation of art whatsoever and who proceeded to warm me up nice and proper, accusing me of practising witchcraft. They said no one on earth, short of of using witchcraft, could have so accurately portrayed not only the chief, but also his servants, in clay. After the beating, I was hauled off to the chief's village after being told that my offence was very grave indeed and that I might be lucky to get away with my life once I was brought to Mazolwandle.

When I was brought before the mighty chief I was almost dead with terror and pain and I saw, through a mist of unbelievable anguish the damning evidence in the form of the clay statuettes being placed before the chief by the two elders. Time seemed to stand still while the huge chief examined my handiwork, and then I wet my khaki shorts as Manzolwandle rose to his feet and walked slowly towards me. Reaching down with a huge hand he hauled me to my feet, took one look at the front of my shorts and roared with laughter.

"*Hawu! U Cetshwayo yini? Uyazichamela, mfana?*" roared the chief, his smile as broad as a spring sunrise — "and who told you, boy, that I, Manzolwandle, was a beast to be feared?"

The chief turned upon the men who had brought me before him and rebuked them for having thrashed me. No child should ever be thrashed for doing things of beauty, he said. Then he turned to my aunt's husband and commanded him to see to it that I got a good education at the local mission school. He added that the work I had done in clay would one day make me a great man if I continued with it.[6]

In 1928 Mutwa's father entered the picture again and obtained custody of the child over the objections of his mother. The young lad was obliged to go to the Transvaal with his father, stepmother and their three children. The family moved around to several different farms, and finally settled near Johannesburg where Mutwa's father found a job as a carpenter, working for one of the mines.

Mutwa's father, raised Roman Catholic, converted to the Christian Science of Mary Baker Eddy in 1935, and remained devotedly loyal to that religion until his death. Therefore, as Mutwa remembered, "If we were sick, it was hard for any of us to get medicines." And of course they were not allowed to avail themselves of traditional healers either. The only reading material encouraged by Mutwa's father were the writings of Mrs. Eddy, to which Mutwa himself was never drawn.

He was educated in mission schools, taught in English about Western history and civilization, and confirmed as a Christian in the process. His goal in those years was to become a schoolteacher, and hence he studied his lessons very well.

When I was a young boy of some 14 years, I was made into an altar boy and in the church, the Catholic Church of that time, many prayers were said in Latin and I was fascinated. The Latin language fascinated me as much as the English language had some years before.[7]

In 1943 there began a time of sickness and disorientation for the young man, described in more detail in the next chapter. He was afflicted with dreams and visions, and a strange malaise would often come over him. Young Credo was experiencing the sickness that often comes to future sangomas, initiating their call.

Now there are several kinds of traditional healers among the Zulu. An *inyanga* may inherit the profession from relatives. But a *sangoma* must receive a "call" from the spirits, which seemed to be happening to the young man. At the urging of his mother and grandfather, Mutwa would undergo purification ceremonies, renounce formal

Christianity, and begin to prepare himself to receive the training of the sangoma.[8]

Mutwa has remembered his own call to become a sangoma not so much as a sudden breakthrough, but a gradual one. It began with the illness, growing within his mind as well as body. He became preoccupied by a study of traditional tribal lore and art objects, which he studied without knowing why he was doing it.[9] The illness through which he had passed is called by the Zulus, *ukutwasa*. From his own recollections:

I had a sickness then, which was one of the reasons why my mother recommended that I take my grandfather's profession. It was a very weird sickness which medical doctors did not understand. I felt strange to myself. I was not who I was. Sometimes I had visions of myself being torn apart by great cannibals and sometimes by leopards. I could see through solid objects during the sickness. I remember at one time I was able to follow the progress of my dog through a barrier of stone. It was as if the stones were made of glass. I have since then been cursed with a very strange gift...the gift of seeing things before they happen, which I've been trying to get rid of since then but I cannot....[10]

The apprentice sangoma then, is one who has been touched by this illness, *ukutwasa*, hence he or she during this training period is called a *twasa*. The *twasa*, as Dr. Stanley Krippner has elucidated his role,

must learn how to prepare herbal medicines, how to interpret dreams, how to incorporate spirits, how to diagnose illness, how to exorcise "tokoloshe," frightened ghosts or zombies, how to control weather, and how to foretell the future. In addition the twasa must learn the tribal and community history, mythology, and ceremonies. Because much of their time is spent counteracting the "tagati" or hexes placed upon tribal members by witches, sangomas are often called "witch doctors," a term that many of them take in stride because it does describe one of their functions.[11]

The misunderstood "witch doctor," then, as defined by Mutwa, is not a person who specializes in throwing hexes; rather, the opposite. But the sangoma must understand and to some extent control the same occult forces as does the sorcerer, if he is to be effective in curing a person from the magically constructed spells that have been cast. These are usually initiated by a sorcerer at the request of an enemy, or even a hostile or alienated family member.

But the sangoma's sphere of concern is far more broad and deep that that of the sorcerer. His or her understanding of magic must comprehend its context, its history, and its mythological antecedents. This is a level far beyond that of the mere technician of magic who simply activates its force. In essence the sangoma must embrace the whole inner sense of both the natural and the supernatural worlds as a preliminary to entering into the zone of magical cause and effect. Power is not believed to reside in a single act or ritual of magical efficacy, but in the entire universe, and it is only through knowledge of and orientation within that universe that the sangoma's power may be exercised in a wholesome way; one that heals both the person and his world at the same time, relieving the magical exchange of the reflexive overcompensation of cause and effect.

Having sent my book *The Shaman's Doorway* to the Mutwa in 1989, I asked him if he had found anything from the worldwide pattern of the shamanic initiation in his own experience.[12] He said, "I am positive it is the same kind of thing, sir. You get imbued with a crazy feeling that if you could be sacrificed on some altar, things would come right with the world... I still can talk with wild and domestic animals... It's crazy when one has got to explain it in English but in Zulu it makes a lot of sense."

Credo Mutwa was to prove to be a very succesful sangoma, and eventually was elevated to the rank of High Sanusi, like the Indian *sannyasin*, a holy man who has taken vows. In this way he came to be the leader of well over 500 other traditional healers. "They look upon me as their father figure," was how he put it, "and come to me whenever they have forgotten some aspect of traditional healing.

"When I was made into a sanusi, I took a vow never to reveal my knowledge, never to tell people about my profession or about the sacred artifacts like this one, and many others that I'm entrusted with. But I feel that this vow is a hindrance, and some years ago I decided to break it. The result of this has been that many people have ostracized me and many people have bitterly blamed me for what I had done."[13]

Credo Mutwa very much believes in the value of tradition, but also affirms that we live in changing times. The traditions are to be kept, but their influence is to be made open to a larger audience than the dwindling faithful among the Zulu people.

The keepers of traditional stories are called "Guardians of the *Umlando*" (tribal history), a different but overlapping role with that of the sangoma. This role also Credo has embraced. To become this kind of traditional storyteller requires an aptitude for precise memorization and also the dramatic and artistic recitation of the stories. Some of the tales require as long as a month or more to tell, while others are shorter. In this book we have focussed on the latter.

Political and Social Realities

What good might all the mystical knowledge in the world do for you if you were black and South African, we might ask, especially before the ending of Apartheid? Mutwa has not only been a chronicler of African traditions, but also a political polemicist. His first book, *Indaba My Children: African Tribal History, Legends, Customs and Religious Beliefs,* was published in 1964 in South Africa and in England in 1985. It is a vivid, evocative recitation of the great legends, both mythic and historical, of the Zulu people. "Indaba" was the phrase with which the traditional storyteller would begin his recitation of those events that belong to the myth time — "the dreamtime of the ancestors" — as the Australian Aborigines call it. The book is a call to his people not to forget their traditions.

But Mutwa's second book, *Let Not My Country Die,* which was published the following year, is an impassioned plea addressed to his contemporaries. For Mutwa has encountered the social agonies of Africa personally. Simple human insensitivity and bigoted racism he acknowledges as the primary demons, and his chapters recite the daily humiliations and frustrations of a subjugated people. A "second class" person could have obeyed all the rules, and still achieved nothing. "South Africa," he wrote, "has been cursed with some of the most arrogant and insensitive bureaucrats in the world...."

It is very common to see white or black bureaucrats standing about and chatting for hours behind their desks while the
silent queues get longer and longer.... When black people ap-
plied for a pass-book, they had to wade through the coals of
hell itself before they could hold that cursed little book in their
hands. Blacks had to go from office to office, stand in queues
for days and even weeks on end, spend money on train and
bus fares day in and day out and return home empty handed
each evening. By the time the people made any progress they
were usually heavily in debt, because of having to borrow
money from neighbors and friends to travel to town and stand
in queues of misery.[14]

The sadistic rigamarole was enforced by raids on one's home in
the night or early morning hours by armed police to check permits,
and beatings or detention for the failure to produce one. Then there
has also been the random violence in the streets from reactionaries,
as when Credo and a black friend walked through a suburb that
they did not know had a particular "day of hatred" toward blacks.
The two men were cruelly beaten, forced to strip, and made to go
on their way naked.

But there were also continual slurs, deprivations of educational
opportunity, access to medical treatment or other necessities. Credo
Mutwa believes racism to be an unconscious reflex that demeans
not only the object of discrimination, but the holder of such atti-
tudes. "It is utterly bizarre and indescribably obscene," he says in
Let Not My Country Die,

to see modern men — men who have seen their brothers walk
on the moon and in the starry void of space, men who have
seen the miracle of organ transplants and men who have looked
into the fiery hearts of atoms and stars — killing and maiming
their brothers and sisters over beliefs and creeds spawned in
the minds of half-savages, dead and buried a thousand centuries ago.[15]

The remedy for the problem, as he believes, lies not in revolu-
tion, but in education. There is a fundamental understanding and
mutual affection that can emerge naturally between human beings

when they learn more about each other, and discover and acknowledge the commonalities of their experience.

Mutwa tells the story in his book of John Langabilele Dube, one of the founders of the ANC (called in his day The South African Native National Congress). Unable to obtain the kind of education he needed in South Africa because of racial discrimination, Dube did an audacious thing, a veritable leap into the unknown. He decided to get an education in America. Dube stowed away in the hold of a freighter bound for the U.S.A. As Mutwa tells the heroic story:

> He would have died of thirst or hunger had not a couple of sailors discovered him in the hold. They frogmarched him, more dead than alive, to the captain's cabin. The captain at first did not know what to do with John Dube...should he clap him in irons or throw him overboard? Finally it was decided that the young Zulu could be useful aboard the ship and that he would work his passage to the USA as a stoker — feeding shovelsfull of coal to the roaring and ever-hungry furnaces of the great vessel.
>
> "Ye're as ugly an' black as the very devil, my bhoyo," said the captain to John Dube. "An' by the Virgin Mary, ye're agonna work like him!"
>
> John Dube finally reached the U.S.A., the land of Booker T. Washingon and other great men, and there, after great suffering under which a lesser man's spirit would have broken, John Dube at last received the type of education that his heart desired. Some years later he returned to South Africa with an impressive list of degrees behind his name and was immediately seized and thrown into prison by Lord Kitchener as a "dangerous and troublesome native."[16]

Finally gaining his release, "Dube went on to become one of the brightest black stars of his time in the South African firmament." He founded the Ohlange Mission College in Natal, and went on to found the first Zulu language newspaper in Natal.

Mutwa has been a great admirer of the African National Congress's stand on racial equality; but he fears that sweeping social reforms could ignore, or trample under, in the service of progress, some of the traditional and spiritually-based values of his culture. New forms of fundamentalism, including Christian and Islamic, also threaten to ignore what he feels is the spiritual heart of Africa, the deepest roots of his people.

Mutwa has always spoken out against violence — in the service of whatever ideal. His feelings were deepened by painful personal losses. His fiance was killed during the Soweto demonstrations; and his son, young Mutwa, a sweet-tempered young man, who showed the most aptitude for following in his footsteps, was killed just a few years ago by the horrible method of "necklacing," in which the person's head is tied into a tire filled with gasoline, and he is burned alive in this fashion.

Mutwa himself was attacked by activists as a traditionalist, out of keeping with revolutionary principles, and his right arm and hand slashed with axes. This was doubly pernicious, the Mutwa observed, because these men knew that as an artist (painter and sculptor), his right hand was his means of making a living in the world. Likewise, "necklacing" is horrible to the African traditionalist, because it is believed that if a person dies in this manner, his or her very soul, as well as the body, perishes. Mutwa feels uses of terror of this kind in the service of any ideal sullies that cause.

It is not easy to stand witness to the collision of blind and violent forces and not take sides, yet this is what Mutwa has done. Astonishingly enough, though he has always suffered from the leaden indifference of the government to the plight of the black man in Africa, and revolutionary violence has struck close to his heart, his solutions still are grounded in forgiveness and mutual understanding, and his fond wish is that out of much suffering may come the dawn of a new age of cooperation with mutual respect between the races. "There are things in this world against which the force of arms alone are useless," he has written, "things that can only be defeated by weapons of the soul."[17]

"The black man of South Africa does not know his true greatness...." Mutwa has written,

> he does not know that there are things the white man has only recently discovered that his forefathers knew about hundreds of years ago. He does not know that within him lies coiled a beautiful serpent, a golden dragon which could, if released, soar

to the stars tomorrow and make the black people of our culture as respected and powerful as the Japanese.[18]

This last is addressed to a recognition of the psychic forces that lie within each human being; but how may a disadvantaged black man acquire the internal wisdom and force to meet the more powerful whites on their own terms? Credo Mutwa's best solution, really, is taken from his own story:

If any Black man with a little knowledge of English, French or Portugese wants to study the White man — as I have done — all he has to do is to go into the nearest town and become a regular customer of one of the second-hand bookshops there. He must buy and read no less than twenty different kinds of books and magazines a month for a period of no less than ten years. He must read classics, philosophical works and even cheap murder mysteries and science fiction. He must read Homer, Virgil, Aristotle and the rest. He must turn the pages of Walter Scott, Voltaire or Peter Cheyney. He must read the newspapers with great care.

Gradually, as the years pass, he will gain more or less a clear understanding of the White man, his way of life, his hopes and ambitions. But few White people have ever bothered to study the African people carefully — and by this I do not mean driving round the African villages taking photographs of dancing tribesmen and women and asking a few questions....

There can be no understanding between them so long as neither has a clear picture of the other, what it really thinks, believes in, hopes for, and why. You cannot found a friendship on faulty guesswork, because guessing breeds suspicion, hate and bloodshed. And there is much that is guesswork between Black and White.[19]

If there is one traditional voice that comprehends not only the collision of races but of cultures and of deeply-embedded value stances in South Africa today, it is Credo Mutwa's. It is a voice resonant with the most ancient languages we have, and yet with a kind of celestial laughter. Enjoy its poetry and its power, and learn from its wisdom.

STEPHEN LARSEN

Credo Mutwa with Sangoma women

To the goddess Amarava,
whose luminous form
ever brings spiritual inspiration,
and to that loveliest of her great grandaughters,
my wife Cecilia

Credo Mutwa with bronze sacred ceremonial objects

1

The Way of the Witch Doctor
How I Became a Sangoma

You get imbued with a crazy feeling that if you could be sacrificed on some altar, things would come right with the world. You also journey to strange places where you see very ancient gods who tell you what you must do. You find that you can even talk to animals...

My becoming a Sangoma was but the first step on a long journey which eventually led me to many parts of Africa — a journey of searching for the great truth, a journey of being healed by greater healers than I, of my many ailments, and also, eventually, of healing others of my people when I myself became a fully-fledged healer.

The Illness

The story started long ago when I was studying to become a schoolteacher way back in the 1930s. In those days school teaching was an honorable profession amongst the Zulu people. If you were able to read and to write, if you had been trained to stand in front of a classroom full of children and teach them the miracles of writing, reading and arithmetic, you were a greatly honored person. I had desperately wanted to be a teacher, had studied hard and was close to reaching my goal.

About a year before these events that I am about to relate, my mother's relatives had contacted me and told me of my mother's wish that I should return to the land of the Zulus and start training as my grandfather's successor. I had at first been most unwilling to obey this command because I knew that to become a healer, I must

2 ◈ The Way of the Witch Doctor

leave my white man's education and follow the ways of the old people, my mother's people. I had told my uncles, my mother's brothers, that I was not at all prepared to abandon the path of Christianity and return back to what I had been taught to believe were the ways of ignorance, the ways of hedonism, the ways of the Devil. The missionaries had taught us that those of our people who still followed the ancient ways were the Devil's people, whose souls would not enter the sacred gates of Heaven after death. And I was not prepared to condemn my soul to eternal damnation just to please my mother.

So, I had carried on with my studies to become a schoolteacher. I wanted to show my father and the rest of my family, who tended to look down upon me, that I could become a teacher and bring great honor to my father's name. But one day while I was walking to the mission school, I was attacked by a sudden weakness, a feeling of nausea and dizziness that was like no other feeling that I had ever had before. I suddenly felt very weak, and I sat down on a rock thinking that the feeling would pass away, but it didn't. I became weaker and weaker until things went dark; and when I regained consciousness, I was back in my father's *kraal* (an African home made out of grass and mud) lying on a grass mat. My father entered the hut and told me that I had been found by schoolchildren, lying unconscious on the side of the footpath.

He asked me how I was feeling, and I told him that I was still feeling rather weak — perhaps I was coming down with influenza. My father, who was by this time a follower of the strange Christian Science philosophy of the American, Mary Baker Eddy, told me roughly that according to the writings of the sacred white woman, Mrs. Eddy, all illness was an illusion and that it was my duty to fight this illusion and not allow it to gain the upper hand over me. With that, my father left the hut and returned a few moments later with a bottle full of clear water over which he proceeded to mutter a long prayer, and he gave me this water to drink at regular intervals.

Then he went out of the hut to go about his daily duties. I drank the water that my father had prayed over but I felt no better. In fact the feeling of great weakness and dizziness returned, and once more I slipped into the valleys of darkness. It was to go on like that for many days until I was a very sick person indeed. My father's neighbors suggested that I should be taken to a witch doctor, and this my father scornfully refused to do. One of the teachers from the mission school who visited me — a senior teacher at the school where I was studying urgently advised my father to take me by ox wagon to the local town where he advised me to see a white doctor. This again my father angrily refused to do. Do not the Christian Scientists teach that the taking of medicine is a great sin? Do they not teach that all illness is error? And nothing, nothing could sway my father from this position. He firmly believed in the teachings of the holy woman from America.

Almost every day in those days that marked the beginning of my great illness my father used to sit next to me as I lay under blankets sweating and feverish, and he used to read to me the writings of the American lady, Mrs. Eddy. I remember distinctly that one of the books from which he read was called, *Science and Health with a Key to the Scriptures,* and it is one of the main books of the Christian Science philosophy.

In spite of my father's reading, in spite of the large quantities of holy water that he made me drink, my illness went from bad to worse and other symptoms besides dizziness — great weakness and fever — began to manifest themselves. There were pains in my ribs, there were rumbling sounds in my bowels. There was a mysterious lump in my throat and a constant low, nagging headache to which was soon added a strange feeling at the top of my head, a feeling of numbness which later changed into a feeling which I can only describe as that of a huge, dark, metal nail being driven into the top of my skull. I was a very sick young man indeed.[1]

These symptoms were accompanied by constant nausea as well as loss of appetite and constipation. My hands became numb with a tingling feeling in them. I began to suffer from great thirst and sleeplessness. I could stay awake for the whole night while other people slept soundly all around me. There was a constant dull pain in my spine just in the region of the lower-most ribs and this pain was one of the sources of my misery. It was always there, ever there, dully throbbing, and within a short while that area became quite tender to the touch. Then one day I found that I had lost all ability to walk.

My body felt numb from the waist downwards. I was completely helpless; I could no longer move my legs, my toes, my thighs. There was just what I can only describe as a deadness in the lower regions of my body.

I now had to be carried like a child by the few kindly relatives I had. I had to be carried out of the hut when I needed to relieve myself. I could see my feet and legs, but I could not move them. It was a terribly embarrassing thing. The feeling of helplessness nearly caused me to lose my last residue of courage, the final shreds of my determination to fight this persistent and debilitating illness. During the time when I was completely paralyzed from the waist down, I became aware of a new and extremely disturbing phenomenon. I began to have visions, visions of fantastic places, of impossible landscapes and unearthly animals. I began to have visions of people — very old, old people, gray and wrinkled people, people who spoke things to me which I could not understand. I also had visions of fearsome monsters which often changed into people, some of whom I knew and some of whom I did not know.

I suddenly found myself being swallowed up body and soul by my dreams and visions, by day as well as by night. People spoke to me, telling me things I could not understand — people I did not know — people wearing skins, some of them wearing strange clothes of a type I'd never seen before, all during my waking hours as I sat helplessly in my hut bathed in pain and misery. I began to become aware of the fact that I could see through people. If a person appeared before me, if a person entered the hut in which I was, I could look through that person and actually hear his or her thoughts. I began to see that every person and every animal, such as my dogs and my cats, were covered by a faint but definite nimbus of light, something like a halo, which, however, covered the entire body from head to toe; and I saw that each animal and each person had a halo completely different in color from any other animal or any other person.[2]

If I was being carried out of the hut on really dark nights to relieve myself, I found that when I looked in the direction of my father's cattle corral, I did not see the cattle because of the darkness, but I could see their lights, a huge lake of definite but dim mist-like light where the cattle were lying or standing. If one of the animals moved, if it detached itself from the rest of the animals and moved to a corner of the corral, it was as if I were seeing a faintly glowing ghost with horns and a tail and hooves moving across a deep field of intense darkness. I found to my amazement that if a person who came near me had an injury or a pain of some kind anywhere on his or her body, I could actually see it.

There was a gentle aunt of mine, Anastasia, a half sister of my father, who made it her duty to look after me, to nurse me, to see that I was fed and bathed. She loved me dearly, this sad woman, and then one day while she was pressing a bowl of soup to my trembling lips, I suddenly turned my head aside and said, "Great Mother, you are not well." The woman was very startled. She said, "What do you mean, son of my brother?"

I said, "You care for me, Great Mother, but you need more help than I do."

She said, "Why?" I said, "There is a dark cloud, a dark patch in the region of your heart. I think your heart is giving you trouble."

Anastasia was so shocked by this that she actually recoiled as if I had struck her, and the clay bowl of soup smashed against the hard mud floor of the hut. She looked at me for a long time, her face gray with fear. She said, "How do you know that?"

I said, "I can see, Great Mother, I can see, don't ask me how, but I can see."

Anastasia then laughed. She said, "You are right, these last few weeks I have been having strange palpitations in my heart. My heart speeds up and beats at a rate I've never felt it beat before. You are quite right, little Mutwa, I am a sick woman, but you know your father. He is very stubborn where illness is concerned. He says we should not go to doctors."

I said to her, "Great Mother, I think you should go to a doctor, a white man doctor, because if you don't, you might not be alive next year."

For a long time Anastasia said nothing, just kneeling there in front of me in the slowly darkening hut. And then she said to me, "You can see my illness little Mutwa, but do you have the power to take it away?"

I said, "I don't know, Great Mother."

She said to me, "Can you try?"

I said, "How?"

She said, "Can you do what Jesus did? Can you place your hand over my heart?"

And this I did. In my days, adult people were sacrosanct and it was forbidden for a young person to lay his or her hand on an adult person for any reason, but Anastasia took my hand and placed it between her ample breasts and for a long time there was silence. Then I heard myself say, "Great Mother, I think the pain in your heart, the speeding of your heart shall no longer trouble you. The dark cloud I see in this region is dissipating; it is still there but it is dissipating."

Then Anastasia laughed a little, stood up and went out of the hut. She returned with a candle, lighted it, and then went out again without saying anything. Several days passed and then one morning Anastasia said to me, just after she had finished bathing me with blue soap and water, "Hear me, little Mutwa, you have a great power, a power to heal people, a power to take away the sickness of people, and many people are going to come to you as a result of this."

I said, "My father would kill me, Great Mother. He would never allow me to heal people. He says that all that is something from the Devil. You have heard my stepmother. She tells everybody that I am not sick, only possessed of devils."

Anastasia said, "Little Mutwa, listen to me. You have taken away my illness; my heart no longer troubles me as badly as it did. I don't know why, but I am going to do something about your illness. I am going to help you too. I'm going to write to your Uncle Anthony in Durban, and he must come here so that we can discuss what we are to do. You must be helped, little Mutwa. You cannot be allowed to waste away as you are doing. I'm sure that there must be a doctor or a witch doctor who will be able to help you some way. I am going to help you."

"Great Mother," I said, "please promise me that you will never tell anyone about the fact that I'm able to heal people. I am afraid of my father."

"I promise, little Mutwa," she said.

But Anastasia was one of those women who just cannot keep a secret. She revealed my secret to a friend of hers who told another woman in the area and very very soon people were beating a path to my father's *kraal* and demanding that I should touch them. People with constant headaches, people with aching limbs, and one very fat man who insisted that I should touch his private parts because they were not functioning properly. And all this touching and healing was done only on days when my stepmother and my father were not at home.

But the secret was bound to come out sooner or later; and it did when a relative of our tribal Chief fell ill and a message was sent to my father ordering him to prepare for the reception of this relative of the Chief, who, my father was bluntly told by the elders, was coming to be touched by the sick boy who could not walk, who was wasting away in my father's hut — namely me.

I had never seen my father so furious in my life. He was beside himself with rage; and as for my stepmother, one of the most rigid people I've ever had the misfortune to know, she became totally hysterical. She said that Christian people should have nothing to do with a Devil-possessed thing like me. But whether they liked it or not, my father and stepfather were forced to receive the relative of the Chief. An ox was slaughtered and there was much eating and drinking in my father's *kraal*. And this relative of the Chief, a young man, demanded that he should be allowed to sleep in the same hut in which I was so that I would touch him every morning. He stayed for ten days — I remember — and every morning at sunrise and every evening after sunset I had to touch him.

Meanwhile my strange talents developed further. I began to sense when people were coming to my father's *kraal*. Somehow I used to see these people coming long before they arrived; and I even knew what sex they were, and how many they were, and I used to tell my Aunt Anastasia each time people were coming. The relative of the Chief told my aunt that I had a great gift and that this gift should be developed and that my father was a wicked and a stupid man for forbidding me from receiving proper treatment. The relative of the Chief told my father bluntly that I had healed him and that the terrible weakening illness that he had contracted while working in

Johannesburg had completely disappeared thanks to my hands.

"You must save this son of yours," said the relative to my father. "You must!"

I don't know what my father said to the man, but all I do know is that after this more and more people arrived at my father's *kraal*. And then my stepmother started talking about us moving out of the district and going to live elsewhere.

It was then that my father's brother, Anthony, arrived and be-tween them — Anthony and Anastasia — they persuaded my father to allow me to go to Durban with them, where they had their home.

"Are you trying to trick me, Anthony?" I remember my father asking angrily. "Are you trying to take this little wretch to witch doctors or to white doctors?"

I remember Anthony saying, "My brother, my elder brother, since when have I ever been false to you? I believe that what Credo needs is a change of atmosphere. I believe that the sea air in Durban is going to do him a lot of good. I've got a little house in Catomanor (which was a suburb in Durban where Indians and black people lived side by side). I will look after Credo but I will give him no medicine whatsoever, this I promise you. And you will be free to visit him any time you wish."

My father agreed, albeit reluctantly, that Anthony should take me away to Durban with him. I remember the long journey first by train and then by bus. I remember our arrival in Catomanor. I re-member the sheer strangeness and over-crowdedness of the place. Street after street of unbelievable hovels, some built of corrugated iron and some built of wood and cardboard. I remember the filth, the stench, and the noise.

Beginning the Cure

Once I was living with my uncle Anthony and his family and aunt Anastasia, Anthony decided to break every promise that he had made to my father. He said that he just could not as a Christian stand by and watch me sicken and possibly die of my strange ill-ness without doing something about this. He said that my father was stupid, shortsighted and crazy; and he had ample support from both Anastasia and his wife Johanna. Johanna was a well-educated woman who worked in a laundry in Durban. She said that I must be taken to Western medical doctors, as well as to any other healer who could free me of my wasting illness, because by now I was almost like a skeleton.

Anthony took me to several Hindu doctors, but it was of no avail. He bought for me every patent medicine that the chemists of that time stocked. I drank this or that blood mixture, I was rubbed with this or that until I smelled like a laboratory; and always always my strange visions were haunting me.

Each night my mind would take long fantastic journeys to unknown lands and to times in the remotest past. One moment I would see myself sitting inside a hut built entirely of what appeared to be decaying grass surrounded by unbelievably ancient men and women, some of whose faces and bodies were one mass of wrinkles. These people were telling me things, they were telling me about herbs that could cure and herbs that were poisonous. They were telling me about medical preparations which I had never seen in my life.

At certain times I experienced what could only be described as nightmares. In these nightmares leopards attacked me, tore me to bits, devoured every scrap of flesh I possessed on my body. I could actually feel my limbs being torn away from me by these awesome beasts. I could actually smell the animals that were devouring me, but always somehow I came back to life again. These were the most horrendous of the visions that visited me at that time.

On several occasions I had visions of myself being killed by men wearing skins, men carrying shells and battle axes as well as spears. I could actually see them stabbing me time and time again. I could feel the impact of their weapons on my body and I could feel the terrible pain. At one time I underwent the most fearsome nightmare vision of all. Unknown people, whose faces I could not clearly see, were dragging me along the ground. I could feel stones cutting into my back. I could feel my limbs being stretched by the cool hands that were dragging me along the ground. I could feel my head bumping against stones. I could feel myself bleeding. These faceless people lifted me up forceably and tied me to what appeared to be a gigantic, very old and dry tree of some kind. And then other equally faceless people began cutting my body open. I could actually see my bowels flowing out of the terrible cuts like water. I could see the blood, I could hear myself screaming.[3]

These were dreams which were so real it was as if I was actually experiencing these things. I remember one other vision that occurred after a particularly violent one, in which I was laid upon a flat rock and again disemboweled, again my entrails were dragged about upon the ground by faceless people whom I could not clearly see. Now a very very beautiful vision visited me. It was a vision of a woman, a woman with an orange-brown skin and greenish black hair and black eyes. This woman, unlike the Zulu women of that time, was not wearing a skirt of cowhide, but she wore some type of grass skirt or a skirt made of fiber of some kind, a skirt dyed red with some kind of clay; and I remember this mysterious creature saying to me, "Do not be afraid, for I am your bride, and Amarava is my name."[4]

When I woke up from this vision, it was early in the morning. I was feeling particularly weak and ill; but the strange name, "Amarava," haunted me for the rest of that day and for many days to come. "Amarava": This did not even sound to me like an African name, though later I would find it was. Again, I was to be haunted by visions of strange and beautiful women, one of whom called herself, "Anana."[5] I did not know what to make of these things.

The difference was that this time, in my uncle's home in the slumlands of Catomanor, I was not alone. There was Anastasia, big and gentle. There was Anthony, short and fat and ever smiling. There was Johanna, very efficient, very educated, very clean. And all these people not only looked after me in my great illness, but to my surprise, they wanted to know as much as possible about the strange visions that I was having. Unlike my father and unlike my stepmother, these relatives of mine wanted to know as much as possible about what was troubling me.

Then one day I had another vision which persisted for several weeks. This was the vision of a tall black man, by attire obviously a

Zulu, and judging by the black ring that he wore around his head, obviously a king from somewhere in the last century, somewhere in Zululand. This king used to appear to me again and again, continuously every night for well over ten weeks, and his appearance and the words he spoke were always the same. In one hand he held a shield such as Zulu warriors used to hold in battle long ago, and in the other he held not a spear but a round-headed wooden battle club. I saw each time that his body was covered completely with awful gaping wounds, none of which were fresh and all of which appeared to be septic, because I could actually see fluid streaming out of some of them. This king — who was later identified by my mother's father as King Shaka of the Zulus — used to say one sentence to me. He used to say, "You are named Vusumazu, awakener of the Zulus, and you must help my people to awaken." Over and over and over this ghostly chieftain with terrible wounds on his body, with shield and battle club, used to appear before me, fix me with a burning gaze like that of an eagle, and say, "You are named Vusumazu, which means awakener of the Zulus. You must awaken my people, the Zulus."

It was this vision that forced my Uncle Anthony — a confessing Catholic, a true Christian — to seek the advice of an old witch doctor who was the night watchman in the factory at which Anthony worked, a factory which manufactured steel rope for the great mines in Johannesburg and other cities in South Africa. The old witch doctor told my uncle that the man whom I saw again and again in my vision could have been none other than the famous Zulu emperor, Shaka, and that my sickness was really not a sickness at all, but rather I was undergoing the great illness which all sangomas-to-be had first to undergo. The old witch doctor told Anthony that if he wanted me to survive, he had to stop stuffing me with Western medicine. He should rather take me away to someone in Zululand who would duly initiate me. Anthony thought of one person — namely the father of my real mother, my maternal grandfather [Ziko Shezi, see *"Editor's Introduction,"*] who lived in Zululand many miles away from the city of Durban.

One day Anthony contacted my mother's relatives by letter and their response was amazing. They came to Durban, took me away to Zululand, and there a completely new life began for me. I met my mother who had been abandoned by my father while I was yet a baby; and many were the stories that we exchanged. My grandfather told me that I had to accept treatment by him without question. "You must obey me without question if you wish to live," said the old man. "I have seen your type of illness many times before and I will heal you of it."

My treatment began. I was given baths of steam, my body was rubbed by powerful Zulu hands until it felt almost raw. I was given purgatives and emetics, and I had to drink bitter-tasting traditional tonics and stimulants, all prepared by the hands of my maternal grandfather. Deep in my Christian heart I had no faith in all this. I said to myself, "How could these people succeed where Western medical doctors have failed?" But within about six months I began to see strange results, and the first one was that I was able to take slow, painful steps with my feet for the first time in almost two years; and the more I underwent treatment, the stronger my feet became, until I could walk fairly normally. When he was satisfied that my paralysis was gone, my grandfather ordered that I was to dance — a drum was to be beaten every day and I was to be taught how to dance. It was my mother who assisted me, together with a relative of hers, Mynah. Mynah was a fully fledged sangoma and it was she who led me into the whirlpool of dancing such as only sangomas know. She sang songs which were strange to me, and beat the drum.

At first my weakened legs, which had not walked for so long, could not stand the pace of the rhythm, and I used to collapse exhausted, but the regimen did not let up. I had to dance and dance, and gradually I became stronger, more agile, and I was swallowed up by the very rhythm of the dance. We danced at least twice a day, early in the morning after my bath in the cold waters of a nearby stream, my daily emetic, and my daily steaming with herbs and water. Gradually my condition improved. The constant headache was gone. Mynah's snuff-like powders consisting of finely ground herbs of different kinds saw to that. My grandfather's steam baths made my body feel like that of a bird — light, and full of energy. His tonics and stimulants worked their wonders too.

I began to ask myself, "Do I know the Africa that is my mother? Do I really know my people?" The answer was "No! You do not know your people, you do not know their greatness. Look now where Christian religions have failed and where European type medicine has failed. You have been made well by herbal medicine in which you had not believed."

The Sangoma's Apprentice

Mynah and my grandfather between them taught me how to refine my skill of healing and divination and diagnosis of illness. My grandfather taught me the art of the divining bones — bits of seashell, animal bones and bits of ivory, which an African witch doctor throws in order to foretell the future or to find out what the patient's problem is. My grandfather also taught me how to control my powers of seeing and how to sharpen them and to make them more accurate and efficient. He taught me the art of breathing properly. He taught me the secret art of joining my mind to that of the great gods in the unseen world. He taught me how to sit still — very very still — and eliminate all the thoughts from my mind and call upon the hidden powers of my soul.[6]

In short, my grandfather taught me the Zulu version of what is called in English, "meditation." How to breathe softly and gently like a whisper until you feel something like a hot coiled snake ascending up your spine and bursting through the top of your head — a fearsome thing that is known as *umbilini*. This *umbilini*, my grandfather told me, is the source, the primal source of the sangoma's powers. A sangoma must be able to summon this *umbilini* at will through the beating of the drum and through meditation, very very deep meditation.[7]

My grandfather taught me that there are many ways by which one can reach the ultimate truth that is at the full extent of one's mental powers. He told me that I could either do it painfully by depriving myself of food and drink and by causing my body to suffer as much as possible, or I could do it through the medium of joy, of happiness and ecstasy. I chose to experiment with both these two ways. Sometimes I fasted and tortured my body until I felt like a prisoner undergoing savage interrogation. Sometimes I used the joyous way, as it is called, in which I sat down and thought only beautiful thoughts and ate pure food sparingly and drank only pure cool water and that also very sparingly.[8]

Strange vistas opened in my mind. I no longer was afraid of the fearsome visions that I saw; rather I worked with them, and saw them as useful guides which greatly strengthened and broadened my perception, not only of the world in which I lived, but also of the entire cosmos. My grandfather told me that a sar.goma must be able to draw knowledge from what he called "the Hidden Lake." There is, he said, a huge unseen lake somewhere in the spirit world where all the knowledge of the universe — past, present, and future — is to be found.

"Knowledge lives in that lake in the form of little silver fishes," my grandfather said. "You must never never again say that you do not know something. You must just ask the lake, the unseen lake, to provide you with the knowledge that you seek. You are a Child of God, you were created by God. Even the Christians tell you, 'All things are possible.' Because you are a tiny tiny fragment of God Almighty, all things are possible to you also." This is what my grandfather taught me. Even so, to my still-Christian mind some things sounded like blasphemy.

One day I very rudely confronted my grandfather with this question: "How could God be almighty and I also be almighty?" My grandfather controlled his fierce Zulu temper and he said to me, "Come out" and immediately I obeyed.

We went out of the grass hut and my grandfather pointed towards the west and said, "Look over there, what do you see?"

I said, "Grandfather, I see mountains."

My grandfather said, "Yes, you see mountains."

And then he took a piece of sandstone and thrust into my hand. He said, "What is this?"

I said, "My grandfather, it is a stone."

My grandfather said, "Look, this stone is a fragment of one of those mountains. This stone contains within it all the characteristics of those mountains over there." My grandfather knocked the stone out of my hands and then he said, "Come on, follow me."

I followed him. He came to his favorite tree, which was a fig tree that he had planted as a young man and which was now tall and producing a lot of beautiful fruit. My grandfather said, "What is this?"

I said, "Grandfather, this is a tree."

My grandfather struck me across the face and said, "Listen you little dog, this is not a tree, this is a person. Do you understand me? In old Africa, in the land of the ancient Zulus, in my time when I was a young man, we never used to call trees 'trees' but rather 'growing people'. This is a person.

"Have you seen me standing next to this tree on certain days?" he demanded.

I said, "Yes, grandfather."

"What have you seen me doing here?" he asked again.

"Grandfather, I have seen you touching the trunk of this tree, and at one time I saw you taking snuff out of your snuff horn with your snuff spoon and pouring it at the foot of this tree."

My grandfather laughed, a gap-toothed, cruel laugh. He said, "Now what did you think I was doing, you little Christian rubbish? Did you think that I was worshipping the tree? Did you think that I thought the tree was my God?"

I said, "No, grandfather."

Another blow flew across my face and snapped my head back. My grandfather said, "Listen, I *was* worshipping the tree. I *was* talking to the tree. I was sharing my snuff with the tree, and I often share any good news that I happen to have with the tree. I sing to it, I praise it, I thank it — and see the fat figs that it produces for us because I talk to the tree and I believe that it is a person. Do you understand?"

I said, "Yes, grandfather."

He said, "You understand nothing. Let me tell you further. In the old days of our great great grandfathers in my days as a young man, we used to speak with animals whether wild or domestic. We used to sing to our corn. We used to sing to our pumpkins and our sweet potatoes in the field. Even as we planted the corn we used to call upon it to grow strong and to yield more and to give us more food. In the days of the old people you were not allowed to curse or to commit an act of violence inside a cornfield because that would frighten the corn and make it produce little food."

Thus my grandfather began what was to become a very long lesson for me on how to communicate with animals, wild animals as well as domestic animals; how to communicate with birds and with growing things whether edible or not, whether medicinal or poisonous or neither. I accepted my grandfather's teachings because I had suddenly realized that our people possessed knowledge that was earthshaking; and if there is one thing that has haunted my life since my earliest years of childhood, it has been an overwhelming curiosity, a wish, an insane wish to know as much as possible about as many things as it is possible. And so I drank in my grandfather's teachings like a calf drinks milk at its mother's udders.

I learned and learned and learned and learned. My grandfather told me that in 1925 he had gotten into trouble with the local missionary because he practiced the custom of organizing dances by young men and women in the cornfields of the tribe when the moon was high. The missionary had told my grandfather to stop misleading young people, as he said. My grandfather was threatened by the missionary with expulsion from the tribe, and had reluctantly agreed to stop taking young people to the cornfields to dance for the corn when the moon was bright in the sky.

Ironically enough, when I, Credo Mutwa, reached the United States of America in 1974, I found people in Los Angeles buying potted plants from nursery men and with each potted plant there was supplied a printed little leaflet by the nursery men on how the owner of the house plant should talk to his or her plant so as to make it flourish. The thing which was once despised by missionaries when they saw Africans practicing it, which they contemptuously called "a native superstition," has today been accepted by scientists in the United States and other countries, and so it passed on to the common people as well.

My grandfather taught me that a healer without compassion for all life in his heart is like a drum without its skin. He is like a river without water, he is like a human being without reproductive organs. My grandfather warned me against misusing the great power that I was going to have over my fellow people as a sangoma.

During my more than two years of initiation into sangomahood, I was subjected to very, very strict discipline. I had to wake up very early in the morning — some two or three hours before sunrise — and I had to beat my potful of sacred mixture into froth. This was a mixture of ground roots and herbs whose purpose is to clean the sangoma's entire system and to open up his head — to make him even more sensitive, to make him see more — to make his powers of divination even sharper, more accurate than ever.

This mixture is beaten into froth and it is contained in a clay pot with always about four liters of it in the clay pot. Then you drink down this mixture and, using a feather, you tickle your uvula and bring it up again. You do this several times every morning before sunrise. Then you must jump into a stream which is ice-cold, in winter especially, and bathe your whole body in the cold water. Then you must get out and take your clay pot on your head and hurry back home. There you must undergo a steaming ritual, a clay pot filled with a steaming mixture. A steaming mixture is placed on a fire until the contents boil. Then it's removed from the fire, the initiate strips, covers himself with a blanket, and goes on hands and knees above the steaming mixture so that his entire body is bathed in steam.[9]

After that, the initiate must bathe a second time and then go and formally greet his instructor. This formal greeting takes about twenty minutes and words of praise are directed by the apprentice to the instructor, his or her ancestors — those who can be remembered being named by name. Then there is a time when the apprentice must confess to his or her instructor any negative thoughts, doubts, or longings that had crossed his or her mind and a special punishment is meted out to the apprentice by the instructor should the apprentice confess to having entertained proud, insolent or doubtful thoughts. This punishment often consists of extra duties, hard work, or it can even consist of being ordered to dance for two or three hours without stop, to the beating of a drum. It is wrong for an initiate to feel homesick. It is wrong for an initiate to even think about sex. In fact, total abstinence from sex is one of the strictest rules binding an initiate in the art of being a sangoma.

Then, this done, the confession done and the punishment meted out, the initiate must get on with his usual day to day duties, which often consist of assisting his or her instructor in diagnosing patients' illnesses, looking after new initiates, looking after the livestock and so on. While the young sangoma to be is undergoing initiation, he or she must be careful of what he or she eats or drinks. There are certain foods which are forbidden. There is a certain type of bean which Zulu people especially like to eat, but this type of bean is strictly forbidden to young sangomas to be. They must not even touch this bean. Pork must never be eaten by a sangoma either during or after initiation. And the flesh of an animal which had died either from old age or from disease must never be eaten by a sangoma either during or after initiation. And so it goes on.

After I had ended initiation under my grandfather and under my mother's sister Mynah, I wanted to learn more, so I went to Swaziland and studied there under great healers while earning a living both as a healer and as a laborer and sending money back to my father and the rest of my family. From Swaziland I went to Mozambique, which was then under Portuguese control, and there I studied under Mombai traditional healers and under Shangon sangomas and Tsonga *nyangas*. There I learned even more than I had learned under my grandfather. I went on to Rhodesia — today called Zimbabwe. Wherever I went in Africa, there I knelt before great teachers and I learned. I discovered how insignificant my Western education was, and how inadequate and how false in many aspects — especially where knowledge of Africa is concerned.

The Lore of the Soul

The Christians have told us that God created the soul, but our belief in Africa is a little different from this. We believe that the soul is in fact an integral part of God and that our souls came into being when God created Himself. We exist because God exists, and our souls are fragments of this Universal Self.

There are two "souls" in a human being, the *ena* and the *moya*. The moya we depict as a globe or sphere of perfect transparency, which in its disembodied form may fly or float through the air. We say that female souls have transparent wings, like those of a mosquito, while males float, but without wings. Inside each sphere, male or female, are two worm-like creatures, perfectly visible; one is blue in color and the other red; they move around and dance with each other and struggle with each other and are never quiet. We say that these worm-like creatures represent the good and the evil inside a person. The red worm symbolizes all the bad things in a man or a woman — a warped sense of morality, low cunning, dishonesty, cruelty, pride, cowardice, perversity. The blue worm stands for all the good in a person — morality, charity, compassion, selflessness, courage, honesty.

The soul is thus always in balance between good and evil, life and death. A combination of good and evil, equally balanced, is essential. For all souls that exist, neither perfect goodness nor badness can prevail or the soul would find a premature demise. It would be out of balance. That is why some people who are very good die prematurely; the contest is already over, the worms have settled the conflict. In other cases the worms quarrel ceaselessly, and for example if the red worm dominates, the person can develop an evil disposition and begin to do nasty things, abuse people, even steal or murder. If the blue worm is victorious, the person expresses nothing but virtue and becomes almost too good to live on this Earth. This is the lore of the moya.

The ena, which we also call "the self," is shaped like the person but is made out of a spirit substance. Animals also have enas, and these are shaped like the animal.[10] When a child is born, it does not possess an ena. This soul develops as the person develops, out of memories and experiences. If you were to see your ena you might imagine that you saw a ghost of transparent mist that resembles you. What some people call ghosts are thus enas; but this is not the immortal soul — though it may live on some time after the death of the body. In the after-death state, an ena, like a physical person, needs nourishment — and this is derived from the prayers and sacrifices of the living. A sacrificed animal's ena goes to feed the ena of the ancestor in whose honor the sacrifice has been conducted. Even the thoughts of the living, we believe, can sustain the enas of our ancestors; that is why people who do what is called "ancestor worship" are very serious about remembering and propitiating the enas of their ancestors; they also believe that the ena can be consulted in times of trouble or can serve as an intermediary who communicates with the gods on behalf of the people. If we forget about our ancestors, their enas pass into non-existence, and a valuable communication with the gods is also lost.[11]

At the average person's death, the ena wanders the Earth for a while, but eventually dissipates. The moya, however, goes on into other incarnations, other forms. It can be reborn in the form of a human being or an animal. When it takes this new form, it makes a new ena, and the ena is in human form if it is a human incarnation, or animal form if it is an animal incarnation.

People and animals create enas to survive in the world, and I will tell you why. We are all swimming in a great ocean called Time; but our enas are a little bit ahead of the physical body and can actually send back messages to us. An ena can bring back to the body, via dreams, knowledge of what might happen in the future. That is why some people dream of their death, like the American President Lincoln did. But it might also bring back a warning of a disaster, and if the person is listening to this warning, the disaster might be avoided. That is why in Africa we say it is very important to attend to one's dreams, for the ena sends important warnings through dreams. Animals seem to have a much more perfect communication with their enas and get all kinds of messages from them; but humans have lost much of their original senses and have to be trained all over again. This is some of the most important training of the sangoma.

Sometimes the ena knows that something bad will happen, but it is not able to tell the body when the something will come, so the body can be expecting something bad to happen for a long time in a kind of anticipation, but the soul does not know when it is coming. On one level it is as if the bad thing has already happened.

The moya can be trapped in too small a body, or too weak, or sick. We believe that the moya also breaks into smaller globules in a body, so there is a moya of the blood, a moya of the liver, of the stomach of the heart and so on. And if the moya of that part is sick, then the organ itself is also sick, and is not functioning properly. That is why the soul affects the body in such intimate ways. If my heart soul is weak it could affect my heart, but also it could affect the soul of my lung or of my liver. There is a state of mind that goes along with each of these souls, and we believe that courage has to do with the heart soul, for example; and a sangoma will help to work with that portion of the soul that he or she feels is weakened in a person.

We also believe that there is such a thing as soul loss, that one can lose parts of one's soul, or that other people can capture parts of the soul, knowingly or unknowingly, or can damage each others souls by magic or hatred. When a person has lost a part-soul they are very vulnerable to illness, particularly in that part of their body from which the soul has been lost. Our people are very sensitive to the white people's machines, because they fear their souls are affected by televisions, by cameras, tape recorders and other things. They are afraid that pieces of their souls may be captured or wounded. They also feel that the white people's attitude of belief or disbelief regarding whether there is anything valid or important in our culture affects our soul. That is why we are sometimes very guarded or careful around the white people. They mistake it for fear or reserve, but we feel the white people are not as sensitive to things of the soul as we are.

We believe that the soul is also sensitive to projections of evil, or to possession by evil spirits. As a sangoma I have participated in many expulsions of evil spirits from people; and I tell you I still don't like it. There was a man who had a very peculiar and evil habit; he had been arrested for mauling children by chewing on their hands. In several cases he had quite badly hurt the children by this peculiar thing, trying to eat their hands, as it were. I was called in to work with this person, along with other sangomas.

We discovered that he was possessed by one of his own ancestors, a cannibal spirit, from several generations back. It was this wicked creature that was causing all the problems, because he desired still to feast on human flesh. Seven sangomas and I did a ceremony. We built fires all around, and we brought the ancestor forth so we could see who was there, and then we expelled him. A dark cloud and a terrible stink came forth from the man and we sent him on his way, and after that the man was quite normal.

There was another case of a young girl who was possessed by very rambunctious spirits; things would fly around the room and break on the walls or floor, or furniture would move. One time a piece of crockery, a blue mug, somehow lifted up from its cabinet and came out of the locked house where it was being stored and smashed against her head. It was a very astonishing thing, because someone recognized the mug, and we went and found the exact set from which it was missing in the locked house. We had her surrounded by sangomas, and we all combined our powers to work with this spirit that was very strong and very violent. When it came out, there was a stink like I have never smelled before, a truly horrible stench that filled the air. But after that things were more quiet around that young woman.

How a Sangoma Cures

A Sangoma, either during or after initiation, must know how to communicate properly with people. He or she must never talk down to people but must talk to people at their level. A sangoma must never never argue with a patient. If a patient believes for example that he has been bewitched, even if the sangoma knows that witchcraft has nothing to do with this patient's misfortune or illness, the sangoma must rather keep his or her opinions to herself or himself and go along with the patient's beliefs, using them as an effective tool of gaining the patient's cooperation during treatment. These and many other important rules I was taught as a sangoma. I was taught how to recognize certain forms of madness in human beings. I was taught how to recognize an illness, such as the one I was suffering from, which at first glance looks like madness or a nervous breakdown, but which is much more than a mere illness or a mere nervous breakdown; rather, it is an invitation to be initiated as a sangoma.

A sangoma also has to be able to distinguish between a hopelessly mad person and a person who — though very mad indeed — can be saved and made well again. We were taught many ways of dealing with mentally ill people. For example, if a mad person kept on seeing illusions (hallucinations), shouting that there is a dog entering the hut and about to bite him, the sangoma must take a stick and pretend to beat this imaginary dog until the sick person tells the sangoma that the dog is either dead or has run out of the house. In short, the sangoma must use the patient's visions, illusions and delusions as a lever with which to move the patient back to sanity.[12]

Also, the learning sangoma is taught that there are forms of madness which can be cured by certain herbal preparations. There are forms of madness that can also be cured by keeping certain types of metals or substances away from the patient, and there are also forms of madness that can be cured simply by changing the patient's lifestyle or by advising the patient to do a certain thing. For instance, if you find a young man who lost his father at an early age and who, because of his extremely close attachment to his mother, is incapable of forming lasting relationships with young girls, you must advise that patient to marry a woman who is about five years older than himself and who looks as much like his mother as possible in face as well as in figure.

What do you do if you are presented with a person who is afraid of a certain type of animal? For example, if you find a person who is afraid of cats and who wants to be cured of his or her fear of cats, you must expose this person to cats — and it is done this way. A ceremony is made and a goat sacrificed. The skin of a goat is folded into something like a cushion and then the patient is stripped to the waist, placed face down upon this cushion of skin, and held by powerful people, firmly to the ground. Then a cat is taken and placed upon the back of this person. The person will scream and try to struggle but will be unable to breathe properly because he or she is nose down on the cushion of skins. The result will be that the person, unable to breathe, will choose the lesser of two evils and start now not fearing the cat upon his or her back at all. In fact, she will sweat out her fear of cats and never know this kind of terror again. This is one discipline in the treatment of mental illness which is followed by sangomas where a person is exposed deliberately, under careful observation, to the one thing that he has always feared in his or her life.[13]

There is also the matter of diet. If a person is violently mad, you must keep all kinds of copper artifacts away from that person. The patient must never be allowed to wear copper bangles, and, furthermore, he or she must be fed occasionally a diet of boiled fish or tasty boiled goat's brains or cattle brains, and these brains must be cooked just well enough to make pleasant eating.

One very effective method of dealing with homicidal maniacs — of which there are many in our modern townships like Soweto — is to take this homicidal maniac out of the township to a place where a woman is about to give birth to a baby, and then wash his hands thoroughly. Then, just after the baby is born, you must take baby — placenta and all — and place them upon the outstretched hands of the homicidal maniac, who will be blindfolded at this time. The homicidal maniac will often feel sick, tremble, and sometimes vomit after he has handled the baby for a few minutes, and he will never again kill another human being. These and many many other things I was taught.

I also learned about various types of ordinary illness. I was taught about headaches — their causes as known to African sangomas. I was taught about heart disease — its causes as known to African healers. I was taught, for example, that one of the greatest killers of Africans in modern communities — high blood pressure — is due to the very exacting and high speed lifestyle that many of our people lead today. If one is an upwardly-mobile black person nowadays, one sooner or later develops high blood pressure, and we are taught that in order to escape this scourge the patient must either change completely or modify his lifestyle. He must avoid certain foods, especially rich and sugary Western foods. He must avoid eating meat too much, and he must eat a lot of vegetables and boiled cereals.[14]

As apprentice sangomas, we were taught about the awesome powers that lie dormant within the mind of each and every human being. We were taught, for example, that under no circumstances should a man offend a woman in any way. Women possess very potent mind powers sometimes, without being aware of the fact; so great are the powers that some women possess that if they are angry with a man, it is as if they have put a curse upon him. The man becomes unlucky in everything that he does, until he goes back to that woman and asks for her forgiveness. We were shown how one human mind is capable of transmitting thoughts to another human mind, and we were given lengthy demonstrations of this.

We were trained how to locate hidden objects by simply reading the minds of those people who had hidden those objects. We were told that the power of the human mind can be used for both good and evil. You can use your mind powers to heal people as well as to destroy them. And we were taught how to counter the evil wishes that enemies direct at us or at those who had come to us for assistance. We were taught, furthermore, how to distinguish between different types of ghosts, how to distinguish a real haunting from a haunting that only exists in the minds of the people who live in that particular house. We were further told that should we ever at any time come up against a real ghost, we were not to try to bully that ghost or threaten it into leaving the place where it was causing trouble. We had to talk to the ghost and find out why it was haunting this particular place and disturbing these people. Then we had to find a suitable place — somewhere we could persuade our troublesome ghost to go. A traditional African exorcist does not thump Bibles at his ghosts; many times he talks softly to them and persuades them to leave his patients alone and to go to some place where they will feel more at home.

We were also taught how to deal with the most dramatic ghostly manifestation of all — where household utensils are hurled through the house by unseen hands, where people are assaulted by invisible assailants, and where many disturbing things of a noisy character occur. We were told that this type of haunting often attaches itself to a girl in that house or near that house and that it goes with her wherever she goes and that if we remove this girl gently to another place away from the haunted house, the hauntings will stop. And indeed, I have found this to be true in many cases of this type of haunting that I have dealt with since my initiation.[15]

We were further told about extraterrestrial phenomenon — what to do when a flying saucer has landed in a certain place, what rituals to perform there and how to communicate with the creatures inside these vehicles from beyond the stars, should one of them land near where the sangoma happens to be at that time. I was amazed at the vastness of the knowledge that the people of Africa possessed, knowledge which had been driven underground by the coming of Christianity to Africa. And it was this knowledge, this fascinating, amazing storm of truth that suddenly fell upon my head in the days of my first initiation, and that made me want to know more and to learn more, much more.

The Bone Oracle

When a twasa or candidate has passed through a stage of initiation, a feast is usually held, at which a calf or goat is slaughtered. The bladder of the animal is inflated and must be worn by the initiate in his or her hair. This signifies the readiness of the spirit to communicate with the initiate at any time.

The twasa then, on each ceremonial occasion, searches through the ashes of the fire for an unbroken bone. When four of these perfect bones have been found, they are treated ceremonially, cleaned, and carved with sacred symbols on one side only. These are the *dingaka*, or oracle bones. They may be used for many kinds of divination in much the same way as the Chinese or now Europeans and Americans use the oracle book that is called the *I Ching*. The oracle bones may also be used for the diagnosis of illness.

The four dingaka are named *lekwami*, or *lekgolo*, which mean "the old man," *kgadi*, which means "the old woman," *selume*, "the young man," the *koatsane*, or *lengwe*, "the young woman." If the bone lands face upward, it is said to be "smiling." If it lands face downward, it is said to be "sleeping."

When the twasa or the sangoma casts the bones, all aspects of the arrangement are considered carefully. These include which way the image is facing, the distance between the bones, any unusual configurations in the pattern. The bones are believed to detect the presence of spirits around a sick person, resentful ancestral spirits, offended nature spirits, or malevolent spirits which have been sent by a sorcerer against the person. The bones also will hint at how the affliction (of an ill person, or one under a curse) came about. It could be a breaking of taboo, careless or thoughtless actions, a natural weakening of energy, or even "soul-loss," which can be quite serious and lead to wasting illness and death.

As I have said elsewhere, for serious divinations, those affecting life and death, the divination may be done in several different places:

indoors, outdoors, at a sacred site or cave or on a mountain top. If the indications are the same in three of these locations, then one can be extremely confident of the answer.

Where illness or madness have come, the sangoma knows that some power of the universe is disrupted and must be balanced or restored to harmony again. The evil spirits must be removed or returned whence they came; offended nature spirits must be propitiated or pacified; or something as mundane as diet might have to be changed, a blockage in part of the body softened or loosened, or good breathing restored.

Once the diagnosis has been made, a sangoma may apply many remedies, medical or magical. These might include the application of herbs, roots or seeds, or minerals, the bodies of insects ground up, shells, smoke, eggs (for taking away bad energies). Therapies can include massage, herbal teas, salves, snuffs, poultices. Occasionally animal sacrifices may be used; and blood especially is used to placate disruptive spirits.

When the twasa's apprenticeship is complete, an ukukishwa ceremony is held, which welcomes him or her fully to the ranks of traditional healers. I have worked with many dozens of these apprentices, bringing them to completion as fully matured healers. For myself, I cast the Bone Oracle whenever an important decision is at hand.

The Sangoma's Creative and Psychic Powers

The so-called witch doctors of Africa are scientists, psychologists, para-psychologists, and artists. Sangomas are also clairvoyants, as we have seen, diviners, and diagnosers of illness. They play the same role that psychiatrists and priests and priestesses of various religions fulfill in Western and Eastern societies. We were the spiritual leaders of our people in ancient times, and in many ways we still are. We were the people who made it possible for Christian missionaries to operate freely in Africa, because we told our people to accept these foreign men with strange ideas. It was at our sanction and with our permission that they came; but, ironically enough, the very missionaries we welcomed into Africa turned around and started destroying us.

In Africa we have always striven to develop the perfect human being, and the much maligned traditional healers of Africa strive to become these perfected human beings. We try to eliminate from ourselves all base feelings such as jealousy and anger, and within the limits of our tribal laws, we have sorted out the truth — the truth about mankind, the truth about the universe — and we have pursued art in all its forms for many many generations. To be creative, we believe, is also to heal. You can heal a whole community by creating something beautiful near that community, be it a clump of standing stones, a sacred hut or shrine, or whatever. Some of the many paintings that you find in South African caves, and which are attributed to Bushmen were actually painted by black witch doctors. It is my profession that teaches me to pursue art, to pursue writing, to pursue all forms of communication between human beings; because, when you are a traditional healer, you must be able to communicate with people at all levels and in all possible ways.

As for clothing, the sangoma woman wears a kind of dress that depends on what initiation she has undergone; she wears a long wig made of wool with beads on it, which denotes her humility before God. She also wears a headband which denotes the purity of her thoughts. Then she may wear a skirt of leopard skin to denote her honesty and courage. Sometimes she will wear a red blouse to show that she is ready at any time to sacrifice herself in the service of the people. While in ancient times sangomas wore blankets of various animal skins, nowadays they wear a cloth called a *heia*; and the various heias have a symbolic meaning — a lion to show that we are people of courage, or one, for example, with a symbol that shows that a woman sangoma was enchanted first in the land of the Swazis.

First of all let us get one thing very clear. It is not a witch doctor who casts spells, it is a sorceror. If you remember, in Europe there were magicians of the white kind and magicians of the black, the dark forces. The magicians of the white were people like Merlin and other good wizards and witches, but the black magicians used their powers and their talents to destroy other people. And if it was so in Europe, it is still so here in Africa. A witch doctor will never cast a spell upon anybody. He can neutralize a spell, he can stop it;

but the moment a witch doctor harms a person, he is no longer a witch doctor. He becomes a sorceror, one we call *umtagatin zulu allmaloy insone*, which means "a doer of evil deeds."

We all have psychic power, but some use it and some don't. Some develop it, some leave it locked up out of fear. If you want proof of the fact that all of us possess this power, just take a good walk in some very rough part of any city in your country, like Harlem for example, in New York. If you are walking along the sidewalk and you meet a real sinister character, and you pass this gentleman, the moment the gentleman turns around and looks at you, you are going to feel it. The very moment he starts thinking how to knock you on the head and of what he's going to rob you, you are going to feel that, and you might start running faster in the other direction as he comes after you.

Now, this is what I am saying. We all have an inbuilt warning system which many fear to use and few make use of. This system works the more efficiently, the greater the danger that threatens your community (or even your country) is at a given moment. For example, very few prophets can foresee a wedding feast, but many can foretell the coming of an earthquake or a war. Why? Because prophesy is nothing more than man's early warning system, a system that all our forefathers and all our ancestresses possessed in ancient times. There is nothing unusual about it, but let me say something here. People who are aspiring to develop their gifts of prophesy should avoid exposing themselves overly much to electronic devices such as television sets, radio sets, and other electronic gadgets of this day and age because, for some reason, these electronic devices emit an inaudible sound that blankets all psychic power. I have noticed over many years of close observation how difficult it becomes for a witch doctor from Soweto, for example, to foretell events in the future. This is unlike a witch doctor who has lived in an environment where these electronic devices do not exist. So there must be something in our electronic world that is destroying our God-given talents, and I would love to see the day when people stop calling such gifts "supernatural" because the moment they say that, they close the door upon the full and frank investigation of these phenomena.

There is nothing supernatural, everything is natural. We in Africa know — and please don't ask me to explain further — that the human being possesses twelve senses — not five senses as Western people believe. One day this will be accepted scientifically — twelve. So we must not call those as yet unknown senses, supernatural. They are within the very borders of the shining land of nature.

I'm not allowed to say much more, but I can tell you this. Man possesses the sense not only to foresee future events, but also to move out of his body at will sometimes. But this only happens in times of crisis. Man also possesses the ability to influence objects. When I was a youth, I came to the city of Johannesburg and I immediately fell into bad company, and at that time I discovered that I possessed a unique talent that made me many enemies amongst my fellow youths. It was the talent of throwing the dice and winning again and again. But this talent only worked when I was really in a tight corner. I could not summon it at will. It only worked when I was desparate. It is just an example of the thing we wrongly call "the supernatural." It is all natural.

Let us say that a sangoma is about to perform a divination ritual in which she must locate a hidden object or a lost person. That sangoma will first ask her assistants to beat her drum with slowly rising force. Now, the idea behind the drumbeat in this case is to drown out all the other thoughts that the sangoma may be thinking, to surround the sangoma with a barrier of impenetrable noise so that inside this barrier her mind powers are concentrated on one point and one point only, which is to find the lost person. Some will blow flutes, a very loud noise indeed. Now the drum and the flute achieve the same result. It creates a barrier of noise within which all other thoughts are canceled out and the sangoma can concentrate only on the one thing of finding, of seeking out this lost person or object. I believe similar rituals are performed all over the world.

If there is something dangerous involving my people in any way or any people that I know and love, then these things come. It is not something that one can put categories on and say it is like this or like that. It just happens. It's one of those things that just happens. The fact is that this thing is not unique; all people possess it as I have tried to point out. There are those who use it, who develop it.

There are those who don't. It is neither unusual nor supernatural at all. It is part of our beautiful human nature.

The bones of divination are beads of ivory, shell, bone, and other things which are thrown by the sanusi to learn the future of his people or of one person. When they fall, they describe certain mystic patterns on the ground which would take far too long for me to detail here. I may want to know what the future holds for us, whether there is any hope in the situation in which we find ourselves, not only here but all over the world.

The bones must be thrown in three different places: on a mountain, in the open country, and also inside a cave or inside a hut. If the message you receive from these places remains identical, then that is the message that you must accept.

I found that Western education conditioned us to despise Africa, which is why we never realized the tremendous store of knowledge that lies hidden in the minds of those people who are called sangomas or traditional healers. After I had been practicing as a sangoma for several years, my mother sent messages to me that I was to succeed my grandfather as High Sanusi because now my grandfather was no longer well — being old and frail — and I agreed. I became the custodian of some of the holiest artifacts that our people possess, and some of these artifacts, made of bronze, copper, soapstone, and verdite have been dated back to several thousand years ago. I am the custodian of over fifty items of great value, ranging from great copper necklaces once worn by some of our mightiest kings, to stones inscribed with the writing of people who visited Africa thousands of years ago, people who were not of African birth or of the African race.

Ever since then, I have never looked back. I have lived in a great sea of African knowledge, which, could a man but live for a second term upon this planet, I would have been glad to share with my black brothers and sisters — not only in Africa but also in the far away Americas, especially the United States of America. But I am now an old and sick man myself, and I do not think I have much longer to live. Looking back along the long long road of my life, I say that God has been kind to me for having revealed his greatness as well as my people's greatness to me.

I have no one to pass my knowledge on to. My first-born son, innocent Mutwa, was murdered by activitists in Soweto some time ago. He was — of all my children — the best qualified to inherit the knowledge I have acquired, as well as the artifacts of which I am the guardian. He was already thirty years old, and my other children do not qualify for this great task — they are in their twenties or teens — and you cannot take something as important as this and put it in the hands of an immature child. It is my duty — because I have no successor — that many of the artifacts that I'm the custodian of should be buried before I die, because I cannot bear to imagine these great and ancient and sacred things imprisoned in glass cases in some dusty museum or exhibited as curiosities.[16]

And so it is, sir, that I pass on my knowledge to you, who ask questions, who have interest in these matters, in the hope that you will pass them on to others who need knowlege of these sacred things. Perhaps there are children of Africa who live in America, or people of good will, of whatever race, who will listen to my stories and learn from them. Through much suffering and learning I have become the guardian of my people and my culture in a new way. *Indaba.*

2
The Great Goddess

But the Goddess said, "Now look, my dear, look into Eternity, and you will see why you must do as I have bidden you." And Amarava saw a race of human beings covering the Earth — living and loving and bearing children and dying, and she saw that they were her own children. Then she saw a flash of lightning, and heard a voice as faint as rumbling thunder that asked her to accept this destiny. And so it is with all human beings, that often they are asked to accept a destiny they do not desire, and they are helpless to resist.

The Tree of Life

In the beginning nothing existed but the Fertile Darkness, floating on the invisible River of Time. There was no sun, there were no stars, nor the light of the moon; no earth, no place to stand, no vegetation, no waters, no roaring ocean, no brooks or rivers, no animals, no people. Nothing existed but nothingness and a darkness that overspread all.

But there was a trouble, a stirring in the darkness, a desire arose in the River of Time, a desire for something, for the Fertile Darkness to give birth to something out of nothing. It was a strange mating, between Time and Nothing, but from it came one tiny spark of Living Fire.

And the Living Fire was consciousness; it began to know things; and it knew it was alone in the darkness, and its loneliness was like that of every infant whose mother has been taken away; it was like a tiny firefly lost in the caverns beneath the Earth. It was the first Great Loneliness, and all creatures since then share a little in that loneliness, the one that emerges when consciousness sees itself alone in the vastness of everything. It is the part in us that cringes in the dark when the lions and the hyenas howl beyond the tiny village compound. It is the part in us that shivers when it sees the vast blackness between the stars.

"I am," the spark wailed, "I AM!" In its fury and loneliness, it fed upon the Nothing and the Fertile Darkness, and so it began to grow, and it grew into a light, shining in the darkness, and then a great blaze. Nothingness felt this Something, and did not like it, for Something negates Nothing, and Nothing wants only Nothingness; so when it felt a blazing angry presence in its midst that said "I AM!" it wished to destroy it. It gathered the coldness from the space between the stars and sent cold to overwhelm and destroy the spark of fire. And thus it happens that when a child asserts itself too strongly, even a very loving parent may secretly wish to destroy it.

But all living things resist whatever threatens its very life, and so the spark grew brighter, and fought against the cold and the darkness which was its ancient Mother. And the light broke and consumed the darkness, and the darkness the light; and still we see the blazing sparks in the cold black night sky, as a reminder of that first struggle of becoming. And the River of Time, Father to the child, saw the child's Battle with its Mother, the Fertile Darkness, and joined its Cold Eternity to the battle; and since that time, Father Time snuffs every spark of consciousness that comes into being, but the Fertile Darkness secretly holds a mother's compassion, and so she births them again from the darkness of Herself, and so we see beings come into existence and wink out again; and the stars blaze in the sky, or die in a great explosion of fire, which is their scream of "I AM!"

And since that time there is also the eternal battle of Fire and Ice, of light and of darkness, throughout this universe. The Wise Ones know that if the Fire were to triumph, all things would die in a universal roaring Flame, but if the Darkness and the Cold were victorious, all things would grow cold and stiff, and cease to be in that way. And so we balance forever between Fire and Ice, Light and Dark, Heat and Cold. When the Summer sun blazes in the sky, we seek for cool dark shadows and caves beneath the rocks; and when

Winter blasts the Earth with its Icy breath, we crouch by the fire, or shiver to warm our flesh and long for the Sun's warmth.

And the Wise ones know that this is a battle that must always be fought but never won. Only the Great Spirit, *Unkulunkulu*, may watch over such a titanic struggle and remain calm, for the battle goes this way and that, and all life struggles in its embrace, as the flesh grows hot with fever and must be cooled, violent with the heat of passion and must be satisfied. May the Spirit of Life grant that this one Great Battle go on, while all the lesser ones are given up. It is the Great Struggle on which all Life depends.

It was from the still warm ashes of that conflagration that arose the very first Goddess of human shape, All-knowing, Omniscient *Ninhavanhu-Ma*, or *Ma*, as she is called in a thousand tongues all over the Earth. She is the object of every infant's first cry when it feels the cold or dark, it cries out, like that first spark of consciousness alone in the void "Maaaaa!"

It was she who, at the command of Unkulunkulu, placed the Heavens in order, the stars and the Sun, and made the Earth firm to stand upon. Though she is the mightiest and most original of all that wear the human form, *Ma* is called by the Old Wise Ones, "The Imperfect Undying One," and those who carve her form from wood or stone or make her form in clay, know that she must be made imperfect. Her legs or arms are long or short, or deformed, or one breast is larger than the other. For it is from her pattern that all life is formed, and that is why we all are imperfect. She too had those wounds of the soul we call jealousy, anger, misery; she experienced lusts and cravings, she wished for food and for copulation. That is why Ma does not judge our human imperfections like those male gods who oversee Human destiny, for she shares them; and all beasts and humans are her beloved, imperfect children. The imperfect seed brings forth a stunted plant, the limb twists, or drops bad fruit or is too early or too late. The animal is weak or deformed, becomes prey easily, or misses its prey if it is a clumsy lion or leopard; and all human children have faults of character; they howl in the crib until we get angry; soon they think they know everything, and are selfish or spiteful. And the adult often acts like a spoiled child. But still, if the wise know well, like Ma, we are to love them all, imperfect humanity.[1]

When Ma had finished creating the stars, the Sun, and the Earth, she seated herself upon *Taba-Zimbi*, the Mountain of Iron, and a strange feeling came over her; it was the loneliness of the spark of consciousness felt when it found itself alone. She began to weep, a weeping that shook the universe, and from her soulful eyes flowed waters in all directions, streams and rivers, cataracts greater than *Musi-Wa-Tunya* that falls into the great river Zambisi. These waters ran crashing down the mountains and formed a great pool that soon became the salty oceans. Ma wept so hard the stars fell from the sky — just as they continue to do today.

At last the Great Spirit Unkulunkulu rebuked the Goddess, who was in danger of ruining all that she had created in her cosmic temper tantrum.[2] His voice came roaring from beyond the borders of Eternity; like a great tempest howling down the canyons, shaking the mountains, a sound so vast it would dwarf the the thunder on the desert, a sound that caused the first great earthquakes:

"Imperfect Being: I alone understand the purpose for this universe I bade you create; do not destroy it. Bear your loneliness a little longer, and you shall set an example to all creatures. None shall spend eternity in loneliness, and all shall find companions. Hear my words, and cease your lamentation!"

The Great Goddess, hearing the voice of Eternity for the first time, ceased her lamentations and stood in awe before the Almighty. Her tears stopped flowing and Creation quieted. The tidal waves ceased devouring the continents and the volcanoes grew sleepy. The thunderheads of the clouds released quiet rains and their underbellies were tinted red as the Sun descended behind the distant mountains. Ma replied, "Thou hast spoken, Oh Great Spirit, and I have heard."

But as the Goddess thought of Unkulunkulu's words and knew she would have a companion, her luminous golden eyes lit up, and the blood roared hot in her divine veins. Her four immense breasts with their emerald nipples heaved, and her breath came forth as a great cloud of vapor. She seemed to swim in an invisible cosmic joy. "Great Master," she said, "who will my companion be?"

"For now," said the ever-fainter voice that nonetheless shook the stars, "you may only dream of him. He shall bring contentment to you, and you shall bring forth children to fill a world."

Though gods and goddesses do not sleep as mortals do, they dream dreams as vast as the world, and Ma, entering the mountain, dreamed of her beautiful but unknown companion, and waited, impatiently for the first dawn.

But when it came, casting long shadows from the young Eastern Mountains, Ma heard a voice she did not recognize, a coarse voice she had never before heard.

"Come, oh my mate!"

The silvery Goddess arose, shimmering in her splendor, and burst through the side of the mountain, so great was her eagerness. Boulders crashed down the mountain and a cloud of blinding dust arose. When it cleared she held out her arms to her mate.

But the arms that reached for her own — how strange they were — gnarled and twisted, draped with creeping vines. His skin was rough, like the bark of trees, with chunks of granite embedded — a horrible, wonderful display of minerals: iron ore, diamonds, jewels of all kinds. His body was thick like a great Baobab tree, and the Goddess beheld with horror, eyes on many stalks, bloodshot and filled with a lecherous glee. His mouth seemed wicked and filled with pointed teeth, and he had a long green tongue which licked his granite lips. His legs were living roots on which this being scrambled quickly toward her, crablike.

She shuddered as she was folded in those many arms and felt the granite lips press against her own.

"Come to me, oh my beloved, come to me!" said the strange voice of this horrible-wonderful being. "I am *Sima-Kade*, the Tree of Life, thy mate, and I desire thee!"

"No, Release me, you monster!" shrieked Ma, "It cannot be! My mate you are not — my companion — NO!"

"But I've just caught you — you, my heart's desire. I did not catch you only to release you!" And the many arms held her fast.

When Sima-Kade released her at last, Ma fled, shrieking to the Great Spirit to release her from such a terrible mate. But the tree pursued her relentlessly; like young men do to women nowadays.

He had tasted the nectar-filled cup of love, and having tasted, vowed to taste again and again. On she fled, on her swift, silvery feet, over valleys and mountains, through plains and deserts, as he, burning with the fires of love, relentlessly pursued, for years it seemed; until at last they came to the barren lands that would be called Ka-Lahari.

The pursuit went on, until the two came to the shores of Lake Makarikari. Ma leaped into the water and streaked away like a silvery fish, while Sima-Kade waddled like a frog in the mud of the lake. But then when she soared like an owl into the night sky, Sima-Kade feared he would lose her forever. He grabbed a great wad of mud and clay and rock from the bottom of the lake, bigger than Mount Kilima-Njaro, and hurled it at his fleeing love.

His aim was true, and the Goddess hurtled down through the air limp and unconscious, into the many waiting arms of the Tree of Life, who safely caught her. But the missile, hurled with such force, flew into the night sky and began to circle the Earth as the Moon of today. Thus it was that the Great Spirit declared the Moon to be the Guardian of Love, since it helped to re-unite the Tree of Life with the Great Goddess. To this day, the love lives of beasts and men, fish and fowl, and even the gods are regulated by this shining missile. Drums beat and rituals are performed by its light. *Aieee!* Great is the power of the Moon.

The Tree of Life held the Goddess fast, and it seemed an age passed by while she lay in that strange embrace. But then she began to feel movements within her. As time passed they grew until at last she felt an urgency and a tearing pain. Ma cried out as her silvery body trembled and shook, but still the Tree held her tightly. After fifty agonizing years, she freed herself from Sima-Kade's embrace, and rolled on the barren earth, trying to ease her agony. At night she counted the stars, and still many people have a saying, "To count the very stars in pain."

Like many a helpless father since, Sima-Kade kept watch as his mate writhed and wailed through her birth pains. At long, long, last the Great Goddess gave birth to the first mighty nation of human beings who, as they came into being, populated the barren Ka-Lahari. As the Tree of Life watched this miracle, his own strange transformation began. He groaned as green buds burst from his writhing limbs. Clouds of seeds spewed forth and fell upon the rocky plains. Where they landed they took roots in the stubborn rock and barren sand. Soon a creeping carpet of lush living green began to overspread the Earth.

Ages seemed like moments and mighty forests rose against the mountains; great tree roots broke into the Earth in search of moisture. Clouds massed and released torrents of rain that furrowed the Earth into valleys, and nourished the green children of the Tree of Life.

Now a still stranger thing began. While Ma gave birth to human children, from Sima-Kade's roots came reptiles, crawling and slithering. Insects of all kinds came forth in clouds, humming and whining. Then from his branches, The Tree of Life bore living, snarling, howling animal fruit. They fell to the ground with a thud and scampered off into the forests in their countless millions. From great cracks in the trunk birds of all kinds came flying and waddling forth, filling the air with all their love calls; ostriches and ibises, eagles, hawks and flamingoes, and those seen no more on Earth, such as the two-headed talking Kaa-U-La birds.

The song of life began, as sounds of all kinds resounded from the forests and valleys; beasts mating and fighting, birds singing for joy in the deep forests, creature calling to creature, life where there had been no life — and overhead the smiling Sun.

The kinds of animals we see today, in all their kinds though, are but a remnant of the million children of the Tree of Life that were born in the morning of the world, because Efa, the Spirit of Extinction, has done his wicked work. (Legends tell us of three kinds of lion, of which only one, the one we see and fear today, survived.)

The Holy Ones of Kariba Gorge tell us that the first men to walk the Earth were all of one kind. They were of the same stature, and their color was red like Africa's plains. The Wise Ones of the Ba-Kongo agree; they say also that the First People had no hair on their bodies at all; all had the golden eyes of Ma. All the Wise Ones of this Dark Continent agree that the splitting of all Humanity into races: the tall black Wa-Tu-Tutsi, the brown Pygmies, or the Ba-Twa, the short yellow Bushmen of Ka-Lahari, even those lighter-skinned, long-bearded A-Rabi who raided our villages mercilessly for slaves, resulted from one great accident which occurred through the sinfulness of these First Men.

How Evil Came Into the World

Let me relate to the world now, the forbidden story that all wise ones, all witch doctors, know, but were told to keep secret from the strangers — the outsiders; for now the world is changing and there are few, even of my own tribespeople, to keep this secret lore alive. Now the barriers are broken, not by me alone, but by the world, which has demolished the walls that kept peoples apart. May the races be one again, not in body but in kinship of spirit. For this is the story of how Evil came into the world, and Evil is the legacy of all Men.

I shall open my mouth and tell you, so gather around me — "*Indaba*, my children..."

It is said that more than a thousand times ten years went by in which there was peace on Earth, in the scented valleys and over the timeless hills. Only certain beasts were permitted to kill, or to be killed by the Laws of the Great Spirit, in accordance with their victual needs. No wanton destruction of life was allowed. Men did not forge weapons against man. There was no possessiveness, no anger or hatred, no contention, no rivalry. Man breathed peace on the cheek of his brother men. Worry, guilt and sin did not exist.

People walked the Earth without fear of wild beasts, which also had no reason to fear people. Death came like a gentle sister in the night, and was greeted with a smile, for unlike our frightened selves, they knew her for life's Ultimate Friend!

But an evil star was due to rise, and humanity's undoing was nigh. It came to pass like this.

In a cool vine-screened cave, a beautiful woman whom some call *Nelesi*, but whom many more call *Kei-Lei-Si*, gave birth to the first deformed child; but this one was not deformed in flesh alone, but also in his soul. His shrunken body supported a big flat head containing one cyclopean eye. His arms and his legs were shrunken stiff and were twisted like a sun-dried impala, while his mouth was completely displaced to one side in a perpetual obscene leer. His scrawny neck was wrinkled like a starved old vulture, and he had a protruding paunch. Strings of saliva drooled from his sagging lips, and he breathed through only one nostril with a hissing sound.

The name of this very unpleasant monstrosity was *Za-Ha-Rrelle* or *Zaralleli*, The Wicked! And it was he who introduced all evil to this Earth.

Now in those days, whenever a child was born, the Mother would take it for a blessing to the talking Kaa-U-La birds, and she would also ask them to give it a name. These birds were colored like the rainbow and had six wings and two heads that were always in conversation, and they were very wise. Thus it came about that when Kei-Lei-Si brought her terrible offspring to the big old Kaa-U-La bird, who nested not far from her cave, it gave one glance and shuddered. In the deformed child the girl held, the Kaa-U-La bird could see Evil so great that it could threaten the Universe. And the other head of the Kaa-U-La bird saw what evil destiny lay beyond the veil of tomorrow if this thing were not checked.

"*Kaaaaaauk!* Oh woman, what have you there? Destroy it, kill it, without delay!" the heads screeched at her.

"What?" cried the mother in despair, "But this is my baby, my darling child! Where have you ever seen mothers kill babies?" Now Kei-Lei-Si was pleading, on her knees.

"For the sake of Mankind, and for all those as yet unborn, I beg you to destroy that thing in your arms! Though it seems but a baby, its essence is naked evil," said the one head. "It contains untold misery for the Human Race!" said the other.

But Kei-Lei-Si was possessed by the mindless love that all mothers have for their offspring, no matter how bad or good they may be. She turned and ran through the brush, clutching the child.[3]

The Kaa-U-La rarely flew in those days, preferring repose, but now this grandfather rose in pursuit, calling by telepathy for the others to join him. But Kei-Lei-Si ran like an antelope, like a gazelle, like a mother whose child is threatened.

Once only did she pause for breath on the grassy slope of a hill; and the birds descended on her like a terrible rainbow with sharp talons. But she raced for the deep forest where they could not fly, tripping and falling and bruising her legs, but on she ran. Again and again they appealed to her to surrender her child for Humanity's sake.

"A thousand times, no!" she screamed. Into a deep hole that opened before her she leaped, without a moment's thought, and disappeared from view. She fell for what seemed an eternity, and then struck the floor with a terrible shock. They had landed at the side of an underground river that passed through vast caverns beneath the Earth and for a long time lay there stunned and listening to the roaring of the water.

The evil child had twisted in the air so that he fell on his hapless mother, unharmed, while she took the blow of the fall. But she recovered slowly, and for years lived with her malignant son in the bowels of the Earth. They lived on fish, and crabs from the muddy banks, and he grew skilled in catching fish with his long fingers and slowly choking them.

Returning from a crab-hunt one day Kei-Lei-Si saw her son sitting near the fire humming a happy tune to himself. She was greatly surprised because he had never spoken a word.

"My son!" she breathed, her soul overflowing with joy, "You are singing!"

"Shhhhhh..." he said, and Kei-Lei-Si saw him staring stonily at some iron ore she had brought to the cave to strike with flint and kindle their small fires.

She froze with astonishment and then fear as she saw the iron turn soft and begin to flow under that terrible gaze. It grew and began to form itself into something. In a few heartbeats she saw two bright stalks tipped with small blood-red eyes emerge and a hungry looking mouth, already snarling at her, displaying razor-sharp teeth. Kei-Lei-Si shrieked in terror when she realized the tune her son was singing was a magical incantation that brought the lifeless iron to life. As she watched spellbound, legs like those of a grasshopper took shape — then came pairs of dragonfly wings and a rat-like shining metal tail, with a sting, a crystal sting with dark green poison!

"My son!" she cried, "What...and how...and why?"

"This," he said, to her astonishment speaking perfectly, "is one of my weapons of conquest!"

"Conquest? Conquest of what, my son?"

"Of everything — the Earth, the Sun, and the Moon!"

Now the insect-like horror was complete. Zaralleli turned his cold eye on his mother, and smiled a twisted smile.

"I want to try it out!" He gestured toward his mother with a deformed limb. "Seize her, drink your fill!"

The horror leapt upon the startled woman, seizing her with his insect-like legs.

"My son, my son, what have I done that you should do this to me? I am the woman who bore you, and brought you up!"

"I know very well who and what you are — but nobody asked you to bear me and rear me, and least of all did I."

"I saved you from the big birds who wanted to kill you, my son!"

"All that I know," said Zaralleli calmly. "It was only the instinct of a female beast, and you were obeying a natural law."

"Have mercy, my son," cried Kei-Lei-Si.

"What is this thing called mercy? You are of no use to me any more. I have now grown to full independence, and I no longer need your protection. All I need now is nourishment for my new servant, the *Tokoloshe*, to grow and reproduce its kind."[4]

From the mouth of the metallic creature protruded a long needle structure with which it pierced her chest and heart. And as it sucked it grew.

Through the mists of her last agony the mother saw her son's outrageous future; too late she appreciated her error, and knew that, after all, the talking Kaa-u-La birds were right. Her mercy had saved her child who was himself without mercy. Her dimming eyes saw the creature withdraw its probe, and it began to lay silvery eggs. "Farewell, Mother," Zaralleli said contemptuously.

Soon hundreds of *Tokoloshes* were hatched. The winged metallic beings were utterly obedient to their evil creator.

The fantastic reign of the First Chief on Earth — Zaralleli, sometimes known as *Tsareleli* or *Sareleli*, was about to burst upon the world. He was the deformed incarnation of naked evil, like a glittering poisonous flower. Oh Woe, oh woe, to all those as yet unborn!

Zaralleli the Wicked emerged from the tunnels borne aloft by a litter of four of these metal things, while all the rest of the metal Tokoloshes came swarming behind in a vast and glittering cloud, awaiting his word to enslave and to kill.

The first battle was with the two-headed talking Kaa-U-La birds. From miles away came the sacred six-winged birds, like a flying rainbow of righteousness to stem the tide of evil. A mighty aerial battle took place that lasted more than a hundred days without pause, and it was watched in fear and amazement by men and beasts.

The birds inflicted a great deal of damage, tearing and ripping with talons and beaks. But the poisonous stings of the metal things caused havoc among the attackers. In their hundreds they fell down to earth, followed to be sucked of their blood; for as fast as these metal things nourished themselves, they produced more and more of their metal kind. For each one destroyed by the Holy Birds, a thousand took its place. After a hundred days, the birds were defeated, and the survivors flew to the ends of the earth, crying, "All is lost! Woe to mankind — woe to the World."

After his victory over the Kaa-U-La birds, the deformed offspring of Kei-Lei-Si descended with his victorious hordes (the first poisonous insects) and promised the First People a new life of plenty, of luxury and peace, and limitless pleasure. At first he told them he was sent by The Great Spirit to vanquish the evil Kaa-U-La birds which had been keeping all mankind in savagery and ignorance. He told them that he would deliver them all from poverty and disease if they followed him humbly; that the world would become safe for mankind since he would exterminate all dangerous beasts. People would not have to till the land any longer, nor harvest crops, for the metallic slaves would serve them. Thus the First People fell into greed and error, blindly following the advice they received from an evil master, the great Deceiver.

Zaralleli plumbed the secret of immortality as well as domination, and when two generations of humans had passed, he ruled the most fantastic Empire the world has ever seen. It was the empire of *Amarire*, or *Murire*, of which the legends tell. People lived in shining golden huts that moved about by themselves at the whim of their inhabitants. The metallic Tokoloshes served these humans in every way. They tilled the earth and stored the grain. By Zaralleli's magic one could command the food to boil in the pot, so there was no need to gather wood or keep a fire. People could wish themselves to places so they didn't have to walk; even the vessels of food could be commanded to rise and pour their contents into mouths almost too lazy to chew.

Then the High Chief Zaralleli gave them powers to wish the food right into their stomachs — no more need they bruise the gullet with swallowing too hard. And the result was inevitable. For every unnatural power the magician bestowed, the people lost their own natural powers — of arms and legs and mouths — and they even began to feel that begetting and raising children was too much of a strain. These self-indulgent humans were losing the powers of reproduction, and still they thought their life the best the world has ever known. Soon all were sterile save the singer, the beautiful *Amarava*, she who is soon to become central to our story.

The evil tyrant-magician passed to his sterile subjects the secret of Immortality, so they could live forever under his dominion. Then he turned his mind to Secret Knowledge and Forbidden Things, those very things which the Great Spirit has forbidden us to seek. And thus, so imbued with his power was he, that he began unknowingly to sow the seeds of his own destruction.

Thinking himself the equal of the Most High, he sought to change Creation itself. He sent the Tokoloshes to seize the animals of the forest, and, crushing them into pulp, he created new forms, shaped like human beings, to be slaves and workers in his ever-expanding empire. Like kaffircorn cakes, he made thousands more of these lowly creatures, called *Bjaauni*. The legends say that they looked like giant, hairless gorillas; but, fashioned of dead flesh and blood, they were greenish brown, like rotten flesh, and emitted a putrid odor. They had no power of speech and could not think for themselves, dumbly and blindly obeying their red-skinned masters. If you asked them to drink the river Zambesi, they would drink until they burst and died. If you asked them to carry stones, they would build a mountain. But strangely, unlike their sterile masters, the Bjaauni could reproduce their kind.

One day the Tree of Life sat with his Goddess wife looking down at creation. He did not like what he saw.

"Ma," he said, "our children live selfish and useless lives, depriving existence of its very meaning. They enslave others and distort Creation itself. What kind of beings did we bring forth? They no longer even beget their kind. Perhaps we should destroy our first effort and begin all over again."

"No," said the ever-compassionate Goddess, "they have just been led astray by that evil tyrant who thinks he is a god! Let us send them a warning first!"

Sima-Kade, The Tree of Life, then ordered rain clouds to gather and cover the earth. They crowded into great thunderheads with lightning crackling about them. Dark tornadoes, like cruel and violent children, accompanied them. Then began the most frightening deluge the world had ever seen, with winds and rain and hail.

Soon the degenerate empire with its mighty glittering cities was drowning in its own offal. Many of the Tokoloshes and Bjaauni and half the human inhabitants of Amarire, helpless as they were, perished in that terrible flood.[5]

But the horrible child of Kei-le-si looked on and laughed. Suffering did not bother him — in fact it stirred his appetite for more. The warped Emperor felt no remorse for the corrupt kingdom he had built nor for any of his previous ways; in fact the tragedy vexed his cruel and inventive spirit more. He ordered giant rafts to be built that could ride the waters of the flooded earth, and on them he bade his slaves to build new cities — of gold and glittering jewels, more beautiful than the ones drowned beneath the waves. With his magic power he made an artificial sun to replace the one obscured by clouds. Then he sat back gloating, never asking, in his arrogance, if there were something wrong. Thus he came to his last and most foolish act of pride.

It was a day like others in *Amak-Habareti*, the greatest of the floating cities, which contained the lavish sanctuary of Zaralleli. The misshapen tyrant, draped in a gold kaross embossed with jewels, reclined on a couch of gold and ivory. A self-replenishing vessel of beer poured itself occasionally into his mouth, which then returned to its perpetual leer. Hundreds of his favorite nobles sat around in degenerate splendor and in order of their rank.

They were engaged in their favorite entertainment: watching Bjaauni slaves in a great silver cage disemboweling and dismembering each other, while they, the nobles, feasted and laughed. At last, only one was left, a great hulking creature named *Odu*. This brute climbed over the bodies and the limbs and stood at the bars waiting for his instructions. "Sleep," roared the Emperor, and the creature fell over unconscious, to the amusement of the Amarire nobles. "He is my favorite," said the Emperor. "He always destroys the others, the strongest of all." Zaralleli loved — in fact he feasted on — conflict, battle and pain. Whenever he could, he sowed the seeds of rivalry and envy in his nobles, and since his demise, many and many a tyrant has done the same. And whenever these terrible games of jealousy and "divide and conquer" are played, we say that the spirit of Zaralleli is still present.

Then the Evil Emperor bade his nobles come close and attend closely. He waved his hand and a great silver bowl filled with a dark fluid floated into the room. "In searching for the source of this recent disaster, which of course I have turned to my own ends, I have seen a marvellous thing. Behold!"

He stirred the fluid with his finger, and when it grew still, a fantastic scene emerged. In a garden that seemed Paradise itself, was a mighty tree embracing a beautiful woman — a silvery woman with eyes of smoldering gold, four magnificent breasts with nipples of emerald. The tyrant leered with an unnatural lust they had never seen before. "Behold!" cried the Emperor, "my enemy and my new bride. The legends tell of Sima-Kade, the Tree of Life, and the Great Goddess, Ma, mother of all the Amarire. Is she not beautiful? I intend to wrest that beautiful Goddess from that Tree by force and make her my own bride. In this way I shall assume my rightful role as Lord of Creation — Master, not only of the Universe, but of Eternity itself!"

Some of the nobles gasped with astonishment, others laughed nervously at the audacity of the Emperor's plan.

Thus it was that a sacrilegious war was commenced. Millions of giant insects of metal were created, with terrible poisonous stings, razor-like claws, and serrated teeth. The awe-struck population of Amak-Habareti saw them assemble in the city square and then suddenly vanish, as Zaralleli sent them by his magic to the World that lies beyond the River of Time, to the Spirit World that is forbidden to humankind until they leave their earthly bodies! Together, gazing into the magic bowl, they saw the ferocious army now assemble on the plains of the Spirit World.

Then they marched forward at a secret order from the demented Emperor and began to attack the Tree of Life himself. When the Tree recovered from shock at the blasphemy that was occurring, lightning flashed from his eyes, destroying legions of his attackers. But on they came, impelled by the sorcery of Zaralleli, in their thousands and tens of thousands. At last the Tree himself became weary, for he was sorely wounded by the metallic monsters, and his business was the creation of life, not destructive battle. Half the army was destroyed, but still the metal monsters marched.

Eternity wept in shame, and Zaralleli, peering in the magic bowl, shrieked with demented delight. Four of his metal slaves were ripping the Golden-eyed Goddess from the Great Tree's hold and bearing her away in triumph, while the Tree still battled with the army.

By the time Sima-Kade had destroyed the rest of the army, the four Tokoloshes with their prey had crossed the plains of the Spirit World. Then they vanished and emerged in front of Zaralleli's palace with their silvery burden.

The citizens of Amak-Habareti came by the thousands to gaze upon the Mother of Humanity in all her divine, radiant beauty. But their gaze was the gaze of vulgar curiousity. They had no reverence in their hearts, having long since lost their appreciation for Holy Things. Ma, the Mother of All, in turn, regarded them with great sadness in her liquid golden eyes: her children, fallen into this state of forgetfulness.

But now the Divine Order had been broken by blasphemy; the River of Time that separates this Earth from the World of Spirit had been violated in the service of greed and violence. Even as the people stared, and Ma gazed sadly back at them, something unforseen was happening. The radiant heat from her body was working upon them. They screamed as the skin was blistering from their bodies and their eyes were melting. They turned and ran in a vast stampede, leaving a trail of death behind them.

"My children! My children!" lamented the Goddess, "You whom I bore with such pain — doomed you are, my children!"

With these words, a mighty earthquake shook the world, and the scowling clouds lashed the heaving earth with torrents of rain and giant hailstones. Lightning crackled and fires from the underworld broke forth in fissures that overspread the Earth. The world became a boiling cauldron of molten mud and roaring steam. Whole continents vanished beneath the steaming waves, and new ones appeared from below; great plains tilted on their sides and capsized like wooden boats, forever entombing countless millions of animals and men. Great mountain ranges split asunder and howling hurricanes ravaged the steaming Earth.

The shining cities of the Amarire were swamped with boiling water and superheated steam, melting the metal and the rock.

And glittering Amak-Habareti, Zaralleli's great capitol, fared the worst. Now let me tell you what happened in its shattered streets. The order of things was overturned by the Tyrant's sacrilege, and the Bjaauni — those strange servants of the Amarire made from crushed and tortured animals — when they saw their panic-ridden overlords fleeing, felt the blissful kiss of Rebellion within their heart! Led by Odu, the Killer, they rose in their countless thousands and fell upon their masters, killing those who had so abused them, with a great delight; they knew well how to disembowel and behead, and now they did this to their helpless oppressors by the thousands. The Tokoloshes, those metallic engines of death, now released from control, ran amok destroying indiscriminately all who came within their reach as well as each other; and the skies were filled with stinging, flailing metal monsters. (And we think that some of the most annoying insects of today — the mosquitos, gnats, and stinging flies are the diminished descendents of those wicked tokoloshes.)

The evil Zaralleli witnessed all this from the safety of an indestructible shelter he had made, watching impassively as his subjects died by the millions. He remained unmoved, even when his artificial sun exploded into a million burning fragments and plunged the World into apocalyptic twilight. The insolent monster was confident of his own ability to rebuild his world again.

Ma stood sadly in the sea of blood, her eyes still pleading as her children died; If Zaralleli would relent, some might be spared; but the Tyrant merely smirked.

Suddenly an astonishing apparition appeared: a huge green giant with bloody axe! It was Odu, the killer, the last of the Bjaauni to survive the catastrophe. The smirking Emperor came forth, wishing the Goddess to see that he too could create something magnificent. It was as if all the race of Bjaauni had come together in Odu; and for the first time, Odu spoke.

"I...kill!" bellowed the giant.

"Oh yes, you do that very, very well!" laughed the Emperor; and he thought of a magnificent joke to enact before the Goddess.

"I am your God — your Creator," the demented being laughed, "and now I command you to kill yourself! KILL YOURSELF!"

The creature stood absolutely still, and his brutish gaze locked into the compelling eyes of Zaralleli master, as he understood his master's truly evil nature for the first time, and what he was being asked to do.

But the spell of control had been broken. Odu roared and seized his master's throat. Zaralleli's one eye opened wide in disbelief, then dimmed as the Bjaauni crushed his windpipe and ripped out his lungs. Thus was justice accomplished — the evil creator was destroyed at last by his own creation. And thus ended two hundred years of tyranny and miscreation![6]

Alas, but we know it to be true, that though his warped and twisted body died, Zarelleli's cruel spirit lives on, and infests humankind! Whenever people are ambitious, and love intrigue, power, domination, bloodbaths; whenever the spirit of discord arises between parent and child, between husband and wife; when bloody wars start between religions; when people intending good do evil — Zaralleli is present.

The Tree of Life witnessed all these things, as sadly as did Ma, for of all the children they had created, only one remained. Beautiful Amarava — she who was not sterile — and the strange Bjaauni,

Odu, who was created by Zaralleli, but from the bodies of animals created by Sima-Kade, the Tree of Life. So there was both good and evil in Odu.

"Spare them, oh my love," Ma said to Sima-Kade, "and they shall be the ancestors of the Second People!"

As Amak-Habareti, the last of the cities of Murire, tilted and slipped beneath the waves forever, the real sun broke through the dissolving clouds and turned the sea to molten copper.

Amarava, and the Second People

The beautiful, heavy-breasted, narrow-waisted Amarava was to become the mother of the Second People, my children; but not before many strange things befell her in the morning of the world. This red girl, destined to become a goddess, was floating on her mat at the moment that Murire was destroyed.

A horde of subhuman Bjaauni in a terrible killing mood came toward her; and the leading one, a great hulking brute whose body was covered by a thousand battle-scars, seized and would have killed her — when a voice of divine authority rang out: "Release that woman!" It was a towering silvery form, with four emerald tipped breasts, who emitted an aura of unearthly light. Odu fell immediately to the ground, and Amarava, released, also fell to the ground. She looked up at Ma in worship.

"I am *Ninavanhu-Ma*, the First Goddess, the eternal mate of the Tree of Life," said the radiant figure.

"Forgive our sacrilege," wailed Amarava, while the Bjaauni grovelled in terror.

But the celestial apparition bowed low to the startled girl. Her divine hands lifted Amarava, and she kissed the frightened human's quivering breasts and her belly.

Ma spoke kindly to Amarava, like a mother to a daughter, and with much solemnity: "Out of this city, you alone will I spare, and you shall be the mother of a new humanity which will inherit the new Earth when the waters have subsided."

Then she raised the terrified giant Bjaauni, Odu — for it was he, the executioner of the tyrant Zaralleli. "And you," she said, "spared alone from all your race, shall be the Father of Future Races."

A wave of revulsion swept through *Amarava* as she stared at the sub-human creature. "Oh no!" she wailed, "anything but that!"

But the Goddess said, "Now look, my dear, look into Eternity, and you will see why you must do as I have bidden you. And Amarava saw a race of human beings covering the Earth — living and loving and bearing children and dying, and she saw that they were her own children. Then she saw a flash of lightning, and heard a voice as faint as rumbling thunder that asked her to accept this destiny. And so it is with all human beings, that often they are asked to accept a destiny they do not desire, and they are helpless to resist. And Amarava was the first woman of the Second race to marry a bestial man, and to marry against her will — but she would not be the last.

"Goddess, First Mother, I promise to obey," she sighed. Then Ninavanhu-Ma placed Amarava's hand on her own blazing thigh, and touched her stomach and her nipples with her finger. "Take the oath again, and know that if you fail in obedience, those places where our bodies touched will cause you terrible pain!"

Amarava said, "I swear to obey!"

Then came a great fish over the troubled waters. The fish, a great shark that was to carry Odu and Amarava to a new land, was a creation of the Goddess herself; and it obediently accepted the couple on its back. "May your breasts be ever full, and your hips be ever fertile," called the Goddess in a final blessing, as the couple rode away over the billowing waves. As the last of the giant cities sank beneath the water, the fish swam through a sea strewn with the debris of a whole civilization: The Race that Died.

For many days the great fish went eastward, toward the rising sun as the seas grew calmer. At night the moon turned the waves silver, and at dawn the torrid sun reddened them, like the blood of Earth's destruction.

At last the fish nosed up the mouth of a mighty river that would bear the name *Bu-Kongo*. Amarava and Odu stood at last on solid ground. If there is one thing that the Bjaauni knew, it was hard work, and so he quickly had created a hut wherein he and Amarava could dwell. Soon after that he fashioned a canoe and implements for hunting, and then there was food aplenty for the couple. And Odu and Amarava repopulated the world with offspring.

Amarava, however, was tormented within herself; her soul was a cauldron of emotions. She knew what she had promised the Goddess, but she also knew that her ape-like, sub-human mate still filled her with revulsion. Commands from heaven warred with her own human instincts. But then a new way of thinking began to come to her. She thought, "What if an accident, something terrible, should happen to Odu?" The Goddess could not blame her for that!

She took her time and waited until Odu slept deeply. Then she nugdged a little coal from the fire until it contacted the grass walls of the hut, which began to smolder. As it roared into flame, Amarava ran from the hut — and ran and ran, for she really did not know whether she was fleeing divine wrath or her own most revolting mate. "At last!" she thought, like many a woman who has fled a brutal husband: "I'm free!"

When she paused to breathe, the glow from the burning hut left far behind, it was as dark as the underworld itself, as dark as the cave in which Zaralleli was hatched, and Amarava did not know where she was.

Amarava spent the night up in a *mopani* tree; but in the morning as she descended to gather food, her breasts and her belly began to sting as if she were bitten by scorpions. As she writhed in agony, she remembered the words of the Great Mother, and knew that in slaying Odu, she had done terrible wrong. She cried out to the skies, begging Ma for forgiveness; but the pain did not abate. She ran in a blind fury of pain until, unknowing, she was in the air, having dashed off a precipice. Then the world went dark for beautiful Amarava.

When she came to consciousness, Amarava lay in a dimly lit cave, surrounded by three creatures, each more hideous than the last. Were they frogs? crocodiles? They stood on their hind legs like men but were taller, with green protruding bellies and strange glittering eyes.

"Who are you?" she asked weakly.

"*Gorogo!*" said the leader.

The strange, intelligent Frogmen pondered all the night about what to do with the female human they had found. Their own race, they knew, was doomed to extinction, because their own females, like those of the First Race, had lost the ability to bear children. Then they decided: Gorogo should try to mate with her!

As they stood in discussion, Amarava seemed to divine their intention and took flight; but soon she was recaptured. Now, my children, you should know what we mean by "a Frog's Bride" — From the Xhosa to the land of the Baganda, "a Frog's Bride" means a forced marriage; a girl is thrashed into marrying someone she does not love. But a strange destiny was at work in the world; Amarava grew great with many eggs, which, in time, she laid; and from them came a people that some have seen as frog-like — little and yellow — the Bushmen and the Pygmies.

But soon the Frogmen were struck by disaster. In those days all men reached maturity in only a few years — for all beings matured faster in the morning of the world. Amarava awoke one day to a terrible noise — a battle was taking place, and the air was filled with dying croaks. Her offspring were now armed with bows and arrows; and the sharp arrows were tipped with a deadly paralyzing poison.

In no time the Frogmen were exterminated, and the last to fall was Gorogo, their Chief.

Imperfect man had made his return — destructive, homicidal man!

Amarava had grown to like the intelligent non-human Frogmen, and her grief welled up inside her. Her own children, a wild and brazen-eyed naked rabble, stood some distance away, while their mother cursed their precocious violence. They fled wildly into the forest as Amarava left the killing-grounds of a second race. She wandered over the earth in the deep despair of depression — of one who has seen too much wanton destruction.

Then one day she came face to face with the very creature she thought she had murdered: Odu the Bjaauni, the man made by Zaralleli. The hulking creature explained in his poor words that the Great Mother had warned him in a vision of Amarava's murderous plan; he had merely feigned sleep, escaping in time from the burning hut.

By now Amarava had had adequate time to repent of her murderous urge, and she had seen the terrible deeds of her offspring. She knew the battle with evil in the human race was only just beginning, and she had seen it in herself. As she looked at Odu, she saw no rancor, no blame, just sadness in the man-thing's eyes, as he himself knew that she found him repulsive; and knew equally well that he found her beautiful. And Amarava's heart began to soften.

Odu brought her to his kraal which he had built, and to Amarava it looked strong and beautiful compared to anything she had seen in the land of the Frogmen; and Odu himself somehow seemed less hateful. He sat her down on a lion skin, and tenderly fed her morsels of food (though in one version of the story, it is said he spanked her soundly for trying to kill him; and she accepted the spanking, because it eased her guilty conscience).

It is said that the Great Goddess herself appeared to them and now encouraged the two to live in harmony. No one should try to defy the destiny laid on them by the gods, she said, and she hoped that Amarava had learned her lesson.

Now you remember that Ninavanhu-Ma had had to marry the Sima-Kade, the Tree of Life, a great many-limbed thing, with roots and stones in his bark, whom she originally found very repulsive. Likewise Amarava had been obliged to marry Odu. My children, I think this is a very ancient theme that shows up in the European fairy tale of "Beauty and the Beast." Over the centuries the story emerged from an ancient ancient epic of the origins of humanity, that something like an angel marries something like a monster or something bestial, and this is essential to our nature. For the soul of a human being contains, as we have seen, a mixture of good and evil.

This theme belongs to the most ancient stratum of Goddess worship, and there is a ritual connected with it. You know, in Africa when a woman wished to become a priestess of the Goddess, she had to defile herself by marriage or relationship to a horrible old ogre, an old man or a woman whom she would serve. And only through this service would she come to wisdom and an understanding that there is a secret relationship between ugliness and beauty;

inside the light is darkness and inside the darkness light. If she wished to be a servant of the Great Earth Mother, she had to meet the three aspects of the Goddess: the Beautiful Maiden, the Matron, and the Old Hag.

The Childhood of the Second People

The legends tell us that Amarava, the immortal, lived happily with Odu for one hundred thousands years, and presented him with five-thousand sturdy sons and daughters. Soon their grandchildren numbered twice ten-million souls. Now some of these Second People were black as a much-used pot; some were brown, or yellow-brown, some were tall as a young sapling tree, others as short as the sage-brush. Some were as thin as the bullrush reeds, and some were fatter than a hippopotamus, even fatter than me! They were wise and foolish, brave and cowardly, pleasant and evil-tempered, resembling present day humanity in all its bewildering variety, as unlike each other as the First People had been alike. And now humanity is a very diverse pageant indeed, as any city dweller can tell you.

Odu and Amarava are called the *Mamaravi*, the Mothers of all humanity. They tried to be the wisest parents and elders possible to their children and grandchildren. But finally, even they, the last of the immortals, began to grow tired of life. One night when the millions of their descendants slept secure in their beds, Odu crept into the sullen darkness and began to travel eastward on a journey that was to last a hundred days. At last he reached the snow-capped but still active volcano, Kilima-Njaro. When Odu, the giant creature of most humble origin — he who had outlived many of his own children — got to the crater, he contemplated with both sadness and joy the bowl of bubbling lava he had chosen for a grave. Then with a prayer to the Great Goddess and the Tree of Life on his lips, he dived into it, and found at last the rest his soul craved.

In her lonely hut far away in the West, Amarava sat up with a pang in the dark. Her heart told her of the death of the strange husband she had come to love. Seizing a bronze dagger, the immortal woman attempted her own suicide. But her grandchildren, *Zumangwe* the strong Hunter, and *Marimba* the beautiful Singer, the first Bantu poetess, from whom Tribal singers claim descent, prevented her.

"You are the star that lights our way along the path of life," they told her. "Please do not remove yourself from us or we will lose our way!" But the wounded, grief-stricken Amarava ran away from the village compound, out into the brush.

It is said that thousands of trackers, her children and grandchildren, pursued Amarava, led by Zumangwe and Marimba; and they pursued her for months before they made a startling discovery: a monster also pursued the Ancestress.

At last a great confrontation took place, as the monster cornered Amarava on the mudbank of a great river, and the grandchildren came up but were separated by water from what was taking place. They were astonished as well as horrified when the scaly creature spoke to Amarava in a terrible voice.

"Now, you are brought to justice at last, and you will be relieved of your horrible burden!" He clutched Amarava in his great claws, but did not harm her, only held her.

Then the monster turned and addressed the people standing there in wonder, "You should learn to base your judgements on more than appearances; now see the truth that underlies them, see what has inhabited your beloved ancestress!"

Even now Amarava was transforming. Her color changed from red to gold, her breasts sprouted udders, and her hands turned to terrible claws. A lion's tail curled from her backside, and it lashed angrily as the astonished people stared.

"The Spirit of Evil, who long ago incarnated as Zaralleli, and now is called *Watamaraka*, has been with Amarava for a long time, since the early days. You saw, but did not understand her uneven temperament — how sometimes she seemed the most beautiful of mothers, but at other times was a terrible demoness!"

Marimba and Zumangwe and all the people nodded dumbly. "This then is the explanation. I am the sacred messenger of Ninavanhu-Ma."

The demoness, for so she now appeared, was writhing, spitting, and cursing at all of humanity, in the grasp of the monster-messenger. Then suddenly, both of them vanished in an unearthly flame.

And that is why, oh my children, we, who are the descendents of Amarava, have in us something wonderful and something terrible — a soul that is split in the middle between evil and good and are always in conflict. Amarava had carried with her some of the evil of the First People, and it was present, but less potent, in the Second People.

Zumangwe and his followers founded, near that place, the first village in the country of *Tanga-Nyika*. But they were ashamed at the revelation concerning their ancestress and agreed to keep the knowledge secret, so that the name of the ancestress of humanity should be honored. And so it is that some people to this day are ignorant of this story and do not know that to be human is to hover between good and evil. If you doubt this secret, oh my children, do not take the word of old Mutwa for it — just observe your neighbors, and see how they behave; see if there is a struggle in their souls. And most of all, oh my children, observe yourselves, and see if a single day passes in which your own soul is free, blissfully free, from all conflict.

Now the creature brought Amarava to Ninavanhu-Ma; and there the Great Goddess, who ever loved Amarava as a beloved daughter, removed Watamaraka from her soul and cast the Spirit of Evil into outer darkness. And great was the healing of Amarava, whose original nature shone forth then, as red-gold as the Sun, and she no more carried that terrible darkness within her. All who beheld her felt reverence for her, and so she was, indeed, transformed into a goddess; and Ninavanhu-Ma bade the gods take her up to the constellation called "The Net of the Heavens," and she became an immortal among the stars. She is still worshipped in the Ka-Lahari, and in Natal, and among the Swazis. We call these stars among which she dwells, "the stars of Amarava." One of the brightest of these stars is the one that the white people call "Alpha Centauri."

In our lore, we say that all creatures are connected in a great web of life and of evolution; and that from the different human races come some of the greatest of the spirits of the universe: the *Abangafi Bakafi*, "The Undying ones of Eternity." It is the task of these Undying ones to make us understand the deepest things of the Spirit, and they are the ones that guide human destiny and the destinies of other races of the stars. It is they who remember what must remain even when this world has passed away. They belong to that region, the Stars of Amarava, and she is the goddess who guides that process, for they are human beings from whom, like Amarava herself, all traces of evil have been removed, or have been vanquished; and so they are fitted to the great task of guiding all of our souls, still caught between good and evil.

When the white missionaries first came among the traditional people of Southern Africa, we thought that the Jesus Christ of whom they spoke so often must have been one of the Abangafi Bakafi, for he seemed to be a great holy one who was guiding all of humanity. But the white ones were not interested in our story; they just wanted us to learn theirs. Their Jesus Christ was all that they knew, and they did not care if he belonged to the Undying Ones or not. They thought that he must be the only one that guides the destiny of human beings of this Earth. But maybe if the Christians could see that their Christ is but one of many beings of wisdom and of light, the Buddhas and the Mohammeds, who have guided and do guide humanity, their religion could find its way to more kindness and humility than it now has, and the different religions could live together in brotherhood. I think it is so!

As for me, a very strange part of my life concerns Amarava. In my youth I had not really known very much about her; but in my dreams and in my visions was a figure who kept appearing to me — a beautiful woman with a red skin and greenish hair. I didn't know what to do, and I wanted this woman to stop bothering me and go away. But I never told anyone about it. I was praying to be released from these disturbing visions. Then, to my astonishment, a man from Australia, a Mr. Crowley, showed up in my life. He had been contacted by a psychic woman from the "Outback" of Australia. In her own visions, a woman with red skin and green hair had been appearing, a woman like a goddess, who called herself "Amarava." This woman told her to send word to a man named "Mutwa" in Southern Africa, and gave him some idea how to find me.

I was astonished when this Mr. Crowley came to me, but even more so when he told me what his message was: to stop denying my visions. How could this woman in the outback of Australia have known that I was having these visions of a woman with red skin and green hair, and that I should open myself to them?

Of course, my life changed when I opened myself to my own visions, and now Amarava is one of the most important figures in my inner life. It is she who has been telling me to transmit these secret teachings, the legends and mythology of the Zulu people, to the rest of the world, so that they may not wither away, and so that all of humanity may learn of them. And so, this book is dedicated to Amarava foremost; and may she bless the transmission of her story beyond Africa, so that all Men and Women may learn from it. Indaba, my children!

3
Of Goddesses and Gods

My children, in Africa we find many stories which seem at first glance rather childish and primitive but which on closer examination are revealed to hide mind-boggling facts about the depth of the knowledge our forefathers possessed. It is quite common for us arrogant modern people to look upon our remote ancestors as having been simple minded, unthinking, primitive, half-naked children of nature, who lived by hunting and gathering, who dragged their women into their caves by force and who were always carrying a heavy club upon their shoulders. We are therefore surprised many times when these long forgotten people reveal in stories wisdom that they have handed down to us over the missed centuries. The fact is that in many respects they were wiser than we are and possessed knowledge regarding things of which we are only now becoming aware.

In this chapter I will tell stories of the goddesses and gods; and you know, for our tradition, the goddesses are often as great as or greater than the gods, because they come first, in the same way that all human beings, male and female, come from mothers. We begin with a tale that has many variations in other cultures around the world, I am told; but our African version is very old, and very beautiful in its own way.

The Four Winds of the Goddess

One day the Great Mother Goddess looked upon the Earth and found that human beings were abusing every bit of knowledge that she had given them. She had given them metals and they were using them to make spears — to kill other human beings. She had given them fire, and they were using it to burn other people's villages. She had given them grains and they were making beer so that there was drunkenness and fighting all over the world. And her great heart filled with sadness at the ways of her children, though she loved them still.

And then the Great Mother knew that she had made a mistake by creating human beings and therefore that soon she would be put on trial by the Seven Judges of Eternity, the *Abakulu*, as they are called.

Now these Seven Judges of Eternity peer into the visible universe from a space outside — they do not enter into it; and they are so austere and terrible that even the gods tremble before them. So when the Great Mother Goddess was brought into their presence, even she felt fear in the depths of her ancient soul.

And the Abakulu frowned at the Great Mother: "Oh, Imperfect One," they said, "you have created an imperfect species; as we knew you would — and so be it. You, being who you are, could not do otherwise! But that does not pardon you from our sentence. You must serve a penance in the Underworld, where lives your sister, the Goddess of Darkness, *Nomhoyi*."

"Oh, not that!" begged the Goddess, "her ways are pitiless and unrelenting!" But the judges were not inclined to be merciful.

She who was beautiful, who loved the Earth and the sunlight and the air and the trees and the sweet song of the birds, was taken and bound and blindfolded and brought down, down, down through dark and damp corridors that seemed endless, twisting and turning until it seemed that the whole mass of the Earth lay above her head, into the most forbidding realm of Nomhoyi, her dark sister.

Oh, Nomhoyi was pleased indeed to receive her new guest, for she had long languished in hatred and envy of her bright sister, who had brought into being a world far more beautiful than her own and who was her opposite in every way — oh, yes, she would make her sister welcome, all right!

Where the Great Earth Mother was generous, Nomhoyi was stingy; where she was loving, Nomhoyi hated; where the Earth Mother created boundlessly, and all her children loved her, the Underworld Goddess had a population of dark minions who served her in hatred and fear.

There in the wailing darkness, the Great Earth Mother was stripped and cruelly tortured by dark Nomhoyi.[1] But Nomhoyi did not torture her body alone. Oh no! her cruelty far exceeded that! Her bright sister's soul suffered the greatest tortures. With glee the Underworld Goddess brought forth one of her most loathsome servants — a foul monster, ugly without and within, whose stench was terrible and whose body was repulsive even in the darkly glowing light of the underworld.

"This is your new husband!" smiled Nomhoyi wickedly; and then and there conducted a wedding ceremony, while the horrid creatures of the darkness leered with knowing smiles. After the ceremony the goddess was carried off by this monster and laid upon his noisome wedding bed, and had to endure his most intimate caresses and his slimy loving kisses.

Then the goddess was forced to wait upon his every whim, like the lowliest of servants. For three months the goddess endured this torture, until her soul became as sick and weak as her body, and she longed for nothing more than death. But now a strange and terrible thing began in the world above, for the world that the Great Earth Mother loved and that she had left, itself became sick! First, all of the green things began to wither and to perish; the grasses were blighted, and the leaves fell from the trees, even the lowly mosses and lichens parched and died. Then all of the animals and humans sickened in turn and began to die; terrible plagues began to scour the Earth. The world was rapidly becoming a desert!

Then a great convocation of all living things (who were not too sick to attend) was called. The beasts all whined and howled for sadness, their heads drooped, their once glossy coats were dull and tattered, and those that could weep, wept in their way, as they remembered how they loved their Mother and how much they missed her bountiful presence. And they spoke, whining and growling and bellowing to each other, about what they should do; for if they did nothing, they would all soon be dead.

But then an astonishing thing happened, for the birds of the world — all the eagles and hawks and all the vultures and ospreys, but also all the sparrows and the many nameless songbirds (for they are all the Mother's children) — came together and made a great prayer by flying across the sky with their many thousands and millions of wings. And as they prayed, flying back and forth and then in circles, they created, with the motion of their wings, four great winds.

Now the four great winds — the ones that we call tornadoes nowadays — began dancing across the lands, as whirlwinds do, humming and roaring and immensely powerful, and they swept up trees and houses and stones, and towered and thundered across the landscape until they came, humming and roaring, to the very entrance to the Underworld.

Now even dark and terrible Nomhoyi was frightened by the appearance of these tornadoes, and she sent her servants to deter them, to keep them away; but those servants were snatched up like dark damp leaves by a tempest, and whirled around and dashed against the rocks until they perished. Then the four great whirlwinds wrenched loose the gates to the Underworld, and, without even asking permission, entered dark Nomhoyi's realm.

There was a shrieking in the tunnels of the underworld such as had never been heard before, as all the tubes and chambers in which the creatures of the underworld dwelt began to howl like a great organ played by an insane organist. The very rocks and minerals began to vibrate powerfully with the terrible noise. Nomhoyi covered her ears, at this thing that had never happened before; fresh air from the upper world blew into her domain. Air that had been still and dank for a thousand years now whirled in gusts, beating against the stones of the underworld.

This whirling, whistling invasion was something dark Nomhoyi had never expected, and She who was Fear Itself became frightened. She, the torturer, now was tortured by those four winds of irresistable dancing power! These whirlwinds, like living things, knew their mission: they seized the Earth Mother in an embrace most tender for such terrifying energies; Ma felt like she was carried on a zephyr, a gentle sweet summer breeze, in the heart of the whirlwind, while the outer cone shrieked like a demented demon of the upper air.

And so they bore her, whose essence is beauty and light, up through the endless tunnels and corridors. But, being winds, they were full of dust and sand, since that was their nature; and the Goddess became thirsty — and then thirstier. She had not tasted water for so long. At last, overcome by thirst, she asked to be set down so that she could drink a little — just a little — of the Water of the Underworld. This she should not have done, for it is a rule of all Eternity that whosoever drinks of the Water of the Underworld, now should have to return there until the end of time.[2]

But the four great whirlwinds carried the Earth Mother back to the surface of the Earth, and it was good. When their job was done, they dissipated into fast-growing clouds. And all creatures sighed with relief as the rains began to fall and cleanse the Earth of its blighting. And the streams and freshets flowed, and then the mighty rivers carried the water to the ocean; and so the Earth became green again. And the Great Earth Mother stood in that cleansing rain, and the water ran down her hair and her cheeks and all over her body, cleansing her of the taint of the Underworld; and she drank her fill of the fresh clean water, and knew happiness again.

And the birds of the air dived and swooped for sheer joy all around the Great Earth Mother, and gave forth their cries; and she laughed and blessed the children who had saved her.

But now, for a portion of every year, the Earth Mother sadly withdraws from her creation, and once again takes weary steps down and down into the Underworld. And when She is gone, all of creation weeps and slumbers until She returns again to bless the World with Her presence; and so it will be until the end of Eternity.

Now the Earth Mother is really three goddesses in one, my children; in one aspect she is a beautiful maiden, in another aspect she is the great fat queen mother, in her third aspect she herself is Nomhoyi, the ugly old evil goddess who dwells under the Earth and represents death and decay.

The first name of the Goddess which applies when she is a maiden — a beautiful girl — is *Nomkumbulwana*. This is her name when she is the beautiful maiden who personifies the dawn. As the

Great Earth Mother, the Queen Mother of creation, she is known as *Namubunde*. As the ugly old queen of decay and death she is *Nomhoyi*.

People used to speak of gods and to give them shape, all the better to love them, all the better to respect them. For many many centuries the black people of Africa have believed that the Earth was a woman, a living, merciful entity, a Great Mother who allowed us to dig deep into her sacred flesh in search of minerals that ensured our survival in this world. And so intense became this belief over the centuries, that the people of Africa used to do something the likes of which was never done in other countries on earth before. After the people of Africa had dug a mine and worked that mine for several decades, when the mineral they had been digging for was exhausted, the African people used to undertake the great task of refilling that mine back again. It was a process that took even longer than the digging of that mine, because not only had each tunnel to be filled, but the main shaft too had to be filled with material. This is why, when the prospectors of the last century arrived in many parts of South Africa, they found that nearly all the ancient mines that had been worked by black people had been sealed afterwards. It happens because of this belief that the Earth is a gigantic woman whose wounds have to be healed and whose skirts have to be arranged after each outrage by human beings.

In fact, let me in passing tell you about something. It is this: You've often heard that in the mines in many parts of South Africa terrible fights often breakout between miners of different tribes. I have been a miner myself and I know that those fights are due to a deep-rooted feeling of guilt, not to tribal animosity. Because each black miner who goes underground has deep within his mind a feeling that he is committing a sacrilege. He feels guilty of rape, of incest, because he, being a man, should really not be allowed to enter the biggest woman of all which is the Earth. This is why in African tradition most of the mining was done by barren women, because only women should injure the greatest woman of all.

This belief, that the Earth is in the shape of a woman, caused our people to take very very great care of the enviroment around them. In fact, the first conservationists of wild animals in Africa were black people, because each tribe had its custom, its totem, and the totem was usually an animal of some kind roaming around in the bush. And if your tribe for instance had the zebra for its totem, you were not allowed to harm a zebra anywhere where you found it. So the zebras were automatically protected in your land. So modern people should learn from the ancients, that all life is sacred.

How the Birds Saved the Earth

Now here is another story, my children, of how the birds, who are revered in Africa, saved the Earth in a time of terrible blight; and it is a story whose implications are amazing!

The story is this. In faraway days, long before human beings appeared upon the face of this planet, the birds and the animals were the lords and masters of creation. They were the rulers of the world, and the gods had given them the power of speech, a power that we are told they lost when human beings suddenly appeared on the face of the globe.

It is said that for many years there had been drought in the land. The forests were dead, the rivers dry, the tall mountains devoid of snow; the grass was brittle, sand-blasted and dead under foot, and hot winds, that made the drought even worse, blew across the face of the planet. The animals and the birds had forgotten how beautiful a rainy day felt, for the drought had persisted for generations. Animals had been born, grown old and died without ever having felt a raindrop upon their fur. Birds had been hatched, grown old and perished without ever having smelled the beautiful scent of rain falling upon the parched forests and upon the windblown plains of the sandblasted land.

It is said that this situation continued for so long that eventually, in one part of the land, the chieftain of all the birds called a meeting. He raised his voice and sent forth a hoarse cry and he said, "I, the fearless vulture, emperor of all the birds, call this great meeting. I call upon everything that has feathers and wings to attend this meeting, on pain of death."

It is said that the birds gathered upon the slopes of the great mountain Kilima-Njaro in their thousands, and when the birds had assembled and the skies were dark with them, the great vulture stood up and raised his voice above the hubbub of the multitude. He said, "The drought has persisted for so long upon this Earth that now I feel that desperate measures are called for. We the birds must send an emissary to the Land of the Gods far far beyond the sky, and this emissary must go and tell the Great Lord of the Heavens our desperate need: that the world needs rain or else all life upon its face shall perish.

"I call upon you, oh wisest of the birds, I call upon you oh owl that sees through the deepest darkness. Stand forward and tell us how we the birds might be able to reach the land of the gods."

The owl, who is known for his wisdom about things that are hidden from other eyes, stood up in the meeting and swiveled his head this way and that, beholding all the birds with his great golden eyes. He said, "Oh vulture, Emperor of the Birds, this is what I propose..." and the owl told his plan before the vast assembly of birds.

After the vulture had heard the details of the plan, he turned them over in his mind and found no fault with them; and then, because he was the Emperor with whom no one was allowed to argue, he said, "I, the Lord of all the Birds, decree that it must be as the owl has spoken! You, fish-eagle, step forward." A great white-headed, golden-bodied fish-eagle waddled forward and stood before the vulture, king of the birds. "Extend your wings," commanded the emperor. The fish-eagle did as commanded.

"Dove, pigeon of the wilds, come out of hiding," cried the vulture. "Come out of hiding and climb on top of the back of the fish-eagle and also extend your wings." The dove did as commanded; he climbed onto the back of the fish-eagle, opened his wings and silently waited for the next command. Then the vulture said, "Sparrow," and out of the assemble of the birds there emerged a sparrow. The vulture said, "Sparrow, get on top of the shoulders of the pigeon and extend your wings." The sparrow jumped to obey. He climbed on top of the pigeon and extended his wings, and the vulture said, "In the name of all the birds and in the name of the Great Earth Mother and of the Sky Father I command you three birds — one riding on top of the back of the other one — to fly now and go and reach the Land of the Gods. Go!"

The fish-eagle took off, his mighty wings beating the air. On his back rode the dove on whose back in turn rode the sparrow. Up, up, up into the sky soared the three birds. Up beyond the clouds and far far above them into the deep darkness of the void beyond the clouds. The birds flew and flew and flew.

The eagle flew until he felt his great wings weakening and then he said to the dove, "Carry on oh pigeon, carry on with the flight! I can no longer fly, I am exhausted."

So, with the sparrow on his back, the pigeon lept off the eagle's shoulders. While the eagle dived towards the earth far below, his task performed.

The pigeon beat the air valiantly, bearing the sparrow on his back. Up, up, up he went and then he made the mistake of looking down at the earth far below, and his sharp eyes saw something that tore his soul in two. Down there upon a tree far far below, he saw his wife of many years being unfaithful with another pigeon; and such was the shock that the pigeon's heart stopped, his wings folded and he plummeted to the ground, dead long before he struck the Earth.

It was the sparrow that carried on with the last stage of the flight. It was the sparrow that reached the great village of the Father of the Sky. It was the sparrow that stood at the feet of the great Sky Father and appealed to him to bring down rain upon the rain-hungry Earth.

It turned out that the great God of the Sky had been asleep all these many years and in his sleep he had allowed the clouds to go away from the heavens and the rain not to fall at all. When the great god realized what had happened to the Earth, he blew a trumpet and summoned all the clouds from the edges of the world. The clouds gathered and a great rain fell — a rain that was to last for many days and many nights.

The world recovered and became green once more, while the sparrow returned home to his wife and children and to the acclaim and the gratitude of the other birds. It is said that after this the world never again knew a drought such as the one that had prompted the birds to take this desperate measure of sending a direct emissary to the great God of the Skies.

Even today some tribes in Southern Africa honor the sparrow and will never injure it, and if they find it caught in a snare, they rescue it, mend its injuries, and send it on its way because of this beautiful story of how the birds flew on each other's shoulders to call upon the great god to bring down rain.

This is the story, oh wise ones, of lands far away. It sounds a simple and childish story, but is it? Let me ask you, there was a time when writers of books and great scientists believed that if human beings wanted to travel to the moon and the nearer planets in future years all they would need would be some fantastic spacecraft with jet pipes blazing and curved wings slicing through the air. They believed that such a spacecraft could take off, fly to its destination and return on its own, but harsh reality has taught them otherwise in the course of time.

But now we have found a solution which is like the owl's: We have found that if people want to get into space, they require a three-stage or even a four-stage rocket to do so. One of the most efficient means of reaching outer space these days is what is called a "space shuttle," which consists of a spacecraft, not unlike a bird in shape, which rides upon huge tanks filled with fuel as it leaves the earth assisted by great boosters. These tanks fall away once their fuel is expended and the spacecraft carries on and reaches its destination in space. Then it turns around and returns on its own, this time to land safely on the ground.

Now my question is this — all seekers of the truth — how did our forefathers know that deep space was so far away that in order to reach it from the Earth you need three vehicles riding on each other's shoulders? How did our forefathers know that you need a three-stage contraption in order to reach outer space? There are many stories of this sort in Africa, stories that prove that our forefathers were greater and far wiser than we are willing acknowledge.

Ngungi, the Crippled Smith of the Gods

This the story of the god with one leg, *Ngungi*, who is also the blacksmith of the gods and the God of Iron. Now Ngungi is a maimed god, for in addition to being lame, he also has only one eye. But this strange impaired being is also a great creator who fashions palaces and chariots and works of art and weapons and utensils and all kinds of things for the gods.

Ngungi's mother was *Nananana*, the beautiful goddess who was the mistress (but not the wife) of God the Father. Unknown to the Great Earth Mother, God the Father would go out and make love to Nananana in secret places. This is why the God of Iron was born in a swamp — the Okazango swamps in Botswana, South Africa. So one of Ngungi's other names is *Okazango*.

When she learned of this love affair, the Great Earth Mother wanted to kill Nananana for falling in love with God the Father, and so she was hiding amongst the reeds when she gave birth to Ngungi. But Nananana discerned the presence of the Mother-Goddess and just barely escaped with her life. Poor little Ngungi remained in the swamp and probably would have perished, but for the fact that he was found by hippopotamuses, and those great swamp-dwelling beasts were kind to him and raised him, so he always had an affection for hippopotamuses.

When Ngungi was a boy, he was very stupid; and God the Father took pity on his little bastard child. He sent him to look for knowledge, because whether he found it or not, the journey would test the child. Ngungi travelled far and wide and had many adventures; and then he found the Old Man of the Sea. Now that Old Man, who has scales like a fish, and who always lives near a body of water, is full of knowlege and wisdom. He taught Ngungi many things, including how to be a good blacksmith, for which he expected a bountiful payment of many white cattle (which were the clouds). But when the education was finished, the young god found he could not pay. The Old Man of the Sea said, "You said you would pay me with many white cattle! Where are those cattle?"

Ngungi went in a great hurry to find the cattle of the sky, but the sky was empty, and nothing but the invisible wind, blowing strongly, was present. Ngungi returned to the Old Man in great fear.

"Aiiee, oh Great one," Ngungi said, "The wind has taken them away!"

And then the Old Man of the Sea grew angry. He said to the young god, "I am going to eat your left eye, like a fruit, as a payment for your education!" And he seized the terrified Ngungi and scooped out his eye and devoured it with a hideous satisfaction. And so when Ngungi returned to his father, he had only one eye. And that is why to this day blacksmiths have a tatoo made out of white clay on their foreheads, to show that they were the servants of the God with One Eye.

And now I will tell you how Ngungi lost his leg. After his encounter with the Old Man of the Sea, Ngungi was no longer stupid, and he had learned to make all manner of things. First he made a hammer for himself, and this enabled him to make a number of other beautiful things for the gods.

But one day the jealous Crocodile of Darkness conceived a desire to have Ngungi's hammer, with which he made so many beautiful things. One night, for he could see in the dark, he crept in and stole Ngungi's hammer and carried it off to his shadowy, polluted lair.

Ngungi went to look for the hammer, and finally learned who had taken it. He sent word to the Crocodile, but that mighty and arrogant creature refused to give it back. Then Ngungi became angry and went to confront the Crocodile in his dark lair. An enormous battle took place then, in which Ngungi killed the crocodile, but it bit off his right foot and part of his leg. Ngungi returned to the Land of the Gods very, very angry.

Then God the Father looked for a replacement for the young god's leg, but he couldn't find one at that moment. So he set out on a search mission. Then he found the foot of a buffalo and thought that it would suit, so he sewed that onto the leg of his son. To this day Ngungi is depicted as having one normal foot and one foot of a buffalo, and the buffalo foot is shorter than the normal foot, so he is lame, and he is angry, always angry.[3]

The Gift of the Magic Flower

My children, the short story that you are about to hear now is a story with a moral in it, and the moral is that if God blesses you with wealth, if one day you become a rich person and no longer know the pangs of hunger in your belly and the chill nakedness of poverty, oh remember, remember, never to lose that which is beautiful within you. Do not allow earthly wealth to take away your humanity. Do not allow riches to corrupt you.

This is a story that my father told me at one time, a story that I in turn have told to my children and grandchildren and which now I am telling to you.

It is said that somewhere in Africa there lived a man who was very poor, a man whose children walked about naked in the light of the sun, a man who very often found that in his home there was not a single scrap of food with which to feed his wife and sons and daughters.

Like many poor people, this man was a good man, and he never ceased praying to God to come to his rescue — to make him wealthy and able to support his family properly. As the years went by, the man's prayers became more and more bitter as anger against the Almighty mounted in his heart. The man blamed God for his poverty. He called God cruel and uncaring. He called God a monster who created things and then abandoned them. But somewhere in some great place, unseen by human eyes, the All Highest was listening to the prayers of this man.

Then one day, while the man was out in the bush gathering wood to warm his home, he happened to pass by the bottom of a tall cliff, a mighty rock face that towered to the very skies; and at the bottom of this cliff his attention was caught by a beautiful flower, a colorful flower of a kind he had never seen before. He was a man who loved all growing things, and immediately this flower attracted him, and as he stood looking down at the flower, his bundle of wood resting upon his shoulder, he heard a voice saying to him, "Put down the wood you are carrying, oh man, and pluck this flower which is like no flower you have ever seen before."

The man placed his bundle of wood upon the ground and reached out for the flower and then he hesitated. He said to himself, "The voice says that I should pluck this flower, but if I should do so, then I will never see such beauty again because it will not be long before the flower will fade in my hand and become as nothing."

"Do not concern yourself with that, oh man," said the voice. "Pluck the flower out of the ground and do as you are told."

Reluctantly the poor man plucked the flower and held it in his hand. Then the voice said, "Strike the rock face, oh man, with the flower that you hold in your hand. Strike it three times."

And the man did that, gently striking the stone face of the cliff with the flower, and to his great surprise a huge portal opened in the side of the cliff. Inside the door were cattle, sheep and goats, ornaments of copper and gold — all the wealth that a man of Africa could dream of — wealth such as he had never thought to see.

The voice said, "Go inside, oh man, and drive out the cattle — the sheep and the goats — for they are yours. Also, remove the ornaments and the other treasures that lie within the cave, for they have been given to you, but do not, in removing these things, forget the flower that is like no flower on earth."

The man drove out the fat cattle — the hairy goats and the woolly sheep. He drove out the chickens and he scooped the gold and copper and silver ornaments and placed them under a tree. And as he scooped out the last of the ornaments, he inadvertently left the flower that was like no flower upon a stone, a rock, like an altar which stood in the center of the great cavern which had been opened to him, and he did not remember this flower until the magic door had closed behind him.

Then he said, "It does not matter. The greatest wealth on all Earth is now mine. I have forgotten the flower that was like no other flower, but I have gained great wealth. I shall go home and call my sons and daughters and they shall assist me in bringing this treasure to the safety of my home. I am wealthy beyond my wildest dreams." And he ran home to his family and he told them of what had happened and the children followed him to the bush where he said the treasure was, but when they came there they found nothing but piles of lifeless rocks where the cattle should have been and heaps of dried twigs and other rubbish where he had said the ornaments had been piled.

"But father, there is no treasure here," said his first-born son. "This is all rubbish."

The children turned away from their parent, who now had all the appearance of a hopelessly mad human being. They turned away and deserted him, and he was left there alone in the bush mad, hopelessly mad, to the ending of all his earthly days.

Remember, my children, do not curse the Almighty when you pray to him for something, nor revile the Earth when you ask her for any form of assistance; and above all — as I have said before — if God gives you a little wealth, never never, lose the good that is in you, the real humanity that lies within your heart.

Yes, my children, Africa is one great story. Very often she is a story that tells a story, a story within a story. In Africa a story is a very important thing, a means of instruction, a means of enlightenment, a means of showing the deepest friendship to one's fellow human beings. It is no surprise and no coincidence that some of Africa's greatest kings and queens were at the same time accomplished storytellers and orators. Did not our people say that the story is the footpath that leads you into the depths of a fellow human being's heart? It is indeed so. Indaba!

Somanga, *the Sun God, above doorway to ceremonial hut built by Credo in* Bophutatswana

4
Tales of the Trickster

Since the inception of the human race on this world (or any other where man may have had his origin), people have always tended to form things into definite shapes. Of something like the universe, of such a shapeless vastness, a person living in a cave, a person wearing skins, cannot even remotely conceive. But take that idea and give it the shape of a dark, sleeping goddess with a body of ice, floating in the vastness of nothing, then you have got something that appeals to the depths of that person's mind. He or she is now able to see the universe in his or her mind's eye as a huge slumbering goddess who is busy dreaming of you and me and other things on this and on other worlds.

In this chapter I recount just a few of the tales of that scurrilous fellow, *Kintu*, a being loved not only by children, but by people of all ages. You see, the wise among us know that creation is not perfect, and that we all are prone to mistakes; therefore a hero who is also a fool is very much loved by all the people, because we can find ourselves in him. And this is the kind of a fellow Kintu is. These stories go on and on, and nobody ever wants them to stop, unless their sides are splitting from laughter, such are his antics.

I know there are tricksters in other traditions around the world, too, for I have heard some of the stories of those tricksters. In this first story is also another trickster, *Mpungushe*, the jackal, who is very much like that doggy person, the coyote, among our red brothers, the Indian peoples of North America. He is an eater of dung, but his nose is nonetheless keen, and he can find trails that are invisible to us.

Along with his equivalent, who is called, *Anansi*, the spider, who weaves the very web of creation but still is full of many tricks, we find tales of the trickster Kintu all over southern and central Africa. In the language of the Inguini people he is called *Ntu*. Many tribes believe that this Kintu, this funny hero, was our first ancestor, our first king and throughout African continent the name of Kintu is remembered with amusement.

The Theft of Fire

The law of our forefathers governing the sacred art of storytelling is that every story should be introduced with a song. The song says, "Here is the story, come hear the story, *I am a story*, my children!"

And now my little ones, come and listen to the beautiful and yet sad story of *Mpungushe*, the jackal. How Mpungushe stole fire from the village of the great gods in order to warm the cave of the first man and the first woman upon this Earth. The name Mpungushe is Zulu for jackal.[1]

Come, my children, and hear how the jackal risked his life and endured many dangers to obtain fire from heaven, so that the first parents of the human race, Kintu and Mamaravi, might survive. It is said that had the jackal not stolen fire for us from the skies, there would be no human race on Earth these days. It is said that this incident took place in those faraway days when creation was young, when the countless stars were like millions and millions of smiling babies shedding their tiny lights, and when the Sun was still a young being, sending his life-giving rays like unseen arrows to warm the bosom of the Earth. At that time we are told the Earth was a young bride, newly married to the Lord of Day.

The Sun and the Earth had a daughter, a round-faced, fat, little virgin who was called the Moon. The Moon was a cunning little girl in that she often stole her father's light in order to illuminate her mother's house, especially when she went inside that house, or when she plaited her mother's green hair. This stealing of the light of the Sun by the Moon often caused a lot of quarreling between the Sun and the Earth in their house, because, like all young married couples, the Sun and the Earth had their bright moments as well as their dark moments — their bright moments when they made love pas-sionately, causing the blue skies to smile and the clouds to dance, and their dark moments when they quarreled and fought and screamed at each other and storm clouds overspread the Earth; and we are told that very often the Moon was the cause of all this domestic squabbling.

It is said that one day, while the Sun was sitting outside his great golden hut, his stomach was full of good beer and well-cooked meat. He was drowsy, but just as he was about to fall asleep, he heard voices talking inside his hut. The voices were those of the Moon and her mother the Earth. The Moon was saying to the Earth, "Oh mother, will you look outside at father. See how he sits upon that stool snoring, fat and lazy and doing nothing. He never helps you with the household chores. You and I, Mother, have to work our hands to the bone to keep him fed, and all he does, is to emit that light from around his head day after day after day after day. Does he catch fish for us? No. Does he hunt for us? No! What good is our father, Mother Earth?"

The Earth, who also had reason to be angry with the Sun, said to her daughter, "Oh, my daughter, do not talk to me about that fat lazy one out there. There are many things that I thoroughly dislike about your father, and really, if there were other men in this dark and empty void, where only the little baby stars dance and smile at us from above, I would divorce your father and go and become the wife of someone else. Your father — as you say, my daughter —is a useless, fat, old fool. He is lazy, shiftless and furthermore, he is a dull-witted idiot. When I ask him to kiss me, he kisses me like a wet sponge, spraying saliva all over my face, his thick, heavy lips smothering mine. His fire burns my eyelashes and my eyebrows, and when he makes love to me, he behaves as if he were a rooster and I were a hen. He seizes me like a stolen goat, makes love to me for a few minutes only, and then it's all over. Satisfied, he abandons me there, and starts snoring away under the blankets of cloud as if he did not have a single care in all eternity. Really, my daughter, I wish the gods could have given me a better husband than that ugly thing out there."

The Sun was so badly shaken by these words that he heard being spoken about himself that fiery tears streamed down his cheeks. He said to himself, "I never knew that my wife the Earth had such a poor opinion of me as a husband. She says that I make love like a rooster. She says that I kiss her like a wet sponge and that my lips are thick and blubbery and wet with saliva. What kind of ugly things are these for a wife to say about her husband? But wait. I am going to teach this wife of mine a lesson, and I'm also going to teach our fat little mischief of a daughter a lesson. I'm going to show those two that without my light they are nothing. I'm going to show them that they need me even more than I need them. The Sun can shine in the dark void amongst the stars without the Earth to dance around him, but can the Earth live without the light of the Sun? I must be cunning though. That wife of mine is very sharp-witted. She will easily see through any deception that I may come up with for withdrawing my light from her. What shall I do?"

For a long time the Sun sat in deep thought, and then he came up with a very very beautiful ploy. He would pretend that he was sick and that his light was dimming, day by day, and then the Earth would start to freeze because it could no longer receive the life-giving heat from the Chieftain of the Day. Thus it was that some days after this the Earth noticed that the Sun was not going out of his house to sit outside the hut and warm the cosmos with his heat. She went into the hut to investigate and found the Sun lying under many cloud blankets, groaning gently to himself. "What is it, my husband?" said the Earth. "Are you unwell?"

"Yes my wife," said the Sun in reply from underneath the blankets of cloud. "I am most unwell."

"Why? What's happening? Where do you feel the pain?" she asked him.

"In my stomach," said the old pretender. "I have a terrible pain in my stomach, my stomach is rumbling, my stomach is paining me. I have never felt such pain in all my life. Ohhhhhhhhhh," he said.

The Earth suddenly realized that the inside of the hut was cold and that she was beginning to freeze because the Sun was hidden under many blankets through which his heat could not penetrate. She said, "My husband, shall I find you a herb to cure your stomach ache?"

He said, "Yes, please, please."

And hurriedly the Earth went away to look for medicine in the forest to cure her husband. And when she came back, his condition had taken a turn for the worse. Quickly she prepared the herb that she had found, boiling it in water in a large clay pot, and then she gave him the herb to drink and then sat down outside the hut hoping for the best, but the best did not occur. In fact the Sun's condition appeared to deteriorate even more. In fact his illness grew worse as the days became months and the months became years.

And the Earth herself began to stiffen from the intense cold. There was now frost in her hair and icicles dangled brightly from her eyelashes. She began to tremble as she fought with all means within her reach to bring the Sun back to life again. In desperation she even summoned three very wise stars from the sky. These three stars are always seen together and are known as "the three healers" by our people. She appealed to them saying, "Oh great healers of the skies, please dance the healing dance for my husband. He is not well and he is weakening fast and I am most worried about him. His heat has cooled and I am freezing. See how my hair is now white with snow and see how ice has formed in my eyes and upon my eyelashes. Please, oh three stars that heal, dance my husband the Sun back to health again."

The three healers performed their healing dance. They danced and they danced and they gyrated and they stamped and they leaped with shining masks upon their faces. They performed every one of the seven dances that were required by law so that a sick person might be brought back to life. But it was all in vain. The Sun's condition grew even worse than ever before. The Earth began to freeze. The Moon began to tremble with cold and there was misery in the heavens and misery upon the Earth itself.

The Sun no longer rose in the heavens; only the Moon — a dull and darkened orb — still showed her stolen light briefly and occasionally in the skies. The forests were dark, brittle and frozen. The plains were covered under a thick blanket of rock-hard snow. The streams and the rivers no longer flowed, being held captive. Under great snarling boulders of merciless ice, the waves of the ocean were frozen and the sand of the coasts was hard, cold, and cruel with ice.

The animals were in hiding, and those birds that still survived no longer flew through the air but cowered in caves and holes in the ground living a miserable and shivering existence. The animals no longer grazed upon the plains of the Earth but starved in caves and in caverns deep under the ground.[2]

In a cave at the base of a great mountain upon the once green and fertile Earth, there were two people — a man and a woman — cowering in the rocky womb of a cave, fearful of the biting spirit of cold which was sweeping through the night-shrouded land. Kintu and Mamaravi shivered in cold misery. Kintu had done his best to keep his precious wife Mamaravi warm with fleeces of sheep that he had slaughtered, wild sheep that he had hunted in happier days upon the mountain slope. But still the merciless cold was penetrating even the fleeces; and the beautiful Mamaravi — mother of the nations — trembled and wept under the fleeces.

"What shall we do, oh my husband," she whispered. "This cold penetrates to the very roots of my soul. Every bone in my body appears to be covered in ice. We shall not be long alive, father of my unborn children," she said.

"Keep hope shining within your heart, my wife," said Kintu. "We must place our faith in the gods and in the merciful winds of fate."

"But I have faith, my husband," said Mamaravi to Kintu, her man. "I have faith in the great gods and in the great Earth Mother who created us. I know that the Great Mother will never abandon us although I am weak with cold and stiff with coming death. There is still hope in my heart that all will be well in the end."

"Yes, my love," said Kintu. "Hope is a star that no dark cloud can dim. And if we keep that star in our hearts we shall yet survive this angry and icy night. Have faith my love," he said to her, drawing close and holding her tightly.

Just then there was a commotion outside the cave. A loud animal yell tore the cold night to bits and an animal burst into the cave fleeing for its life. A fierce roar shook the interior of the cave. Kintu leapt to his feet and saw in the darkness that a great lion had pursued a thin and mangy jackal into the cave. Although most animals were starving and dying, the lions and the leopards were alive in the darkness outside, for they fed upon other animals. They raided caves, rooted out the cowering grass-eaters and devoured them. Sometimes, when a lion could not find a grass-eating animal, a zebra or an antelope, it sated its hunger upon jackals and hyenas or any other lesser animals that it could bring down.

Now Kintu was a fearless man, and lions and other such vicious creatures held no terrors for him. Here was action and he leapt to. From a corner of the cave he seized a huge stone, and he hurled it at the blazing eyes of the lion with all his might. Straight and true it flew. The blow was fearful, and the lion died with an ugly sound.

"Here is meat, my wife," said Kintu to Mamaravi. The lions eat animals, and we, to prevent starvation, must eat this lion."

Kintu rummaged in the cave seeking his stone knife; he found it, and with this knife of sharpened stone he got to work upon the dead lion, stripping it of its great pelt and exposing its flesh. He butchered the lion, which he and his wife ate raw, wolfing the warm flesh like the wild animals that they themselves — though human — had now become.

It was only when his stomach was full of warm, bloody meat, that Kintu began to wonder about the other creature which had burst into the cave. "Where is that jackal?" asked Kintu in the semi-darkness. And to his great surprise he heard a trembling dog-like voice saying, "I am over here, mighty one. I am Mpungushe, the jackal."

"Ha! You can talk, can you?"

"Yes."

"Then come out of hiding, oh jackal," said Kintu. "Let me look upon a jackal with the gift of human speech. Come jackal," said Kintu. "Eat of this meat. There is plenty here for all of us. The lion wanted to eat you, and now you must eat the lion."

"Thank you, oh Kintu," said the jackal. The jackal ate and ate and ate until his stomach was as tight as the skin of a drum and as round as the belly of a pot. And then the jackal sat back in the semidarkness and said, "Oh Kintu, do you not think that the world has come to a sorry pass? We who are wise and strong cower inside a darkened cave, bitten by the demon of cold and tormented by the bats of hunger. I feel we ought to do something about this. We must find some means to make us warm, but I do not know what," said the jackal.

"Wait," said Kintu. "I once heard a wandering god telling me that the gods in heaven in their great village of light keep a certain thing that they call "Fire"; and this thing can warm you and also cause light to shine inside any cave. The gods have not given us human beings the secret of this fire, but I understand that they keep it in their village, and very often they play with it, and they hurl it around from cloud to cloud during a thunderstorm, for it is the same thing that we human beings call lightning. If only I was not so consumed with cold, I would try and reach the village of the gods and steal this thing that they call fire and bring it to Earth to warm my wife. She is expecting a baby and this cold is not good at all for her."

In the darkness the eyes of the jackal suddenly blazed with inspiration. A great idea had suddenly blossomed within the caverns of his mind. He said to Kintu, "Listen Kintu, the Village of the Gods, I understand, is protected by fearsome monsters; and a human being like you would not be able to get within twenty paces of the sacred village. I have been told that even the road that leads to the village of the gods is heavily guarded by ogres and great serpents, merciless and incredibly strong. But tell me, do you know the way to the village of the gods?"

"Yes," said Kintu. "The travelling god to whom I spoke some years ago gave me clear directions as to how one could get to the village of the gods, but strangely enough he told me nothing about the great beasts that you say guard the approaches to that village."

"I think the god was laying a trap for you, oh man," said the jackal. "But listen, give me the directions, and I the jackal will easily find my way into that great village. Nobody will notice me, but they would certainly notice a gigantic human being like yourself. I am small and agile. I can hide behind the smallest rock, and if anyone is capable of reaching the village of the gods, then I am that person, oh Kintu."

Kintu told the jackal how to get to the Village of the Gods — which ice-covered river to cross and what crystal mountain to climb. And immediately the jackal prepared himself for his long and hazardous journey.

But just as he was about to depart, Kintu said, "Oh jackal, you are risking your life to obtain this precious gift for us. What payment do you require in return for what you are going to do for us?"

The jackal thought for a long time, his ears drooping and his eyes downcast, and then he said to Kintu, "Oh Kintu, my wife was crushed by a rock some two months ago and I am a jackal without a mate. All I would ask in return for the fire that I will bring from the village of the gods would be that I spend a night with your beautiful wife, Mamaravi."

Kintu was startled by this, but then, hiding his real feelings about the whole thing, he said to the jackal, "Oh jackal, if you return from the Village of the Gods with this sacred thing called fire, then you shall spend a night with my beautiful Mamaravi."

The jackal was so delighted by this that he said to Kintu, "Oh Kintu, it is not good enough for me to plan only to steal a little flame from the fireplace of the gods. I shall steal their secret of fire-making from the village of the gods, because he who has only a small flame to warm his cave will be warmed for a day, but he who has the means of making fire will keep warm for the rest of his life. Do you not think so my friend?"

"Indeed I agree," said Kintu, elated. Here was salvation for himself and his wife and for many countless generations of human beings as yet unborn upon this planet. "Let the jackal take the risks. Let him bear the hardship. He shall be the instrument of my desire," said Kintu in his heart. "For am I not a human being and is he not but a four-footed, wretched, mangy, stinking little beast?" He watched as the jackal slunk out of the cave, a dark, lean shadow soon swallowed by the blizzard-torn night outside.

The wind howled, the ice blew, and from the dark roof of the cave a broken icicle fell and glittered upon the frozen floor of the cave. But within Kintu's heart and within the heart of Mamaravi his wife, there burned that fragile thing called hope.

The jackal did not immediately go upon the great journey that was to lead him to the Village of the Gods. He first went to his cave far away, a cave which he had shared with his mate who now lay dead. From the interior of the cave, jackal retrieved his few possessions. He took his brown skin blanket and wrapped himself around in it, and then from under a rock he dug out his clay pipe, for this jackal had discovered the secret of the hemp plant, the plant known as *marijuana* in the Americas, and as *kif,* or *ganga,* or *hashish,* in other places. Mpungushe always smoked it whenever he was feeling tense and apprehensive and restless. So, tying the marijuana pipe to his back he set out on his epic journey to the Land of the Gods.

He went down a hill into a very deep and menacing valley, a valley haunted by nameless terrors, "The Valley of Nameless Evil," it was called. If you made your way through this valley, you could sense hideous shapes watching you out of the darkness. Every rock and every shadow of this valley was filled with menace, and a stench of fear and corruption lay everywhere. Jackal went through this valley at great speed, among the many apparitions that gibbered and screamed at him; and he went up a tall mountain whose slopes were of wind-blown crystal. Up and up the crystal mountain went jackal.

Look at jackal, look at the brave and the cunning one. Look at the four-footed hero struggling up the slopes of the transparent mountain of crystal. See him upon ledges where the wind threatens to hurl him into oblivion far below. See him scrambling amongst razor-sharp shards of crystal. Higher, ever higher, he fought his way upon that slippery mountain slope upon which not a single plant grew — upon which there was nothing to be seen but snarling, broken crystal everywhere; and as he rose higher and higher towards the unseen heavens, he noticed that the sky was beginning to lighten, that there was a source of light somewhere far away which was lighting up that mountain of crystal. He climbed and climbed for what seemed like hundreds of years; and then, when he reached the slippery, razor-edged summit so unfriendly to the paws of the poor beast, he saw far far away across a very deep and dark valley a sight that very few have ever seen.

It was the home wherein dwell the everlasting gods, the kings and the emperors of the stars — they whose word is unquestioned, and at whose feet a million worlds bow like cringing slaves. There it was, a huge village with a dark wall of obsidian stone encircling it, and thousands of dwellings made, not of perishable grass, but of imperishable gold, and studded with precious stones of all colors.

A great bright nimbus of light hung over the village and all around it. It was huge even at that distance.

"Yonder lies my destination," said the jackal, "and between my destination and this mountain is the Valley of Eternal Night. How shall I cross that fearsome valley where nothing living can venture and survive? I must think," said the jackal. "I must use my mind, for am I not the jackal, the master of all cunning? Am I not the one who has survived many perils? Down there in that terrible valley lie nameless dangers. Down there lie rivers of fire, down there lie lakes of blood. Down there are deep and terrible holes which, should one ever fall, it would take a thousand years to strike bottom. I, the jackal, shall not take my chances with those unknown perils. I must think, but what am I going to do?"

The answer came to the jackal out of the skies. It came huge, fiery-eyed, dagger-fanged and bloody-clawed, with huge wings like those of a bat, beating slowly at the airless air. It was a dragon returning to the Village of the Gods, and it drew near to him.

"Greetings, great dragon," said the jackal. "Greetings, mighty messenger of the gods. How majestic you are, as you fly towards your destination," said the jackal. "How beautiful is the red blaze of your eyes and how bright are your scales like green and living gold in the light of the distant village of the gods. Great dragon, there is no one more beautiful in the air than you."

The dragon turned and looked at the little jackal on the summit of the mountain. "Do you really find me beautiful?" asked the dragon.

"Yes, great dragon," said the jackal. "I find you beautiful and majestic. I find you strong beyond all strength and I find you powerful beyond all power."

"What is your name, little creature?" asked the dragon, pausing in its flight.

"I am known as a jackal, great one," said the jackal in reply. "I am by profession a poet and a singer of songs. Do you want to hear one of my songs?"

"Yes," said the dragon, "but let it not delay my flight more than is necessary."

"I shall sing but a little song in praise of you, great one. From underneath his blanket the jackal took a reed flute, and he began to play a beautiful tune upon it, and such was his skill that the dragon was hypnotized by the unearthly sound. It filled the heart of the great reptile with a nameless longing and an indescribable joy.

"Little beast, what can I do for you in return for what you have done for me?" asked the dragon.

"Oh dragon," said the jackal, "let me but know what it feels like to fly upon your mighty shoulders, to ride upon you as you fly through the air towards the Village of the Gods."

In this way did the jackal trick the dragon into carrying him across the valley of great danger towards his destination. When the dragon was close to the village of the gods, the jackal jumped off the dragon's back, spun through space for a few long moments, and yet landed safely on all fours not far from the great wall that protected the village of the everlasting gods.

Unlike the barren, snow-bound Earth that the jackal had left far behind, the Land of the Gods was fertile, green, brightly lit and fragrant. There were flowers and trees everywhere; there was soft, bluish-green grass at the foot of the great wall that surrounded the Village of the Gods. Butterflies flitted this way and that across the face of the fantastic greenery. The sky was a dark purple; it was a land of breath-taking beauty, a land that had mothered the eternal lords and ladies of creation.

For a few moments jackal was captivated by his surroundings — and that very nearly proved his undoing, because all of a sudden he heard the sound of massive steps behind him, and then a fearful voice spoke out, "Stop creature! Stop in the name of the gods. Who are you and what do you seek here, you four-footed, wretched trespasser?"

Jackal spun around and saw a sight that froze the very marrow in his bones. Towering over him was a huge giant made completely of metal. Far up in the air above massive, gleaming, bluish metal shoulders was a face with burning red eyes and grinning yellow teeth as sharp as newly-whetted spears. "I said, who are you, creature?"

Jackal said, "I am known as the jackal, my lord."

"What do you, jackal, want in the Land of the Gods?" demanded the giant of iron. "Do you not know that nothing that is flesh and blood may invade the sanctity of the everlasting ones? You, jackal, are going to die."

The giant stooped and a huge hand of metal reached down and seized the jackal firmly by the tail. He was swept into the air head downward and for a few blood-chilling moments he stared into the eyes of his terrible captor.

"Have mercy upon me, great lord, have mercy, Guardian of the Gods. I will do anything that you require of me, but please do not kill me," quivered the jackal.

"I will not kill you until you have answered all my questions," said the giant. "I am *Ngozi*, the dangerous one, and I am the guardian of the southern gate of the Village of the Gods. What is this that you have got tied to your back?" demanded the giant, seeing jackal's marijuana pipe.

"Oh great one, this is but a pipe with which I amuse myself when I am worried," said the jackal. "This little thing can bring great peace!"

"What does the pipe do?" demanded the giant.

"Well, I smoke this thing," said the jackal. "Do you want me to show you how? It's very interesting, really."

The giant said, "Very well, show me how this little pipe can bring you peace."

Jackal was released by his metal captor, and he set about lighting up his pipe, at the foot of the giant, who watched from his incredible height very very closely indeed. Jackal lit the marijuana and began to smoke, the pipe emitting a bubbling sound; and then he began to appear very drowsy.

"This is a pipe that gives me great dreams, oh giant," said the jackal. It makes one feel like a god. It makes one exhilarated. Would you care to try it, mighty one?"

The giant scratched his huge hairless head, and then he said, "Very well, I shall try this pipe of dreams." And jackal added a secret herb that he kept in his little bag of medicine. This herb induced very heavy sleep within moments of being smoked, and this was the herb he lighted and respectfully offered in the marijuana pipe to the giant of iron.

"Are you sure that this thing will make me feel like a god?" thundered the giant.

"Yes, yes, great one, try it."

The giant seized the pipe and began to smoke. The more he smoked, the more drowsy he became, until in the end he crashed full upon his back with a thunderous noise, and lay still, snoring hideously towards the sacred skies.

Jackal lost no time in retrieving his pipe. He climbed onto the chest of the great giant and from there he jumped onto the very top of the wall of the village of the gods and jumped down the other side. Now he was inside, a daring trespasser in the great garden of the Queen of the Gods. In front of him he saw three huge huts made of living gold, enormous structures surrounded by a rainbow, and towards these he made his thieving way.

He entered the largest of the huts like a hairy, malodorous shadow. He found himself within the fragrant interior of the cooking house of the Queen of the Gods. There, upon a mat, he saw fire sticks, and there upon a mat he also saw a stone, which, if you strike it with another stone, emitted sparks. All these the daring thief quickly seized and wrapped in his skin blanket, tied the blanket to his back, and made off towards the wall that surrounded the great village.

Suddenly behind him he heard a voice shouting angrily, "Stop, you stinking thief! Stop, I say!"

And when he threw a guilty glance over his shoulder, he saw the beautiful Queen of the Gods standing at the entrance of her hut, shouting at him. But the jackal was unstoppable. He had come so far, and had gained what he had come for, and now was the time for him to leave, posthaste! He climbed up a tree whose flowers filled his nostrils with a heady smell and from this tree he jumped onto the wall, like a mangy bat from the pits of darkness; and from the top of the wall he jumped all the way to the ground to race down the slope of the Sacred Mountain of the Gods, running like black lightning itself. Nothing was going to stop the daring jackal who had stolen the fire sticks of the gods.

He fled from the city — while sounds of rage rang out behind him. He ran for what seemed like a hundred years or more; and as he went, the terrible darkness closed all around him, and hideous shapes — huge flying reptiles — swam through the darkness, their bellies lighted by the fierce flames of the rivers of fire that snaked through the Valley of Eternal Night. Jackal had reached the most dangerous place in the Universe.

Terror became his companion and fear his friend, as he made his way through that terrible valley for what seemed like an eternity. At one point he nearly fell into a river of liquid fire. Another time he was nearly devoured by a rock, which, when he ran past it, suddenly developed a huge and hungry mouth with fearful fangs that threatened to chew the life out of him. Another time he very nearly plunged to his death when a huge hole opened up almost at his feet and it was only by jumping higher and farther than he had ever jumped before that he was able to escape this danger. Another time a fearful creature — half-bird and half hungry reptile — stormed out of fire-lit heavens towards him. It chewed off one of his ears before he managed to bolt into a small cave, from which he was immediately evicted by a huge, white, four-armed creature like an ape, which showed every intention of tearing him to pieces.

Many, oh many, were the perils that jackal endured as he made his way through the Valley of Eternal Danger; and when at long long last, with parts of his body torn and bleeding, his hair scorched here and there by fearful flames and one ear missing, jackal at long last reached the mountain of Crystal.

But he said to himself, "He who has endured the horrors of the Valley of Eternal Danger surely cannot be afraid of the slopes of the Mountain of Crystal." He climbed and he climbed and he climbed until once more he gained the summit of the great mountain. Once more the cold and the wind and the blizzards almost claimed him, but he was triumphant. He climbed down the other side, and after what seemed like a thousand years, he reached the foot of the mighty mountain.

He had succeeded, and his sense of triumph gave him renewed endurance. Many days later, he appeared at the entrance of Kintu and Mamaravi's cave, and he called out to the first man and the first woman in the world, "My friends, I bring the secret of the gods. Are you still alive?"

"We are still alive," replied Kintu, his voice faint and weak with cold. "Do you have the fire?"

"Yes!" cried the jackal; and they quickly gathered dry, dead wood, grass and other refuse. Using the stolen fire sticks of the gods, jackal soon had a huge fire going in the center of the cave. The fire crackled and danced, and smoke spewed out like a white mist filling the interior of the cave. Kintu and Mamaravi sneezed as the smoke invaded their nostrils and soon the cave began to warm, and a pleasant heat, a life-giving warmth, filled its interior. From the roof of the cave the icicles melted and fell to the ground, and water ran freely where ice had glimmered before.

"The secret of the gods is ours," cried Kintu. "We are saved, my wife! We are saved, oh Mother of the Nations. Oh thank you, thank you, wise jackal, for what you have done for us. Thank you a thousand times."

"Very well, my friends," said the jackal, "but do you remember what our agreement was? Namely, that if I returned safely with the fire sticks of the gods, Mamaravi would become my wife for a night."

"Yes," said Kintu, "I remember now."

"Don't tell me you had forgotten, human being," said the jackal, his eyes gleaming in the firelight. "Don't tell me you had forgotten."

"How could I forget?" asked Kintu angrily, stung by the words of the jackal. I swear to you that tomorrow night my wife shall share her love mat with you," said Kintu.

"Very well, human being, I will hold you to your word," said Jackal. "For the first time, I see what a beautiful woman your wife is. She is as beautiful as a star, and it would be a great thing for me to make love to such a beautiful creature. Kissing her will ease the pain of loneliness that has haunted my hut since my mate died."

Then jackal slunk away and went to sleep on a pile of old grass at one end of the cave, leaving the human beings to enjoy the fire for quite some time before an uneasy sleep claimed them.

Now Kintu was a worried man. The idea of sharing his wife with a stinking, mangy jackal filled him with absolute horror; and needless to say Mamaravi was not enamored of the idea either. She protested in a whisper to her husband, and Kintu said to her, "I will not let this dirty animal touch you, my wife. Somehow we have got to do something."

Then Kintu remembered a gift that the traveling god he had once met had given him: a whistle which emitted no sound but which the god had assured him would summon any god within reach should Kintu but blow it when he needed assistance from the everlasting ones.

Kintu sneaked out of the cave, out into the cold darkness, and he placed the whistle to his lips and blew a silent blast. Three times he blew the blast, and then he crept back into the cave again. Some time passed; then Kintu sensed an awful presence in the darkness outside the fire lit cave, and a terrible voice roared, "Rrrrrrr, Grrrrrr! Who has summoned me, the dread Avenger of the Gods?" And into the light that spilled out of the entrance of the cave there stepped a fearsome creature, a huge bird bigger than any bird that flew the skies of Earth, a mighty creature with formidable wings made of golden feathers.

The bird had the head of a lion and this head was gifted with the power of speech. "I am the *Nunzu* bird," roared the creature. "I am the bird that punishes those who have done wrong to the gods. Come out you wretched human beings and stand before me," cried the bird.

When the jackal heard the voice of the fearsome Nunzu, he fled into the deep interior of the cave and hid behind a rock trembling.

"Have you summoned me, human being?" demanded the huge bird.

"Yes, great Bird of Eternal Justice. I, Kintu, have summoned you."

"Why have you summoned me, human being?" demanded the bird. "Why have you summoned the one who punishes those who have sinned against the gods?"

"Because, great Nunzu," said Kintu, "We have a sinner with us in this cave. We have the jackal who stole the fire sticks of the gods and brought them here to us."

"Were you party to this jackal's crime?" demanded the Nunzu.

"Oh no, great one!" said Kintu. "This wretched creature asked me if we wanted some warmth and I agreed. Then he said he knew a place from which he could steal the means of making fire. I did not know that he intended to rob the gods themselves. I had not known who possesses the secret of fire. I am not guilty of this jackal's crime and neither is my wife," cried Kintu.

"Very well," said the Nunzu bird, "Let the sinner come out of the cave, that he may face punishment. They who sin against the eternal gods must suffer due punishment no matter who they are. Thus speaks the Nunzu, bird of implacable justice."

Kintu forgot the friendship that had existed between him and the jackal. He forgot all the good that the jackal had done him and his wife. He became a vicious human being, caring nothing for other creatures except for himself. He dashed into the interior of the cave, overcame the jackal after a furious struggle, seized the jackal by the tail with both hands and ran towards the entrance, heedless of jackal's terrified howls. He swung the creature and hurled it full at the Nunzu bird. The mighty bird caught the jackal in its lion-like mouth. "Now jackal," said the Nunzu bird. "Now is your hour of death."

"Have mercy," screamed the jackal.

"But the Nunzu bird shows mercy to no one."

"Don't kill me, I'll do anything," cried the jackal.

"Can you answer the seven questions?"

"I don't know what the seven questions are," quavered the jackal.

"Then you must die, oh Jackal." Then Nunzu seized the jackal in its beak, chewed off its hind quarters and spat them out, and then it went on to chew the head leaving pieces of murdered Jackal in front of Kintu's cave.

After many, many years, a sickly Sun, now recovered from his pretended illness, showed his face over the mountains of the East, and the world was somewhat warmed by the returning Lord of Day. But it was still cold, for a long time still and yet Kintu and his wife were happy in their cave, because they had kept the secret that poor Jackal had stolen from the Land of the Gods. It was a secret that was to benefit not only them, but their children's children's children down to the very days in which we live.[3]

Kintu and the Cattle of the Sun

This story, my children, is another story about that amusing man called Kintu, the great hero of African legend, Kintu the cunning, Kintu the trickster, Kintu the not-always-so-mighty.

This story involves Kintu and the Giant of the South. It is said that one day Kintu was lying outside his cave. His stomach was full of good meat and rumbling, and there was much happiness in his body. The insects were singing a lullaby all around in the bush. Below the cave and above it the trees were smiling and nodding in the breeze, and Kintu was asleep, snoring like a warthog making love in the thicket. He snored and he snored and he turned over and he mumbled. He was quite happy.

Then all of a sudden a terrible light shone all around Kintu, and he opened his eyes with a start, and a little blast of flatus escaped from him, so startled he was! His eyes opened and he looked about him and there, hovering in the air a little above his head, was a shining being.

The being said to him, "Kintu, do you know me?"

Kintu said, "No, lord, I do not know who you are, but you are a fearsome and shining one. You shine as bright as the Sun in the morning. And the heat that comes from your body all but scorches the hair upon my head."

The Sun god smiled, for it was he, *Somanga*, the Lord of Light. Somanga smiled and said, "Kintu, do not be afraid. I am going far to the north across the unchartered lands and the trackless seas. I am going to attend my sister's wedding. My sister has married the Old Man of Ice far far away in the lands where the Sun is not seen for many months on end, in the land of *munyakatela* fishes that swallow you whole, in the frozen oceans where the ice rattles like a drum and thuds like a drumbeat in the darkness. There I, Somanga, the Sun god, am going to attend my sister's wedding.

"Aiee," the Sun god went on, "women are very strange creatures. I cannot understand why my beautiful sister *Nyanaga*, the Moon, decided to marry that ugly Old Man of the North — he with the frozen beard and the crackling bones and the rasping voice and the thin fingers. But I must attend the wedding, for so my mother the Great Goddess has commanded.

"Now listen, Kintu, in the bush over there I have a vast herd of cattle — my cattle, which I must herd through the sky every day. They are as white as snow, every one of them, with shining bronze horns and black ears. One-hundred and twenty-one in number they are, cows and oxen and bulls; and I call upon you, Kintu, to look after these cattle of mine until I return. Do you agree?"

"Great one," said Kintu, "my soul is revealed before you. You know that I am a lazy man, who likes to loll about in the Sun. You know that I am one who just wants to swim about in the pools like a hippopotamus, but I shall look after your cattle, oh Lord, and you shall not be disappointed in me."

The Sun god said, "Kintu, many evil beings would love to gain possession of these cattle that my father, the Great Father of the Sky, entrusted me with. See to it that no harm comes to them. You can milk them all you wish, you can make sour milk out of their milk. You will find it nutritious and full of life. You may, if you so wish, slaughter one of the cattle if you are hungry enough. But, because the forest is so full of game, I do not see why you should kill any one of the sacred cows or oxen or bulls of the Sun. They shall give you milk, they shall provide you with dried cow dung to put on your fire on cold nights. Look after these cattle until I return. Come, follow me, and I shall introduce you to them."[4]

Kintu followed the Sun god, who floated in the air in his shining majesty. The trees bowed before the deity's passing, the wind whispered gently, and the birds twittered and sang when the Lord of Light went through the forest. And then the Sun God whistled seven times, and a great white bull with huge curving horns appeared out of the bush. He was magnificent, he was beautiful, he was a bull of bulls, he was the Lord of the Herds of the cattle of the Sun. He saluted the Sun god, he said, "Ohhhhhhhhhh," and the very forest thundered.

Then the Sun god addressed the great bull by name saying, "*Ntontozayo*, this is Kintu, your new herdsman. He shall help you to look after my herds. I must go now to attend my sister's wedding."

"Go, great Sun god," said the bull. "Kintu and I shall look after your four-footed children. But great one," said the bull, "I do not trust this Kintu. He has got a stomach like a pumpkin and bowed legs, and his eyes are crooked and shifty. But if he does something wrong, oh, Sun God, I shall impale him upon my shining horns."

Then, out of the sky appeared two great eagle-men, men with the heads of eagles and shining wings that blazed like the Sun. And one of the eagle-men took one arm of the Sun god and the other one the other arm and they lifted the Sun god high into the sky until going north his shining presence was lost from sight.

And so Kintu began his new duty as the herdsman of the Sun's cattle. It was going well; Kintu liked to be in the meadows and listen to the lowing of the animals. Many many days passed, and then one day Kintu was lying in his cave. It was cold, and Kintu was doing what he always did best, which was sleeping and snoring his head off. Then he heard a terrible sound at the door of the cave. "Ohhhhhhhhhhh," was the sound. Kintu jumped up, and there was Ntontozayo, the great bull of the Sun, standing outside the entrance of the cave; and to Kintu's great surprise there was a gigantic man riding him. It was a terrible giant, a fearsome cannibal with teeth like those of a leopard, a huge and hideous monster as black as a thousand nights. The monster said to Kintu,

"I see you, little cockroach, I see you little vermin. Wake up! I, *Ningizimu*, the Giant of the South, have stolen the cattle of the Sun with my magic. I have used my magic upon this bull so that he should obey me, as I lead his herd away. As a further insult to the God of Light, I would like not only to steal his cattle, but also his little herdsman as well.

"You poor pathetic little cowherd, did you think that I could not steal these cattle? You are coming with me, whether you like it or not, and I am going to have you for food when I reach my village. When I have done that, I shall call a mighty gathering of all the giants of the South, all the ogres of the desert, all the monsters of the northern lands and the eastern lands, and I shall hold a great feast where we will eat every one of the Sun god's cattle. Is it not said that eating the flesh of these cattle makes you immortal? We, the giants, would all like to be immortal, and we shall devour these cattle in a feast so monstrous and horrible that it will make every god in the skies weep."

"No," cried Kintu. "You cannot do that."

"Why not?" laughed the giant, "Why not? I have stolen the cattle and now, little weevil, I am stealing you!"

Before Kintu could move, the giant made a magic gesture with his hand and Kintu found himself flying through the air; and as he flew towards the giant, the giant took out a huge bag and opened its neck and Kintu fell into the bag, head first. In short, before he knew what was happening, the giant had pulled the drawstring of the bag, and Kintu was well and truly bagged.

Then Kintu heard the giant shouting to the cattle of the Sun, and the great bull, Ntontozayo, upon whose back the giant was riding and carrying Kintu, began to move.

Long, long, hours passed until at last, when the breeze was becoming cold and when the sorrowful insects were bewailing the Sunset, Kintu was suddenly flung into the dust while still inside the bag. And then he heard the sound of many cattle being driven into one place. He smelled the dust in the air for a while and then he heard the giant approaching. The giant seized the drawstring of the bag and opened it, emptying Kintu unceremoniously into the dust. The giant said, "Ah, little Kintu, now is the great moment of my triumph. My friend, I am now going to have supper and you are invited to join me, as part of the menu. But before I eat you, you must go into the bush and gather pot herbs for the cooking of your own self — it will add some flavor to your little bit of meat."

So the giant tied a length of thong around Kintu's ankle and kicked him out of his village, sending him into the bush to go and gather pot herbs. The knot that the giant tied around Kintu's ankle was a magical knot. Kintu could not undo it, so he could only move as the long thong allowed him, and each time he tried to escape, an ugly bird flying above him croaked a warning to the giant, who immediately tugged on the thong, bringing Kintu to the ground. Kintu gathered the pot herbs — a whole bundle of green wild spinach and green vegetables — and he brought them to the giant, and then when he had brought enough, the giant said, "Put them in the pot." Kintu saw a monstrous clay pot bubbling on top of a great fire and he threw the vegetables and spinach into it. The giant said, "It's not enough. I need more. Get out, go. Go and find more pot herbs. And when you have found as much as I need, my friend, you yourself are going to sing loudly and bubble merrily just like the stew in the pot."

While Kintu was toiling in the bush gathering more wild vegetables, he was suddenly aware of an animal sitting on a branch of the tree above him. He looked at the animal and the animal looked down at him. It was beautiful. It seemed to be like a tiny leopard, so cuddly it was, with white paws and a great striped coat. Its eyes were large and yellow and soulful with split pupils. Its ears were pointed. The animal looked full of knowledge, full of cunning; and as Kintu was gathering the pot herbs, keeping one eye upon this fascinating creature, it began to laugh.

"Heeee," said the animal.

Kintu said, "Did you laugh?"

And the animal said, "Of course I did."

Kintu said, "You are a beautiful animal with your big eyes, your little nose and your whiskers. What kind of animal are you? I've never seen one like you before."

And the animal said, "Myoaouuuuuuu, I'm a cat. Many of my tribe live in this forest. Now tell me, why are you tethered like a goat to that long thong and why are you gathering spinach, like an old woman in the bush?"

Kintu sat down, and the tears of sorrow trickled down his eyes and he told the cat everything that had happened to him.

"Aowuuuuuuuu," said the cat, "you human beings are very stupid. Meowwwwww, if you were a cat like me you would know what to do."

Kintu, brightening up, said, "What must I do?".

And the cat said, "Meuuuuuuuu, it's going to cost you! meowwwww."

"It's going to cost me what?" asked Kintu.

"Listen fellow," said the cat, "do you want me to help you?"

Kintu said, "Yes, yes, yes."

The cat said, "Are you willing to pay the price?"

And Kintu said, "I'm willing to pay anything, what is your price?"

The cat said, "You must now decree that you and your descendants will keep us cats happy to the end of this world's days. You, Kintu, must take me to your cave, and after this, keep me in comfort, feed me when I feel hungry, stroke me when I want to be stroked, and give me all the milk that my stomach can drink. Do you agree?"

Kintu said, "I agree. I agree!"

"Now," the cat whispered, "I propose that we trick the giant. Listen Kintu, this is what we are going to do. Take me with you, and on the way back to the giant's village I'm going to give a plan of how to deal with this giant."

"Ha," said Kintu, "you are a very helpful little animal." And as they went together, the cat riding on Kintu's shoulder, it told him what they must do. When Kintu arrived in the village of the giant, he found the fearsome giant's family gathered all around, and his sons and daughters sharpening their teeth with stones in preparation for the feast.

The giant said, "Ah, good evening, dinner! Have you brought enough pot herbs?"

Kintu said, "Yes, Lord Giant."

Then the giant said, "But what is this funny animal that is riding on your shoulder? Get rid of it now."

Kintu said, "But this, sir, is my friend the cat whom I found in the forest."

"A friend?" asked the giant, "do you make friends with animals? Can this animal talk? Cat, can you talk?" demanded the giant.

The cat looked very stupid and sorrowful in its expression, saying, "Meowwwww."

"What?" asked the giant. "This is a stupid animal, that can't even talk! So do you know what I will do? I will eat not only you Kintu, but also this animal as well. Now, do you have any last requests before I eat you? Do you have any ancestor to pray to? Any god to appeal to for mercy, before I cut your throat?"

As the giant spoke, he brought out of his cabot a fearsome knife of black stone. The knife was so sharp and wicked and clumsy that it sent a chill of fear up and down Kintu's spine.

"Do you really mean to eat me?" asked Kintu.

"Of course," said the giant. "Why do you think my wives and daughters are gathered around here? They want to share a spoonful of the wonderful stew that I shall make out of you."

Then Kintu said, "Oh giant, you asked me if I had a last request to make, and I have. Is it not customary for a man who is about to be eaten, to challenge the one who is about to eat him to single combat? And thus I challenge you, oh giant, to fight with me for my life! If you win, you can eat me. If I win, you shall release the Cattle of the Sun and me and this wonderful animal. Do you agree?"

The giant looked at his wives and they all nodded agreement. The giant smiled and said, "Heh, heh, heh! little Kintu; you have challenged me and according to the laws of single combat, you shall choose your weapon from amongst my weapons, and I shall choose my weapon also. So the giant's wives brought out a lot of fearsome weapons: huge stone axes, huge clubs and giant spears tipped with bone and stone. They threw these at the feet of the giant, and Ningizimu said, "Ah, Kintu, choose your weapon."

Kintu said, "But these weapons are very big, how can I fight?"

Then the giant said, "Then lie down and let me cut your throat, you stupid loser."

Kintu said, "But I have a weapon of my own, oh Ningizimu, so let's fight."

"You have a weapon?" asked the giant.

"Yes," cried Kintu suddenly feeling brave. And the giant took up a fearsome stone-headed axe — it was so huge it could have cut a mountain in two. And the giant hefted it in his hands and shook it in the air and swung it in the air until the air whistled like a tempest.

"Now Kintu, you are going to die!" said the giant charging at Kintu. The giant aimed a tremendous blow at him but Kintu jumped aside and the huge stone axe bit deep into the ground and a cloud of dust went up into the air, and then the giant tried again but Kintu managed to avoid the blow. Then Kintu played the trick that he and the cat had arranged.

Kintu threw the cat straight at the giant's head, seizing its tail; and just as any cat would do under such circumstances, the cat, to avoid falling, dug its nails deep into the giant's skull and held on!

Kintu held on to the cat's tail by both hands — and the giant screamed in awful pain. "Don't pull it," cried the giant. "Leave its tail go, let it gooooooo, it's killing me!"

Kintu only pulled harder upon the tail of the cat, and once more the giant roared in pain and the more Kintu pulled, the more the cat dug its claws into the giant's skull. And then when Kintu pulled, a huge piece of flesh and hair was ripped off the giant's head.

Now it is a known fact throughout the land of the black people that these ancient giants were actually terribly afraid of the sight of their own blood; and when the giant suddenly felt blood cascading warmly down the sides of his head and onto his face, he roared with fear. Ningizimu bolted through the bush and ran like nobody's business. He ran with a huge cloud of dust behind him. His wives, seeing his panic, ran after him, and the whole village full of wives and giant children thundered after the howling giant, who was shaking even the mighty mountains far away.

Kintu and his friend the cat finally let go, but the giant's fearsome screams could be heard, far off in the distance.

Some time later Kintu was homeward bound, once more riding Ntontozayo, the great bull of the Sun but now much more happily. The bull was also content, for the ogre's spell had been dispelled from his mind. He was leading his vast herd of white cattle home; and Kintu rode proudly on his back.

Sitting in front of Kintu was the first cat ever to be tamed by a human being; or rather the first cat on Earth to tame a human being, because in the lands of our people we say, "This is my dog, and this is my cat; this is my rabbit and this is my chicken." But we do not realize that it is these animals that are really keeping us.

And the Sun came home, and when he had counted his cattle and found that every one was there, he beamed happily on Kintu, and smiled on Kintu's land and all of his descendants. And in a warm yellow patch of sunlight, first in front of Kintu's hut, and then, later, in front of many of the huts of his children and their children, lay that furry, sleepy creature, who tries never to let on how wise he truly is, but who will trot over gracefully when you offer him a warm bowl of cow's milk, and say "Miaaowr!"

That is the end of the story, my children.

Kintu and the Star Goddess

This is the third story of that funny little hero called Kintu.

Things went along well enough for Kintu in those days, until one day there came something that changed his life drastically. He was attacked, and had to fight for his life against a terrible monster that had come out of a volcano! The fearsome fire monster had tried to devour the people of Kintu's village. But Kintu, who was now king of a large tribe of people, showed courage — which was completely unlike him. He attacked the monster, fought it, and forced it to flee back into the thundering mouth of the volcano.

But Kintu himself was found by his people, lying on the ground permanently blinded, and for the rest of his life Kintu was a blind man. The following story takes place while Kintu was known as "The Blind King of the Valleys."

Kintu now ruled a tribe that spread over ten fertile valleys at the foot of great mountains. He was a wise and much-loved man. He was already old and gray, and he was troubled by the two wives who were his queens. The first of these wives was a huge, fat monstrosity with a very shrill voice and a very bad temper, called *Noku*. Noku was a vicious person. She was cruel to the people; it was said she was even cruel to herself. In contrast, Kintu's second wife —her name was *Kina* — was a gentle, beautiful, though sickly, woman. Although she was a person of poor health, a person of such fragile well-being, Kina had a kind word for every human being and animal in the land that her husband now ruled. She was a good mother to Kintu's many children, treating all of them with equal gentleness. And she was patient with Noku's bad temper. The contrast between his two wives caused Kintu a lot of sadness.

Because he was now hopelessly blind, Kintu no longer was an adventuring warrior, facing strange perils. He had become a musician, a singer of songs, and a composer of beautiful poetry. And he kept the people amused, thrilled, and delighted with his songs, and he moved them to tears with his poetry. And they called him "Kintu, the Shining One." And in the Land of the Gods, the gods smiled down upon Kintu. They loved him, and they kept fearsome monsters and demons away from his people.

Then one day, Kintu was hobbling through the bush alone, followed by his faithful dog, *Sasa*. Sasa acted as a guide dog for Kintu! Whenever he walked alone through the bush, she was at his side; and he held on to one of her ears as she guided him blindly along the way. Whenever he was with Sasa he knew that no leopard, or lion would ever dare to touch him because Sasa was a loyal dog, a mother of many litters of puppies. Her ribs were beginning to show and her muzzle was becoming gray with old age, but she was fierce and faithful to Kintu to the very end.

It so happened that one day Sasa was guiding Kintu through the bush when all of a sudden Kintu heard a sound in the heavens. It was a strange sound, a humming sound.

"What's that, Sasa?" asked Kintu. The sound came again. And then *doooom*, something settled up on the land.

"Sasa, what's that?" And Sasa growled, throwing back her lips, baring her fearsome yellow fangs, one of which was broken. She growled, "*Grrrrrrr. Wowowo.*"

"What is it Sasa, what are you seeing?" Kintu tried to pull the dog forward, but the dog blocked Kintu's way.

"Grrrrrr," said Sasa. "Wowo," she barked again.

"What is it Sasa?" asked the blind king. "What is there ahead of us? Why do I smell something burning in my nostrils? Burning grass? And something that smells like hot copper, what is this?"

"Wo," said the dog. "Wowowo."

"Oh, you want me to wait, do you?" asked Kintu.

"Grrrr," replied Sasa. "Yes."

And then Kintu waited. Long moments passed. And then Kintu heard the sounds of footsteps in the gravel of the footpath. The footsteps were approaching.

"What is it Sasa?" Kintu asked the dog.

The dog growled under her breath but remained still as stone. And then all of a sudden Kintu smelled something — a beautiful perfume, a beautiful scent, the scent of eternity, the scent of countless stars, the scent of those that live forever, to whom the very stars belong.

"Greetings blind man," said a divine voice.

"Greetings, oh eternal one," replied Kintu. "My eyes cannot see you, but the eyes of my spirit can sense you. What can I do for you, eternal one?"

The unseen figure replied, "Blind man, blind king of the people, I come to you in need of assistance. My star thing, the beast in which I travel among the stars is sick; it is fallen here, and it cannot rise again, because it is hungry. It needs to eat something special, and this thing I do not have."

"What does the beast of the stars want to eat, oh beautiful goddess?" asked Kintu.

The goddess replied, "The star beast requires a special type of stone which is as transparent as water, a special type of stone which is harder than anything you can imagine and I believe, oh blind king, that you have such a stone in your bag."

Kintu said, "Goddess, you see everything. It is true that in my bag I have several stones, green stones, pink stones, and one other stone which is like water, so clear it is. I have this 'stone.' He fumbled for his drawstring bag and with an old man's shaking fingers he rummaged in the bag until feeling with the tips of his sensitive fingers he found the stone he sought.

He said, "Goddess, eternal one, is this the stone you seek?"

The goddess said, "It is, oh faithful king. This is the type of stone that my star-animal eats once every four thousand years. Now truly I shall feed it, and I shall return to my village among the stars."

The goddess took the shining stone gently from Kintu's hand and then departed. Kintu heard her footsteps receding as she went towards her star animal, a huge monstrous bird of living gold in whose belly the beautiful goddess travelled through the cosmos.[5]

Then once more, Kintu heard a humming sound, a triumphant sound, a sound of life regained, a sound of eternal joy, as the animal sat there digesting the shining stone that the goddess had fed it. But then, to his surprise Kintu heard the goddess return, and she said, "Kintu, you have helped me greatly this day. Am I not the great goddess *Nananana* who goes where she will in the heavens? Am I not the bride of the heavens? Now let me ask you Kintu, what would you like as a reward? I can give you anything that your heart desires. I can make you the King of the World. I can make you the great Chieftain of the Seas, with the whales and the dolphins and the sharks and other fearsome animals of the deep at your command. I can make you the Emperor of the Heavens with every constellation bowing low before you. Or I can give you *this*." The goddess took Kintu's hand and poured something into his opened hand. It was seeds of many grains, plants which were unknown to Kintu.

He asked the goddess, "Goddess Nananana, Beautiful Bride of the Heavens, what is this that you are pouring into my hands?"

The goddess answered, "This thing that I'm pouring into your hands is a kind of foodstuff that comes from the Land of the Gods. And it produces more of its kind. It is a cereal that can feed many people and give them strength."

Kintu bowed low before the goddess and said, "Oh beautiful Nananana, oh Goddess of Love and of War, I, Kintu, am a humble man. I do not seek to become Chieftain of the Oceans. I do not seek to become Monarch of the Sky, nor do I seek to become Emperor of the Constellations. All I seek is this gift that you now place in my hands so that my people can have this strange foodstuff. For truly something tells me that this corn will bring much health to my people."

"Is that all, Kintu?" asked Nananana.

"Yes, great one, this is all I want. I shall plant this corn in a secret field until much of it grows. Then I shall share it with my people, and I know that great good will come from this. You see, our people live on the flesh of wild animals. They eat too much meat, and the wild fruits and wild vegetables that they can find are few; but these tiny little grains will be the salvation of my people for hundreds if not thousands of years to come."

Then the goddess said, "Oh Kintu, oh man with humility, I, Nananana, draw close to you."

And the goddess drew close to Kintu and she took him in her arms and pressed her breasts against him, kissed him on both eyes and the forehead and she said sadly, "Oh Kintu, although I am Nananana the all-powerful goddess, I have not the power to restore your vision; but know that for all time and for all ages to be, you and your people shall have the love and the protection of the Beautiful Bride of the Heavens against whom no evil monster and no renegade god can stand. I, Nananana, shall watch over your land to the ending of all time. Farewell."

So saying, the Bride Goddess sprang away, leaving behind the sweetness of a thousand flowers; and very soon Kintu heard the sound of the star beast departing, humming with delight, humming with ecstasy, humming with joy, full of redemption, full of well-being. It hummed and hummed and hummed, until it was lost beyond the clouds.

And then Sasa began to wag her tail. After that a strange thing was noticed by the people of Kintu: that their blind king was wont to disappear into the bush for a long long time. They wondered what the king was up to. He used to hobble into the bush, guided by his faithful dog. Many months went by and the people wondered, "Is the king mad? He always disappears into that valley where no one ever went before. Let us follow him, for truly our king will come to harm if we don't look after him."

So the warriors took up their stone-headed spears and their wooden shields and donned their headdresses. Quietly they followed king Kintu and his faithful dog Sasa. The king and his tracks led them to the heart of the valley and there they saw Kintu standing in a huge field filled with a plant that they did not know. "Lord, what is this? What is this plant that grows here? Where did you find it?" asked the warriors.

"My warriors," said Kintu, "you are the defenders of my people. I call upon you to swear an oath of secrecy to tell no one about this secret. This is corn, millet, and sorghum. They are plants that will save the lives of many of our people. They will feed many children. They will make us strong and make us fearless. Now swear to me that you will tell no one about this thing."

The warriors raised their spears and swore to Kintu that they would not tell anyone about the secret of the plants. Kintu smiled and was satisfied that his warriors were trustworthy. But the more Kintu went to visit his ripening grainfield, the more the curiosity of his first wife was aroused. Noku, obsessed with curiousity, followed him, and discovered the ripening grain — and she spoke to him, "My husband!"

Kintu jumped.

"What is this?" asked Noku. "What are these plants? And why are you walking amongst them muttering to yourself?"

Kintu had to think fast to deceive his bad-tempered, fat wife, and he said, "Oh my first wife, these plants are very poisonous, they are deadly, and they were planted here by a demon who wants to wipe out our people. I am guarding them, so that when they ripen, I may burn them with fire. Right now they are still green and will not burn. I did not want anyone to know the secret so please keep the secret to yourself."

Noku said, "I hear you oh king, I hear you, Kintu my husband. The secret is safe in my heart," she lied.

But deep in her heart Noku was plotting murder. As she and Kintu were leaving the valley, she stole some of the ripening grain, she shoved it into her skin bag, and took it home, for she knew that her rival Kina was sick. A murderous plan began to grow in her heart. She would feed Kina this new poisonous plant and slowly poison her.

So, she ground the grain into a paste and she mixed it with water and gave it to Kina to drink. "Now, I'm going to kill you," she said to herself. "You stupid, weak little thing, I am going to destroy you. You are standing between my husband and myself. He loves you more than he loves me."

But, while Kina was lying ill, a fever swept through the village and the first wife of Kintu was stricken by this fever, although she did her best to pretend that nothing was wrong with her. She continued feeding this supposedly poisonous corn to Kina, hoping to see her die in agony; but instead of Kina dying, it was Noku who died — of the fever that was sweeping the village.

And Kina grew so strong because of the healthy paste that the first wife had been feeding her thinking that it was a poison, that she actually recovered and assisted many people to recover by boiling the grain and feeding it to them.

And thus the people discovered that far from being a poison, the grain was, in fact, a wonderful food — a food that had come to them from the stars. They buried the cruel first wife in a gully, and they piled stones over her grave and forgot about her.

And it was not long before every village and every home in the land of Kintu's people was growing the grain which the goddess had given the people. And this is the end of the story of Kintu and the Star Goddess.

The Trickster's Revenge

Listen now, my children, to an amusing story of how Kintu, the father of humanity, saved his people from two giant cannibals when he was already an old, blind man. Because of his great courage and selflessness, because of the many great deeds he had done in his life, the mighty hero Kintu was blessed by the Great Earth Mother with a life that was longer, far longer, than the lives of ordinary people. It is said that he lived for many generations hardly touched by old age, but this story took place when he was already feeling the faint whispers of old age in the forest of his soul.

It is said that one day Kintu was sitting outside his cave, feeling the warmth of the sun upon his body. He no longer could see with his eyes but his sense of hearing and his excellent senses of smell and touch and taste more than compensated for the loss of his vision. He was sitting outside his cave and feeling the happiness all around him. He smelled the different perfumes of the many different kinds of trees that formed the great forest all around his cave. His ears were filled with the music of many birds and the laughter and the singing of the many people with whom he shared the great cave, people whom he and his wife Mamaravi had helped to bring into this world, the first seed of humanity upon the face of this planet.

Kintu heard the laughter of many children. He heard the conversation of many men as they sat under trees repairing weapons or sewing together strips of tanned animal skin to make blankets and loin skins. He heard the sound of women grinding corn — the dull rumbling of grindstone upon grindstone moved backwards and forwards by powerful female hands. He could smell the people. He could smell the grass, the flowers, the trees; Kintu could even smell the rocks. It was a beautiful day and the people of the caves were without a care in this world. Then all of a sudden Kintu became aware of a very strange and somehow sinister smell — a faint smell that invaded his nostrils, a faraway smell which, however, was getting stronger by the moment.

He sat bolt upright, his sightless eyes futilely scanning the surrounding landscape. "Where have I smelled that smell before?" he asked himself. "Where?" He waited, sat dead still, his head turning this way and that. The breeze fanned his nostrils, and he realized that the pungent, terrible, disturbing smell had become stronger. Then he remembered an adventure long ago in which this very kind of smell had played a sinister part. Memories came flooding back into the valleys of his mind, and he identified the smell of man-eating giants. Somewhere sinister beings were creeping slowly towards the community.

Kintu's fingers groped for the horn trumpet he always kept near him. He placed it to his lips blowing two long blasts.

Above the hubbub of conversation from groups of people sitting in the shadow of trees not far away from the cave, the sound of the trumpet soared like an unseen bird towards the blue heavens, alerting all and sundry to the oncoming danger. "AWOOOOOOOOOOO." The sound of Kintu's trumpet froze the marrow in the bones of all and sundry. People leapt to their feet — beautiful women seeking their babies, and mighty men picking up weapons — spears with heads of chipped stone, heavy axes with stone heads, some consisting of a round stone with a hole pierced through it fitted with a wooden handle. These were the weapons of the people.

"AWOOOOOOOOOOOO," sounded Kintu's trumpet again. The people were disciplined. The people had been trained how to react to an emergency. The people had been taught long ago that when Kintu blew his horn it was a sure sign that danger was close at hand.

Men and women and children ran towards the cave, and, as they ran, something monstrous erupted out of the bush some distance away — a lumbering, gigantic form, man-like in shape, with wide shoulders and long dangling arms and a huge hairless head. The creature was as black as coal and its eye blazed red like the glowing coals of a meat-roasting fire. From the creature's lower lip there protruded two fearsome, yellowish-white tusks, like the fangs of a monstrous leopard; its stench filled Kintu's nostrils. "Run my children," cried Kintu. "Run!"

When the people threw glances over their shoulders and saw the gigantic creature coming, they listened to the voice of panic within their hearts. But, while many ran towards the entrance of the cave, towards their "White-headed Great Father" as they now called Kintu, others lost their way, propelled by the demon of fear. They ran this way and that, like frightened chickens. Just then a second monstrous man-like creature appeared from the forest. It roared in fiendish delight. "Ohhhhhhhhhhhhhhhhhh, come to me, little breakfast things. Come to me little human beings; I, *Zimu-Zimu*, King of the Giants, am hungry!"

Fighting its way through the tangle of greenery, the gigantic man-shaped beast reached some of the panicking people; it reached out an arm, and with its huge hand scooped up a woman who was trying to seek the safety of a rock.

"Ha-ha-ha-ha-ha," laughed the giant. "Today I shall eat as I have never eaten before." Her cry of horror vanished down its monstrous gullet. "Aaaaaaaaaaaaaaaaaaagh. Ohhhhhhhhhhhhhhhhhh," laughed the giant, seeking another victim.

It caught a man who screamed in terror as gigantic fingers closed around his running body. "Ahhhhhhhhh," said the giant. "Listen, my little man. Let me, Zimu-Zimu, teach you the meaning of wisdom. "Let me give you a wise saying which your people shall remember for a thousand years. He who is in the clutches of a cannibal should not waste time screaming to the gods for help. Now, I have dinner, little man, and you are invited."

So saying, the ogre threw this man into the air and caught him again in his mouth, swallowing noisily. Then it went about searching for more victims, its feet shaking the Earth and filling the people with yet more panic.

The second giant arrived on the scene, and soon the monsters were feasting noisily upon those of Kintu's people who had been caught in the open. Soon there was not a single human being left insight. Those people who had reached the safety of the cave turned to their great father, Kintu.

"What shall we do, oh, Kintu? It's only a matter of time before those monsters get here. They shall tear the cave open with their hands and we shall be exposed as honeycombs are exposed by the claws of a hungry honey badger. What shall we do?"

"Listen my children," said Kintu. "In this cave there is a secret entrance which will lead you to a still larger cave deeper in the bowels of the earth. Follow me, all of you." The people crowded around Kintu as he made his way to a dark corner where stood a mighty rock leaning against the wall of the cavern. Kintu reached out his hand and pressed this rock which swung aside revealing a dark, yawning entrance behind it.

"Go in there," cried Kintu. "Quickly, all of you. Kingu, you my son, be the leader of the people. I shall stay here and keep those monsters occupied," said Kintu.

"Great father, you cannot do that," cried the young man Kingu, a fierce and fearless hunter, and a very brave warrior.

"Listen Kingu," said Kintu, "you are the blood of my blood, and when I speak I expect you to obey without question. If something happens to me, you must become the leader of the people. Now do what I say, and lead the people into this tunnel quickly."

They poured quickly past the blind Kintu, vanishing into the bowels of the earth, their voices receding as they went deeper. With a sigh Kintu pressed the rock again, and it slid back into place, sealing the entrance.

Kintu stood and waited. He knew that he had done the right thing. He knew that he had to stay there and somehow try to get rid of those man-eating monsters. He also knew that had he fled with the people into the bowels of the Earth, the ogres would have gotten to work ripping the mountain apart until they came to the secret cave in the core, to which his people had fled.

A long time had gone by, as Kintu stood in the cave waiting, when from outside he heard the muttering of angry giant voices. "Where are the rest of these delicious creatures?" he heard one of the giants asking. "My belly is not full. I saw them running into that little cave over there. Come, Sozimu," roared the giant Zimu-Zimu. "Rip up a tree and use it as a digging stick. We shall dig those delicious morsels out, and we shall feast royally as the distant sun sets beyond the mountains."

It was then that Kintu decided to act. He groped his way out of the cave and appeared to blunder towards the oncoming giants. The giants paused in their head-long rush towards the cave, unable to believe their eyes.

"Look, my lord Zimu-Zimu!" said the giant named Sozimu. "One of the little morsels is coming towards us. Do you think he likes to be eaten?"

"I don't think so," said Zimu-Zimu. "I think that little creature is blind. It thinks that it is running away from us and yet it is in fact running towards us. Ho-ho-ho-ho-ho."

A few moments later, Kintu felt monstrous fingers closing around his body. He felt himself being lifted into the air, and he pretended to be very frightened, looking this way and that.

"Look Sozimu," said the giant Zimu-Zimu, "I told you that the little creature is blind — it cannot see, and judging by its white hair, it must be the father of all the creatures that we saw run into the cave. Now listen to me, creature, listen to Zimu-Zimu, my little one. I shall put questions to you, and every one you shall answer completely. Where are the rest of your people?"

"I do not know, great one," replied Kintu. "My people appear to have vanished. They fled into the cave with me but they appear to have vanished. I don't know where to."

"Look into the cave, Sozimu, and see if this creature is telling the truth or not," said Zimu-Zimu. "If it is telling me a lie, I am going to rip out its guts and suck them before I devour the rest of its scrawny little body. Do you understand me creature?"

"I understand you great giant. I am only telling you the truth. My people have vanished."

Some moments later the other giant returned. "It is indeed true, Lord Zimu-Zimu, there is no one inside the cave. I have stuck my head in and have looked — my eyes can see even the tiniest speck of dust — and in that cave there is nothing. And furthermore there is no exit through which the little things could have escaped. There must be magic afoot here, and I, Sozimu, do not like magicians and magic."

"Great giants," said Kintu, "I wish to say something, please."

"You shall only speak when you are spoken to," snarled Zimu-Zimu.

"But please, you must allow me to speak. Because your lives are in danger here."

"Our lives in danger?" snarled the King of the Giants. "What is there in heaven, and what is there on earth that can pose a threat to the life of Zimu-Zimu?"

"Listen my lord," said Kintu, pretending to be thoroughly terrified, "about a month ago a strange creature appeared outside our cave. The creature was very tall, gaunt, and strangely man-like in appearance, with long thin legs and arms and a long pointed head. The creature told us that it had come from the very center of the Sun itself, and that it possessed great powers of magic. Then it proceeded to give us all a demonstration of these powers! It made a large tree to vanish into thin air. It turned a boulder into a clump of flowering bushes. It caused birds to fall out of the sky and to turn into stone, and we were thoroughly terrified of this creature. Then the creature told us that if I agreed to give it the most beautiful young woman amongst my people for a wife, it would not use its great magical powers to harm us, but that if I refused to give it the woman it wanted, it would cause all my people to disappear. Just before you appeared," lied Kintu to the giants, "the creature came, and demanded that I give it the young woman it had chosen, and I, in my great stupidity, refused! I think, great ones, that this mysterious creature is around here somewhere, and I fear that just as it made my people to disappear, so shall it make me — as well as you both — to vanish. I suggest we get out of here with all speed."

"What?" snarled Zimu-Zimu, "Do you expect me, the King of the Giants, to run away from some cheap little magician?"

"Great Zimu-Zimu," said Sozimu, "I think we should do as this little creature suggests. Have you not told me many times before, my leader, that discretion is ever the better part of valor? I, Sozimu, as you well know, fear nothing on this planet, nothing *physical* that is. I fear no snake, no beast — nothing except things that use the powers of magic instead of honorable weapons. These creatures I cannot stand."

"Well, if you think we should run away from here like cowards with our tails between our legs then we must do just that," said Zimu-Zimu. "Let us go, my subject, but we are taking this delicious little human being away with us."

"I suggest we should eat him now, great one," said Sozimu. "Tear him apart and give me one piece of him while you eat the other piece. He is one of most impudent creatures it has ever been my misfortune to meet, and he has told me, Sozimu, something that has made my blood cold — I who fear nothing in this world. For this alone I think we should eat him. Any creature that tells me something I do not want to hear I always devour."

"I think you are right. Here, I will tear him to pieces and give you a piece," said Zimu-Zimu.

"Wait my lord, wait, wait," cried Kintu. "Do not do something that you both might regret."

"Why little one?" Zimu-Zimu wanted to know. "What is it that we are going to regret after we have eaten you? We have eaten lots of your people and now you must follow. So what's all the fuss about?"

"Great Zimu-Zimu," said Kintu, the spirit of cunning working within his mind faster than it had ever worked before. "I am the only one who can protect you against the terrible creature that caused my people to vanish. I am the only one who can recognize this creature. I know for a fact that it can turn itself into anything. It can change itself into a tree, a bird, or even a fish in the water, but no matter how it changes itself and into what shape, I will be able to sense it because I am blind. Do not eat me just yet, because, believe me, this creature is close by!"

"I think you are right," said Zimu-Zimu, "but I promise you, little human being, when we reach my home, when we reach my cave, we shall eat you there — me, my friend here, and every one of my three wives shall have a piece."

Then Zimu-Zimu threw Kintu into his great leather bag and made his way through the dense bush, closely followed by Sozimu, his friend and subject.

As the mountain of the cave in which Kintu's people were hiding receded farther and farther into the distance, Kintu began to pray to the great Earth Mother as he had never prayed before. He prayed that the Great Goddess should give him a means — any means whatever — of getting rid of these two giants so that they would never again threaten his people, and Kintu also prayed for a chance to escape because he did not relish the prospect of being eaten by Zimu-Zimu and his fellow monsters. And he prayed and he prayed as the day grew older and the golden Sun started its slow descent towards the far-western mountains.

Suddenly Kintu felt the giant pause in his tracks. He heard him say, "Sozimu, what was that?"

The other giant stopped, listened, and then said, "I hear nothing great one."

"Listen again you stupid," snarled Zimu-Zimu. "I have heard something behind us. I have a feeling that something unseen is following us." And then a long silence fell.

Then the second giant said, "I suddenly have the same feeling, my lord. I think there is something creeping up behind us from the forest over there."

The two giants tore trees out of the ground to use as clubs against the menace they believed was following them. Long moments passed. Nothing happened. Now, Kintu had received many gifts from the great Earth Mother, and one of these gifts was the gift of throwing his voice so that it appeared as if it came from somewhere else other than from him; and so while the giant and his friend stood about frightened and angry, their red eyes searching the distance, behind them Kintu threw his voice into a tall tree many paces away from the giants.

The giants thought they heard the tree laughing, "Heh, heh, heh, heh, heh, I say — you two stupid stinking, lice-ridden, monstrous beasts — I am the creature of great magic and when the sun sets, I shall close in on you both and do unmentionable things to the two of you. Heh, heh, heh, heh."

"Did you hear that?" said Zimu-Zimu stupidly to his friend.

"I heard it great one," cried Sozimu. And with that he drew back his arms and threw the great tree that he had uprooted with all his power straight at the tall tree from which he thought the voice had come. The missile struck the tall tree, splintering its branches, but the shrill, mocking voice came again.

"You cannot injure me, you pathetic monster, for nothing can stand against my magic. I wish for you to suffer torture in your stupid minds until night falls, and then you will see what I can do! Heh, heh, heh, heh, heh!"

As the Sun slowly descended toward his resting place beyond the very edge of the world, Kintu was aware of the fact that the giants were terrifying themselves. Big as they were, so big was their terror. He did not cease from tormenting them. He threw his voice into any tree or rock that they passed. Laughter screeched at them from the slopes of darkening hills. Threats were screamed at them from the surrounding, slowly deepening darkness. "Ha, ha, ha, ha, ha, ha, ha, ha," laughed the trees. "Ho, ho, ho, ho, ho, ho," laughed the rocks. "Haaaaaaaaaa," screamed the ground underfoot.

Then Kintu realized that Sozimu's skin was beginning to jump with terror, and that within Zimu-Zimu's huge chest the giant's mighty heart was pounding like a thing gone mad.

The sweat of terror was covering the bodies of both monstrous creatures, and its stench was unbearable to Kintu's nostrils, but he did not stop with his game. Threats were flung at the giants from all directions until the monsters stopped in their tracks, turned back to back with huge boulders in their hands, preparing to do battle against their unseen tormentor.

"Heh, heh, heh heh," laughed the darkness. "I am coming, little giants, I am the great creature of magic. I am coming, you cannot strike me with the rocks in your hands. Nor can you brain me with the trees that you uproot, but I shall do unmentionable things to you. Do you want to know what I'm going to do to you?"

And the bodiless voice described in frightening detail the hideous things that it intended to do to both giants, and the giants were besides themselves with terror. The stench of urine filled the night air as they wetted their loin skins again and yet again.

When Kintu was sure that the giants were nearly fainting with fear, he spoke, as if from the bag now, saying, "Mighty ones, great giants, I beg to speak."

"What are you saying, little rodent?" demanded Zimu-Zimu, hardly able to conceal the tremor in his great voice.

"Mighty ones, there is something that I forgot to tell you," said Kintu. "I forgot to tell you that it is me that that mysterious creature is seeking, not you. It is better that I, a puny human being, should perish, rather than you mighty giants. I am old and blind and tired. You are still young with many years ahead of you. I beg of you now to listen to my suggestion! Take me out of this bag which holds me captive, and place me upon the ground, and then turn and run as fast as you can for the safety of your distant homes."

"We have nothing to lose, mighty one," said Sozimu to his king, Zimu-Zimu, "let us do as the little animal suggests. So what if that mysterious fearsome thing out there devours him? We are the giants, and we shall survive. Is it not true that we can outrun any animal that there is on Earth, including some types of birds?"

"You are right, my subject," said Zimu-Zimu. "Although it pains me to leave this delicious morsel behind, let him be sacrificed, that we may survive." So saying, Zimu-Zimu took Kintu out of his skin bag and placed him upon the ground, and then both giants turned and ran for dear life into the depths of the night.

For a long long long time nothing was heard save the thunder of their footfalls receding further and further into the distance, farther and farther away from the danger they so strongly believed threatened them. It was then that Kintu played his last trick. He began to scream at the top of his voice, "Yaaaaaaaaaaaaaaaa, help me, help me, help!" And far away Zimu-Zimu heard the blood-chilling scream and it made him run all the faster, never looking behind him.[6]

As he ran, Zimu-Zimu suddenly felt a deep sorrow passing like a dark cloud over his troubled heart. He was suddenly filled with admiration for the brave little human being he believed had sacrificed himself so that they, the giants might survive. Into the very womb of midnight the giants ran; and when the morning Sun kissed the Eastern Mountains, the giants found themselves safely within the borders of their own territory. But they did not stop running until they were within their own caves surrounded by their wide-eyed children and their gigantic spouses.

They said nothing about what had befallen them until some days later, when Zimu-Zimu called a meeting of all his subjects, and commanded them all on pain of a braining with his mighty club, not to set foot in the territory of human beings again and never again to hunt down human beings for food.

For as he spoke, Zimu-Zimu recalled (with what passes for gratitude in such monstrous bosoms) the white-haired, blind, and kindly little human being, who had bravely sacrificed himself so that giants might live!

Kintu, old and blind as he was, made his way slowly and painfully back to the land of his people. But along the way he was guided by a friendly bird who acted as his eyes, for many creatures loved Kintu. After many days, he managed to reach the cave in which his people were hiding. He groped his way into the cave and pressed the special rock. Then he called out, and cautiously the people came forth, some of the earliest inhabitants of this beautiful Earth. They all came out at Kintu's bidding, and they marveled when he told them of how he had rid his land of man-eating giants.

"I feel in my heart that they shall not trouble us again, my children," said Kintu, once more sitting down outside his cave, once more enjoying the warmth of the mid-summer sun. "Our troubles are over, at least for the time being, but in the future we must always be prepared for any type of danger from any direction. We must be prepared, for are we not the seed of humanity, the future inheritors of the world and all that there is in it, and the protectors of life?"

And are we not all the children of Kintu, my listeners, who is the ancestor of humanity, both wise and foolish, innocent and guileful, cruel and compassionate; the Trickster, whose tales still come down to us, from the Morning of the World?

Credo Mutwa in ceremonial attire

5
The Song of the Stars

*There are things that fly through the night, those you call UFOs, which
we in Africa call Abahambi Abavutayo, "the fiery visitors." Oh yes, Africa
has had her own share of UFOs, and she has for many, many centuries.
Long before they were even heard of in other parts of the world, we, the
people of Africa, had contact with these things and the creatures inside
them, very often. We call them fire visitors. I can only speak within certain
constraints because we are not allowed to talk in any detail about these
sacred things. Our people fear that should we do that, then the star ships
would stop visiting us.*

The Song of the Stars is truly the song of Africa, for you will find
legends and lore about the Sun and the Moon, and all the stars,
throughout this vast continent. And the mythology, and even the
histories of our people, are full of descriptions, not only of the stars
and planets, but of the intelligent beings that belong to them, and
how they have interacted with human beings.

For example, the Dogon speak of visitors that came from what
we call the "Star of the Wolf" *Peri Orifici Orimbisi* (Sirius).[1] We believe that that was the very star from which mankind was driven
away after a gigantic war against the sea-dwelling fish people. We
believe that we were brought to this world inside a hollowed-out
moon by the two sons of *Nommo*, the great and kindly father of the
sea-people of that world, but you will learn more about that story
soon. If you scratch below the surface, all our tribal people have
stories about the stars.

You see, many of the stories about the stars fit together. For example, the Zodiac with all its creatures — the *Mulu-Mulu* as it is
called — is not just groups of constellations going around the Earth,

they are stars from which the various animals we have on Earth somehow originated. We are told that the lions came from the lion constellation. We are told that all the cattle came from the bull constellation, all the sheep came from the sheep constellation, all the grain came from the green maiden constellation, and all the lobsters and all the fishes came from the two fishes constellation or the whale constellation or they came from the sky crab constellation. The water-goat (Capricorn) constellation didn't produce a goat, it produced seals and walruses that dwell in the sea. There is an image which the white people do not have in their Zodiac, of the whole constellation of the sky, which produced all of the many kinds of ocean and land animals that there are.

I tell you these things at the outset to let you know that for the people of Africa, the skies are full of life; yes, even the origin of life may be attributed to the stars! On the plains of Africa, it has seemed to many people, that there are the Herds of Eternity; but really, for the African mind, the living animals of the Serengeti plains are reflections of their heavenly cousins. The Herds of Eternity are really in the stars; there also is to be found the origin and destiny of humanity.

In Kenya there is a nation of people who claim great knowledge about space creatures. These people are the Massai, a very tall warrior people. These Massai people say they were given cattle by a great wise god with a long white beard. His name was *Uru-Wantayi*. According to Massai legend Uru-Wantayi came to Earth from the stars in his gold and iron canoe; and the canoe was full of cattle. And Uru-Wantayi released the cattle upon the plains of Massaimara. There, Uru-Wantayi was met by the beautiful Massai girl called Mara, and into her hands Uru-Wantayi entrusted the cattle, telling the Massai people that they were the keepers of all the cattle of the world. Their cows, which have a very long horn, are called *Ankole*. To this day, even if they are starving and are dying, the Massai will never eat the meat of the hundreds (or thousands, in olden days) of cattle of which they are the keepers and the owners. These fierce Massai people say they must obey that wonderful wise man from the stars called Uru-Wantayi, who told them not to eat meat.

What the Massai *are* allowed to do, however, is as follows: they may make a little cut in the neck of a cow and release some blood, which they mix with the milk from the cow. And then they put in a tiny little bead of the fresh dung of the cow, and they make a sort of sour milk — like yogurt — and they eat this. All you have to do is look at the Massai to know they are healthy. But this is a story which shows how the legends of the star-people affect African tribes.

You have learned of Nananana and Amarava, but there are also other gods and goddesses in our tradition who have commerce with the stars. For example there is *Somnganise*, who is also called "The Paver of the Way." Somnganise also means "the friendly one," the friend of the people. He is the messenger of the gods and carries the word back and forth between Earth and Heaven, and from the Realm of the Gods to other realms throughout the world and the under-world. Somnganise is the father of *Ndeyiza*, who is often seen flying through the sky in a glowing golden basket. Some say he flies through the sky in a golden swing, our African concept of a flying saucer.[2]

One of the least-known facts about the black people of South Africa is that they possessed amazing knowledge of the Cosmos, the Solar System, and even dimensions unknown to man. One of these things that our people knew was that it was the Earth which orbited the Sun and not the Sun which orbited the Earth. And they disguised this knowledge behind all sorts of colorful fairytales and legends.

The black people of Africa in the years when the white people were just coming to the Cape, already possessed knowledge of the fact that the Sun was a fire, which they imagined to be shaped like a morula fruit, and that the Earth went round and round the Sun, under the guardianship of God the Father and God the Mother. Now, our people believed that the Sun, being a male entity, was static, sitting upon a cosmic mountain, and the Earth, being a female entity, danced round and round the Sun, just as the king's favorite concubine always dances round and round the king in the "first fruits" festival in any tribal society.

In our secret tradition we say to the Sun, "We know you are the first... Let it be hidden that we know that you are the First Flower of

God." In other words let it be revealed, but not told to the uniniti-
ated, that we know that it is not the Earth which is the first, it is the
Sun. It is not the Sun that moves, but it is the Earth. And to further
disguise what this whole thing is about, we picture a great mountain of light in the middle of the cosmic ocean and on this mountain
sits the Sun, ever shining, but the Earth is carried around and around
this giant mountain by a great tortoise called *Sixaxa*, who is known
as "the slave of the Earth." "Sixaxa" means "the great, slimy, slippery one."

According to one legend, when God created this Earth, Sixaxa
refused to come and take the Earth on his back because God had
created many Earths before, and then destroyed them for various
reasons. Each of the created Earths had been carried by poor old
Sixaxa on his back. When this world of ours — which is the sixth
world according to African legend — was created, Sixaxa refused
to come out of the sea and carry the Earth on his back and the great
Earth Mother, *Nomcumbulwana*, assisted by her son, the little Son of
God, *Umvelinangey*, made use of the dog of the Sun to force the stubborn old turtle to come out of the sea and to carry the Earth — depicted as a bowl with rivers and mountains on it — on his back.

When the Earth was placed upon Sixaxa's back, he was so miserable and depressed that the Earth Mother brewed him a pot full of
beer and made him very drunk. She said, "Well, he who refuses to
do something while sober, must do it when he is drunk." And thus
we believe that Sixaxa swims around and around the Sun in a
drunken stupor carrying the Earth on his back.

The little boy in the picture, who holds the tortoise, is the Son of
God, sir, the son of God the Father and the Earth Mother. He is the
God of Light, the guardian of the Sun. It is said that it is he who
tends the Sun and keeps it burning on the great mountain.

The dog is the Dog of Light, the guardian of fire. The symbols
show a combination of the spirit of the Earth, represented by the
dog; the spirit of the air, represented by the hawk; and the spirit of
the underworld, represented by the snake.

We portray God the Mother and God the Son. We cannot portray
God the Father because that would be a blasphemy, the Father in
this case being represented by the full Moon over the Mother's left

How the Turtle Was Forced to Work, *painting by Vusamazulu Credo Mutwa*

shoulder. Even though I am painting in the Western style, I must keep to strict African symbolic tradition.

The Earth Mother's sacred name is Ma, the mother, she who originally married the Tree of Life. And the Earth Mother is sometimes depicted in our legends as part woman and part plant. During summer the horns on her head are in flower, and during winter they are just bare wood. Her necklace is the necklace of Spring, which gets stolen by her treacherous second husband in winter.

It was also known by our people that all the stars combined form a gigantic flower-like shape which is ever-spinning. So the people knew in old Africa that stars form galaxies. Don't ask me how they knew. All I know is that they did know this.

The Song of the Stars [3]

This story can take up to two years of telling, each day, by a tribal storyteller. Here I will give you the merest outline of this great story that tells of the extraterrestrial origins of humankind.

It is said that first the gods created humans on a world next to ours, a small world of red sands; and in all African mythology you find a very strange thing: the belief that the first people, the original people who appeared on this Earth, were red, not black or white. This somehow compares with the Biblical notion of Adam having been a red man, hence the name Adam which means "red" in one sense.[4]

It is said that on that Red World women dominated men, hunted them down, mated with them, and then ate them. One day the men rebelled, and a gigantic war took place — a fight between men and women — in which fearsome forces were unleashed, including the terrible star-eating demons who are known as the *gungangu* in our mythology. A great hero named *Moromudzi* and a band of chosen heroes fought one gigantic battle with the demons and drove them from the Red World.

Now Moromudzi had a gentle heart, and did not hate the women, but sought to make peace with them. He had fallen in love with the beautiful *Banu Kimanmireva*. Kimanmireva and other women became pregnant, and then these women, together with a few chosen men, decided to flee from the Red Sand World, which was almost completely destroyed by the battles that had taken place. They wished to flee from the memories of so much violence and hatred.

So Moromudzi and Kimanmireva and the others got into the belly of a gigantic iron dragon that was capable of flying between the stars; and they must have been very brave, for they went out and away from the Sun off into the outer darkness between the stars. And after a long time they came to the star we call Peri Orifici Orimbisi (Sirius), and which is known as *Nalediyapiri* in Tswana and *Nanadiyafici* in the languages of the Shona people of Zimbabwe. It is also called, *Inja*, which means "a dog."[5] Our name for it means, "The Star of the Wolf." There they found a Water World, a planet that circles that star.

It was a beautiful world, and human beings could live there on islands. But the world was already inhabited by an intelligent water-dwelling people, not so unlike our modern day dolphins in gentleness, but also amphibious, and human-like, who received the human beings in friendship, and let them live in peace. The King of the Water People was very wise and much beloved by the Water People, and he was called *Nommo*.

The two races lived side by side in peace for a while, but then something bad happened, something so bad as to constitute an "unforgivable sin" between intelligent races; for the human beings com-

The Firebird's Egg (A Creation Myth), *painting by Vusamazulu Credo Mutwa*

mitted violence. They killed, and then ate one of the intelligent water-dwelling people of that world. It was an act just as terrible as
killing and eating one of your human neighbors.

After a great meeting, the Water People went to war on the human beings, for they now believed that the species was evil. It is
said that during that terrible war, in which mankind was nearly
destroyed, the great lord, *Nommo*, took pity upon the race of humanity and sent his two sons, *Wowane* and *Mpanku* to try and save
the remainder of the human race.[6]

The twin sons of Nommo, almost divine in their powers, flew up
and found a gigantic egg in the darkness of space. This object they
drained of its white and yolk, and into it they loaded the surviving
human beings.

Now the two mighty twins began to roll the egg across the sky of
deep space, where the comets and meteors come and go, back to the
star from which the human beings had come. And we do not know
why — perhaps the human beings begged them — but they by-
passed the Red Sand World entirely and landed on another world,
which seemed habitable, for it had both water and land. When the
great egg arrived in our world, it was hard for the twins to control
it, such was its speed, and it burrowed its way into the underground,
and then the people had to escape and emerge from the underground
to the surface world. There are two holes that may be seen in South

Africa which are claimed to be the hole from which — according to legend — the first people emerged.

When Wowane and Mpanku saw that all the people would be safe, and that this world was both beautiful and habitable, they rejoiced. Then the twins began to roll the egg back up into the sky again. It was pockmarked somewhat from its journey through space, but the twins thought they might return it. Just then, the Firebird, one of the most fearsome entities in the universe and whose egg it was, discovered its loss, and came after them at terrible speed on its fiery wings, through the cold void between the stars.

Wowane saw its approach and said to Mpanku, "My brother, you must get away; you must dive into the sea far below. There you will be safe. And Mpanku dived down. But the bird caught Wowane and took him away. And it tied him to a great big stone, which is represented (in the picture on page 127) as a standing stone, and then slowly it ripped his guts out, while he was tied to the stone. He tore out his liver, his heart, and everything else, telling him that he would scream for many thousands of years, because he had robbed her of her egg. Even to this day, when a person who does something and is punished out of all proportion to the crime, we say that "He has stolen the egg of the Firebird."[7]

After the Firebird had taken Wowane away, Mpanku placed the egg in the sky in such a way that it revolved around the Earth, and that is why the Moon resembles a great pockmarked egg. Then Mpanku dived back toward the Earth and lived in the ocean. There he married a mermaid, and had many children, whom we call dolphins today. We believe that dolphins are people and they are able to talk to us. This is why the Zulu people call dolphins, "*Hlengeto,*" which means "the one who saves." We believe that these creatures are so good-hearted that if you fall into the sea they will rescue you and bring you back to land.[8]

Thereafter, the people began to spread all over the Earth and make it their own. Mpanku was killed some time later, in a battle with a great shark, and all the human beings grieved for the intelligent sea-being who had been their savior.

After many centuries had passed, Nommo, who was immortal, came to visit the Earth with twelve of his wise fellow amphibians.

And he gave our people much wisdom; he taught them how to do things and make things, and he taught them more knowlege of the stars.

Nommo pointed to the heavens and showed them the Inja star where his world was and from which they had come. And he reminded them of many things they had known on the water world, which now has passed into the lore of the Dogon and the Zulu, and many other African people.

He told them that the Inja star had twelve worlds spinning around it; and he described every one of these worlds, and the kinds of creatures that inhabit these worlds. And he told them of the companion of the Inja star which is a star but not a star. It was eaten by a giant evil spirit (gungangu), and this spirit spit out a pit, which was the dark core of the star. And if a man were to land on this star he would be crushed by his own weight, as his body collapsed together.[9]

The great Nommo told our people that we must get rid of war, of hunger, and disease. If we could do this, then Nommo would return again and then show us the way to the stars. Then people would again be able to visit the twelve beautiful worlds, which used to be visited by human beings. Then Nommo explained that the gods used to have a chain which connected all the worlds together, and that one day people could climb up and down this chain, to visit any world they chose, and truly, not just in dreams.

But because of the sinfulness of human beings, who still have not learned their lesson about violence, the great and angry god, Ngungi, who is the lord of all the blacksmiths, had been sent to break this chain, so that human beings would not be able to visit worlds among the stars. So it is said that when human beings become peaceful, less ambitious, less greedy and less cruel, the gods will restore this chain, so that people will be able to visit other worlds in the universe, and the gods themselves, and the intelligent and kindly creatures from other worlds will be able to climb down and visit us, both in our sleep and in the waking world.

I have told you how our folklore hides wisdom. We Africans feel that from our origins, concealed in these tales, is explained the human affinity for water. Because in all nations of the world, even on very distant islands, people have a strange affinity for water, for the sea, for lakes, and for great rivers. There seems to be something magnetic in any great body of water that seems to draw men and say "come here!"

And consider the important part that water appears to play in the ritual lives of human beings. For example, in Jamaica and in other islands in that area, the black people have a ritual in which they plunge themselves into mud holes and then purify themselves under great waterfalls. Now, in South Africa it is a common practice for sangomas and even ordinary faith healers in our townships to pay a visit to the seaside just to take a ritual plunge into the water. The water becomes a vehicle for their renewal and rebirth.

I say that there is a grain of truth in what has been told in these stories. Otherwise why would we blacks imagine such a fantastic thing as a red-skinned people? Why would people who had neither telescopes nor microscopes imagine a world other than this one in which we dwell? Why would people concoct a story that human beings originated on another world? I say there is a grain of truth in this story and that it needs investigation.

The Dogon of Central Africa have some of the best known stories of the stars, and they knew for many years before the white men ever discovered it, that the Star Sirius is attended by a tiny dead star called "the mustard seed," and that it is the presence of this star that makes Sirius move about in tiny movements invisible to the naked eye, but seen by white men's telescopes for the first time not so many years ago. It is the same collapsed star from our legends, that we call the "pit," spat out by the star-devouring demons.

Not only among the Zulu, but the Dogon, and many widespread African tribes, there are stories of the Nommo, who resemble the king of the Water People in our legend. They are said to be intelligent beings who have visited the Earth several times. They are usually described as somewhat like human beings but with skins like reptiles. I have heard them described by some as a cross between a scaly little demon and a dolphin. These wise creatures tell us we are in exile from the society of intelligent beings who dwell on other worlds, because of our aggressiveness.

The *Sikasa*, also intelligen
we, the people of this Earth,
worlds. We did not originate .
as exiles, because of the sins ol
Yes, these things were known

Fire Visitors

Long ago, during the historic wa
going out to attack the Mapepetwa p
was camped near a great mountain in   out of
the sky what the king thought were gi   shields. These
great shields of fire flew one behind the   er — there were three of
them — above the army of King Shaka, in a great circle. And they
flew three times around the mountain and over the army of the
king. Marvellous to say, everyone put down their arms because they
wondered at the omen instead of thinking about killing people.

In the legends of our people, not only unknown flying objects
but also strange creatures sometimes interfered in human affairs. A
story is told of two war-like tribes in Uganda, the Baganda and the
Lunga tribe. These tribes, we are told, were locked in a war with
neither winning the conflict, for well over fifty years; and then one
day while the two warrior armies were facing each other for what
was to be the final battle between them, out of the sky there appeared a great cloud-like creature, a creature which stories describe
as a gigantic mountain of cloud, a jelly-like cloud, yellow in color,
with a huge staring eye in the center of the pile.

It is said that this thing descended slowly and landed in the space
between the armies, and then I tell you a very strange thing happened: Every warrior in those two armies suddenly lost his memory,
forgetting what he was holding in his hands, what the weapons
were for, what the shield was for. The warriors just simply threw
down their weapons and stared at each other, not knowing what to
do. And later the great creature which sat in the center of the two
armies disintegrated, breaking into pieces, and sank into the ground.
After that we are told the two tribes never fought again. This is a
real story, a true story, and in the course of my life I have had a

...es of these unearthly creatures, not only I alone ... other people as well.

...very moving story — a true story — of a beautiful and ... wise Zulu woman called *Mtashana*. This woman was a ...istorical person and she was for many years believed to be a *sikasa* (a human-like alien, described later in this chapter) and the way her life ended confirmed this. Let me tell you her story.

It happened at the time of one of the greatest kings of the *Mtetwa* people in Natal, the king called *Dingiswayo*. A wise man was walking through the bush when he suddenly heard something crying. He went over and he found it was a beautiful baby girl, and he wondered who could have abandoned a baby girl here, but he took this baby girl and brought it up as his own. This baby girl grew up to be unbelievably wise. She could perform miracles. She could cure illnesses of any kind by simply placing her finger upon the forehead of the sick person.

One day she was captured, and the people who captured her tied her to a stake thinking they would sacrifice her. But a great warrior king of theirs, Jama, had been injured. She broke free from the stake to which she had been tied, and walked into the hut where the wounded king lay. She placed her finger upon his forehead, while everyone watched in astonishment. Within a few hours it was noticed that the king's severe injuries were actually healing before their eyes. Soon he was fully recovered.

So Jama was healed by this wonderful maiden, Mtashana, and later she became one of the wives of King Dingiswayo. For a long time she performed miracles: healing the sick, delivering babies, making plants grow very quickly and doing all kinds of other things that amazed people. She taught our people that if a woman had had a very difficult childbirth and was losing a lot of blood they were to kill a calf immediately and force this bleeding woman to drink as much of the fresh calf's blood as possible. And this is sometimes done even now. She also taught people how to use urine to cure certain illnesses, which is still a traditional art kept alive today.

Mtashana outlived her husband and several other kings, living to be well over a hundred years old, teaching and healing all the while. It was after the end of the great wars between the Zulu people and the English that she sought a refuge in my great grandfather's village. One day she suddenly came running into the village. My great grandmother hailed the woman and asked her, "Why are you running? From whom are you fleeing, royal one?"

Mtashana said, "Please hide me, they have come for me at last."

My grandmother thought she had gone mad, and hid her in one of the huts. That night a strange light was seen in the sky. Just before dawn people heard music in the air from an unknown source. The next day Mtashana said to the villagers, "Well, my people have come for me, I must go out to them."

The Zulus were very sad to hear this and they said, "But where are your people?"

And she said to them, "They don't want to be seen by you, but I can see them."

It is said that Mtashana gave away all of her wealth, her cattle, her goats and sheep and chickens. Then she put on her best ornaments and bangles, and in front of well over two hundred people, she walked out of the village in plain sight, about a hundred paces and then disappeared. And there were even (white) gunrunners and explorers who witnessed her disappearance.

You see, all over Africa, when you travel among the tribespeople, you come across a similar mythology (though I think they won't tell it to strangers). The things that they cannot explain, they try to understand them in terms that are familiar. For example, the Pygmies in Zaire believe that there is a god who travels on a swing through the skies. They say that this god brought them knowledge. They say this god flies by on a swing, because to them a swing is the only man made thing that they know that flies. The pygmies call him *Kani* or *Kahani*. This god brought knowledge to the people.

Then there are the Bushmen, who have a god called *Nxunxa*. Nxunxa is said to fly through the air in a flying ostrich egg, a very large ostrich egg in which he rides. It is said that he brought people to this world in one of these magic ostrich eggs. It is similar to our story of Mpanku and Wawane, who brought human beings to Earth in the egg of the Firebird.

One of the traditions is that when a UFO is sighted above a Zulu village, the women of that village must immediately burn a sweet-smelling herb which looks like sage and which the Zulus call *impepo*. And they must burn this herb in the open to placate the little star gods that fly in these fiery disks; because one fact is known throughout Southern Africa where these things have been seen and it is this: That whenever a UFO has been sighted, two definite things happen: One, either the cattle are found mutilated, as I found an old Tswana man's cows so mutilated, or the eldest goat or sheep, or even an old woman, disappears forever without trace. These are facts known to hundreds of people throughout Southern Africa. Not only that, on several occasions people have been taken away, disappeared, only to reappear two or three days later, not knowing where they have been, not knowing what happened to them. And yet these people had disappeared in plain view of many people. And this also happened to me, though it makes me uncomfortable to talk about it.[10]

Like many people, I never used to believe in the existence of either UFOs or aliens, not at all. I was forced to change my opinion by things that happened to me, by my own experiences.

The year was 1951, and we were called very urgently to Botswana, South Africa to a place near a large village where a falling star had been seen. When we arrived there, I found to my surprise that the bush was burning. Now I know it is often the case under such circumstances. The craft, or whatever it was that had brought these creatures, had set the bush on fire. We went into the center of the part which already had been burned, and there was a hut there. At first it was so dark that we saw nothing, but then, maybe a hundred yards away, we saw something. It was about the size of a lorry, but it was round. It was floating in the air.

Then two of these creatures ran out of a clump of trees which had been scorched by the fire and they ran towards this thing very fast. They moved like little children — sort of jumping. They ran not as human beings run; they ran with leaps and bounds, running then jumping then running then jumping. We could see that the creatures were wearing some kind of dark garments, and yet their heads and their hands were bare. There were lights in this thing that was floating above the ground. It lit up the surrounding trees which had been scorched by the fire. The creatures got into this thing — I don't know how — and it just took off and disappeared.

When we approached there, the grass was burnt, and one of our friends had a large paraffin lantern, in which he picked out something which we know to be very dangerous. When one of the these craft which carry these creatures has landed it always leaves some kind of rubbish behind it. This rubbish is white in color. It crumbles like burnt bone, like bone turning to ash, and you must never touch it with your hand or else your hands will get hurt and blister and behave as if they've been burnt. Your hair will fall out from your head and other parts of your body and then you will die. When we see this rubbish, what we do is dig a hole quickly and then we take long poles, perhaps saplings tied together with rope, and we slip this rubbish into the hole and bury it. That is the African tradition.

One day in 1958 I was called again by people in the land now known as Botswana, South Africa. I was summoned by a very wealthy African who came all the way for me to Soweto, saying that I must come and help him because a strange thing had occurred on his farm. We travelled to Bechuanaland as it was then called, and we arrived at the man's farm, and the first thing he showed me was a dog, just an ordinary dog, but the dog was dead and what was very unusual about the dead dog was that the dog was dry and hard. The flesh was hard as if the animal had been dried, but it was not wrinkled or showing the ribs or anything like that. The animal appeared fresh, appeared as if it could stand up and walk on its feet but it was dry and stiff.

I asked this man what had happened, and then he took me to another part of his farm, a part which the Tswanas call *moraka*, which is a cattle camp where cattle are kept in the bush. There in the moraka we saw a number of cattle corrals and this man showed me two cows and they were a ghastly sight: the beasts had been hideously mutilated, as if some savage man had taken a gigantic sword or axe to the animals. I remember distinctly that the hind leg of one of the cows had almost been slashed off just above where the limb bends and is slightly crooked. It was awful. And when I examined the flesh I found that the cut was clean, as if it had been made by a very sharp saw, such as the finest butchers use. So clean-cut also was the bone, the leg hanging by a strip of flesh, almost ready to fall off. The cows were decomposing already.

Then the man took me to a hut, a small mud and grass hut, and inside the hut lay a man, and he said that this was the man I was to help. The man could not talk. The man was an ordinary Tswana, a half breed, part Bushman and part African, a man with a wrinkled yellow face who appeared to be on the border of madness. His eyes were wide with shock, gleaming as if with a fever, and he could not talk to me. For two days I gave this man treatment, nursing him back to sanity; and eventually I prevailed upon him to talk to me about what had happened.

The man told me that one night he had seen a strange thing fall out of the sky, a thing that glowed red like a very big coal from a fire; and he had hurried towards the cattle pen because he had just been returning from the trading store when he saw this thing, and he was worried that a forest fire might be started which could kill some of the cows he was looking after. He ran toward the scene of the blaze, his dog sprinting far ahead of him; then, as he came to the edge of the burning area, his nostrils were assailed by a terrible smell, a hideous unearthly stench that made him retch. And there before him, darkly silhouetted against the blazing trees, was a monstrous thing, and the sight froze the marrow in his bones, and fear imprisoned the scream he felt rising in his throat. He saw that his dog was lying dead in the flaming grass, and close by, towering over him, was a monstrous alien being, just looking at him.

"Could you take me to this place where you saw this thing?" I asked him gently.

His eyes were full of fear, but he agreed to take me there. On the following morning the man led me and a group of three other men to the site, and as we drew near the burned-out area we saw that the trees had been burned, stripped of their leaves and blackened, and a large circular area of the grass had been burned, too. I could still smell, faint but definite, an unusual smell that he had described as "the sickening stench."

Immediately I warned the men not to approach the place any further, because I knew from experience that this could be dangerous to all of us. We scouted around the circular burned place, not approaching its center. Then I saw, fortunately at some distance, a heap of that toxic white stuff I have mentioned, and which has been found at many sites throughout Africa.

Then we camped near the place, and for two days nothing happened. Three days went by, and still nothing happened. And then on the fourth night I was awakened by the shouts of my companions and the barking of dogs. I took my spear and went to investigate.

My friends had all run away, and when I approached the burned-out place something loomed in the darkness in front of me. It did not resemble anything I had ever seen before, so it is difficult to describe it. The thing was gigantic, a huge cylindrical shape without limbs, without hands, without anything — a gigantic walking cylinder that dragged part of itself along the ground. I was accompanied by two of the herdsman's dogs, and the dogs tried to attack it; but almost immediately both were quite dead.

I took a stone and threw it at the creature, and then there occured something that I shall not easily forget. By the light of the moon, that creature turned and looked at me. I saw that, although the creature was without shoulders, without limbs, it definitely had something of a head at its top, and I saw what appeared to be two large glass-like eyes staring at me. These eyes were squarish in shape and the creature wore a sort of a huge metallic cap on its head. I saw no mouth, I saw no protrusions — only that smooth metallic shape. The rest of the creature was a sort of dull purple and there was an awful stench that hung over the entire thing. It was a stench like I had never smelled in all of my life before, as if all the rotten eggs of Africa were gathered together in one place.[11] Around the creature also was also the smell of burning metal. The creature's body had a strange gleaming sheen to it — a dull gleaming. After we stared at each other for a few moments, the creature suddenly rose slightly and turned and moved away, and I never saw it again.

But there is a sequel to this. One of the herdsmen of the cattle, I am told, broke the rule and approached the heap of white stuff about which I had warned the men; and this man, I am told, died terribly a few months afterwards. He lost all his hair, became like an old man although he had been a young man in his twenties, and died vomiting very very badly. I've seen things like that happen many times to people who dared to enter the place where these things have landed.[12]

When you have really seen these creatures, sir, you don't like to even talk about it — because even as we talk, my mind's eye still sees that monstrous thing. Later I learned more about these creatures.

In 1959, when I visited the country which was then known as South Rhodesia, and is called Zimbabwe today, I found a very disturbed community near a little town called Marandellas. There the tribespeople had seen a fearsome creature which they call *Muhondoruka*. This was a creature which frightened them terribly. When I came there, they were collecting copper pennies and were polishing them very very brightly with a mixture of wood ash and milk and metal polish. They were making rings out of these pennies and other ornaments which they wanted to present to this Muhondoruka. They intended to take these polished coins and these rings that they had made to the site where Muhondoruka had been seen, as a peace offering to this fearsome creature.

What is known about the Muhondoruka, and which I have seen, is that the Muhondoruka destroys cattle. It kills goats and cattle, but it is very selective about the animals that it kills. It always kills the oldest cattle in the herd and the biggest of them; and it kills them in this way: It makes cuts on the hind legs of the animal, and the cuts are so fine that you don't see them at first, until you try to move the carcass of the beast, whereupon it falls apart.

Sometimes the cow has been cut open and his stomach removed, but always the hind legs have been cut or the big sinews at the back of the legs have been deliberately cut with an extremely sharp instrument — some kind of saw-like instrument.

The Mashona people of Rhodesia told me also that when this Muhondoruka creature had been seen it was a sure sign that conflict and war would occur in the land. I had arrived in Rhodesia early in 1959, and by February or March violence had broken out.

I was to see a similar creature a second time, this time in the year 1960, also in Rhodesia, and I was told by the black Mashona people that this creature was called the war-bringer. Circumstances were to prove them quite right — that was the year 1960, the start of a long and bloody war in Rhodesia.

Three years later I was in North Rhodesia, now known as Zambia, when a violent conflict took place between the forces of Dr. Kenneth Kaunda and the forces of a black prophetess called Alicia Linchina. The followers of Alicia Linchina were hideously massacred by Kaunda's forces, and I was there in Livingstone, a town in Zambia near the Zambian border, when Alicia Linchina passed through Livingstone and surrendered herself to Dr. Kenneth Kaunda. It was the beginning of the break-up of the Federation of Rhodesia and Nyasaland.

I recall one of my early experiences in Kenya. We were travelling from Lake Victoria to Nairobi. We were travelling aboard a bus that we had hired, with a number of other men, some of whom were merchants and peddlers. I was accompanied by two women, Barbara Karuki and Mitsoni Kiambi. These two women I lived with, because as a senior clerk of a safari company I felt I had to adopt a rather macho image in the eyes of the tribesmen who were my subordinates. And I was living with these two ladies — and a very noisy pair they were indeed — one chattering away at me in Lowo and the other gossiping away in Kikuyu.

As the bus rattled its way through the timeless African plains, night was gathering. The bus was without windows — it was made partly of wood and partly of metal — and it was a real rattlebag that shook every bone in your body. We were travelling very steadily, the engine coughing and sputtering sometimes.

All of a sudden in an isolated road deep in the bush, things seemed to freeze; the bus stopped very, very suddenly. There was no sense of forward movement, there was no sense of applying the brakes, there was nothing — the bus just froze. Our voices froze mid-word and even the goat which had been struggling to escape through one of the glassless windows froze with his head half out of the window. People's movements were arrested. A man who had been reaching for food in his paper bag had his hand frozen exactly where it was. For many long moments we remained like this, like a photograph taken long ago. And then slowly we began to move and looked outside to see what was going on.

At first we saw nothing. I had my gun with me because these were the times when the *Mau-Mau* was still active in Kenya. It was ready in my hands when I left the bus, but there was an eerie silence, a sort of tangible stillness in the whole air. Then all of a sudden we were showered by a burst of light, and, when I looked up, there was a gigantic object standing in the air directly above the bus. I remember that sight as clearly as I remember my wedding day!

The two young Africans who were riding on the carrier on top of the bus were frozen like silhouettes against that brilliant light. The light came from the center of a gigantic disk which appeared to have been made out of some kind of crackly looking metal — I can only compare it to frosted glass. But it definitely was metallic. The light came from the very center of this disk, but there was no globe or fluorescent object that I could see. It was as if the light came just from a hole, a beam of some kind, and this thing lit up the surrounding place in a sort of bluish white light. And I looked at this thing, and I suddenly felt myself going numb. There were lights on the edge of this object. I remember there were about four lights, all of them greenish blue, very bright, and very steady.

Then I saw something else. I saw that floating through the bush were a number of very bright little globes about the size of small footballs. Now these things were just floating around the bush. We stood, and I was very, very scared, but somehow I could not bring myself to shoot at this thing although I was armed. I don't know why, because I was a trained soldier at that time, and we were taught to shoot first and to ask questions afterwards. But somehow my gun was like a useless toy in my hand. I noticed another thing. Although I and the other educated men inside the bus were scared silly, the traditional Africans, the Africans in skins and in long robes, appeared to accept the thing that was hovering above them. They appeared to accept the strange globes that floated above the grass in a steadily lessening circle around us. I don't know how long this thing went on. Was it an hour? Was it only a few minutes? I don't know. But all I do know is that eventually the little globes floated upwards towards this big thing above us. There was no noise, no sound, no hissing, just a deadly absolute silence and the only noise that I heard and which I distinctly remember was the howling of a hyena a great distance away. And that sounded very, very loud indeed.

Then the thing above the bus moved slightly to one side. I remember I was facing it when it moved slightly to one side again without any sound and it stood over the trees some distance away, gigantic, huge. It had no detail. Seen from the side it was like a lens, convex in shape. I could clearly see it and, since I can draw things, I drew it in my mind's eye. The little globes which had been floating around in the bush went back to that thing; and then to our great surprise the thing rose straight up into the sky, straight up without any warning whatsoever, and disappeared. That was one of the major experiences I had with things that are said to come from beyond this world.

At one time in Natal a flying object was seen by a hardened policeman, amongst other people. The policeman reacted in a typical fashion to the sight of this thing which was hovering low over the ground. He drew his pistol and opened fire upon it whereupon the thing flew away and left. And he says — even to this day — that he heard his bullets strike metal as he fired at the object. And black people of all tribes have a long tradition of dealing with things like these flying things from outside the Earth.

The last personal story I have to tell you, I have not told to many people, because I was so certain that educated white people would not believe me, or would laugh at me. But I did tell it to Professor John Mack, in front of the cameras, because he has told me that now there are many white people who have come forward and told their own stories of similar experiences, and so I am willing to tell my own story, unpleasant though it is.

In 1959 I was in the land called Rhodesia, visiting a lady, *Inyangani*, "Little Moon," and I was learning about herbs, so on this occasion I was going into the bush to look for herbs and to gather the ones that could be useful for making medicines. It was an ordinary African day.

One moment I was digging up a plant, the next there was a blue mist all around me, and I didn't know anything. When I next came to I was in a small, unfamiliar place lying on a table. There were five little fellows around me, like little dolls. Their fingers were longer than people's, and they smelled just awful. They were giving me the works, sir! I really could not move, though I was not tied down. They were sticking things in me, up my nostrils, other places, and I was in terrible pain, but could not cry out or do anything. I felt like the victim at a sacrifice!

Then I was drifting in and out of consciousness. They woke me up somehow. There was this other one who looked kind of like a human being — but not exactly. And she made love to me, but there was nothing human or warm about it — it was awful, indescribable. When you are with a human woman there is this sharing, this give and take, and warmth flows between your bodies and your souls. There was nothing like that here — only a feeling of coldness and violation — and it went on for quite a long time.

I was being shown things in a dream-like state in a half-round room. I saw a creature in a purplish liquid moving around like a baby frog. It had a head, arms and legs, but was very strange. I saw people screaming — white, black and yellow people, caught in terrible soundless screams.

After some time I found myself back in the bush again. My shoes were gone and my clothes were torn. I walked painfully through the brush. I hurt inside and out. When I came to a village at last, it seemed that all the dogs in the place went crazy. They all wanted to have a piece of me. I thought I was done for, but people came at last and quieted them down. They looked at me very very strangely.

Then people who knew who I was came. I learned that I had been missing for three days. I had the same feeling that I have heard from other people, that these creatures mark you and follow you around. I know that I was very anxious and uneasy for a long time after that. What are we, sir, to these creatures, that they experiment on us, or harvest us like cattle? Are they as desparate and disturbed as they seem? But I have told you that there are many kinds of the space creatures, some good and some bad. I know that I shudder when I think of these, and of that experience that I had.

Extraterrestrial Beings

Life can take many forms. Look at the forms that life can take on this planet alone. Here in this bush, there are insects you could easily mistake for rocks or for pieces of bark — until one of them stings you, that is. Life does not have to consist of bipeds who move and breathe and smoke cigars as we do. I have said it before and I say it again — the universe is a gigantic chamber of possibility where everything has the chance and the right to happen; and so we must not have cut-and-dry theories regarding just how life should look. Life could surprise us!

There are limits beyond which even a man like myself (who has broken certain taboos) may not go, and so I will discuss these creatures within these limits, because some things I really am forbidden to talk about. We black people believe that a great disaster will befall any person who discusses certain things with foreign people.

I would not like to pretend to knowing the absolute truth on exactly where these creatures could be coming from, but they are there in ancient legends and in recent times too. I am afraid we must all accept that we humans are not alone in this world, nor are we alone in this universe. There are many kinds of extraterrestrial creatures; but I can tell you first some general things about some types of these creatures.

The first one is the well known *Muhondoruka*, the fearsome column-like creature of whom I have spoken, whose appearance heralds violence, and who is hated throughout Africa and feared.

The second is the *Mutende-ya-ngenge*, the grey or white smaller creature with a largish head whose face is chalk-white, with large green eyes that go around the creature's head so that it can look at you over its shoulder without needing to turn its head at all. It is very different from the third kind, the *Mvonjina*, which is also small. Whereas the Muhondoruka stands up to fourteen feet or fifteen feet high and is about two or more feet in thickness, the Mutende-ya-ngenge is about three feet in height, about the size of a young boy with a very large head — it seems almost like a caricature of a white person. The creature is very very slender in build, almost fragile looking; and it has very large hands and large feet.

It is the Balluba people of Zaire who named the Mutende-ya-ngenge, that is, "that white one of the whip," because if this creature is attacked by tribespeople, it defends itself with a whiplike weapon that it carries. This whiplike weapon can sting you very very badly, and can put even the angriest lion to flight. The human being just rolls up and becomes quite helpless, unable to move when struck. Usually this weapon is mounted on the creature where an arm should be. They don't have a left arm but they've got this whiplike thing mounted on the stump of the left arm. You can see carvings of them by the Makonde of Mozambique. The Makonde love to portray such creatures.

The Mutende-ya-ngenge is known in Botswana, South Africa as *Sekgotswana*, "the short one," or sometimes as *Puhwana*. I have seen some of these. They are quite humanoid in shape, with light skin and with long eyes that make it seem as if they are wearing large goggles. The eyes go from the nose almost to the temple, and are covered with a kind of horny black layer. Its ears are very tiny and set low. Where human beings' ears are set high, this creature's ears are set almost where the point of the jaw would be on a human being, and they have tiny little mouths. They have got dirty grayish white skins, and very beautiful, unusual hands. Their hands have six long fingers, with their index finger and the finger next to it unnaturally long. They have two thumbs, not where my thumb is. When the creature grabs something, the second thumb assists the first thumb in grabbing. One thumb is set in the center of the hand. It is very long. This creature is also very thin in body, almost as if it's got tuberculosis.

Now there is a sinister side to this creature, because it sometimes captures human beings for some reason known only to itself; and for hundreds of years our people have been afraid of Mutende-ya-ngenge because it sometimes cuts people open, examines them, and then puts them together again. It also makes children disappear.

People taken by Mutende-ya-ngenge survive but they are never the same again. Their character changes altogether. Sometimes a person who was cheerful, who was lively, becomes moody and very changed and yet is not physically ill. And it is only when a witch doctor puts this person into what we call the *godsleep*, a sort of hypnotic trance, that this fact comes out, that this person has had an encounter with these creatures.[13]

Some of our people believe that these creatures have been sent by evil gods to take parts out of living human beings. We are told that our people learned to commit what is called ritual murder, that is removing organs from human beings while they are still alive. One thing I have noticed over many years of careful study of people who have been cut up by these creatures is that these people all have one thing in common afterward. They become morbidly afraid of going out into the night. When they sleep, they keep a candle burning, which often causes accidents in grass huts. I have learned of about fifty people over the last 30 years who have been victimized by these creatures. These people are always brooding, always jumpy, and all fear the dark, as they become absolutely terrified when night falls.

The Mvonjina is an equally strange, but very different creature. It is smaller than the Muhondoruka and slightly taller than the Muntende-ya-ngenge. The Mvonjina has an unusually large head, is always covered in some kind of shiny skin, and only the eyes and the mouth show, and the mouth is roundish like a cylinder and the eyes are quite large, bulbous, but there are no fingers, no toes visible, nothing. The head of the Mvonjina is about as large as a very large pumpkin and round, like a melon.

Mvonjina is is completely covered by some kind of material, usually of a goldish color. Only its eyes show. The Mvonjina creature is not harmful to human beings; in fact it is one of the creatures that bring knowledge to humanity. It is regarded as a messanger of the gods. In our myths, the Mvonjina is one of the servants of the Goddess Nananana, whose story I have told you.

There is another kind of friendly space creature which looks very much like us human beings. We call it *Sikasa*. This creature belongs to the race of the Goddess Nananana. Visualize a figure, whose skin is reddish, hair usually very black, sometimes with a greenish tinge. But it could, at first sight, be mistaken for a human being. It is a very friendly and good creature, and it is this type of creature that my bronze necklace is designed to communicate with. Sikasas have been known sometimes to marry human beings.

This necklace of mine has a moon shaped ornament, a star shaped ornament, a sun shaped ornament as well as stone ornaments hanging from it, for it is made to communicate symbolically with the star people, especially the beneficent ones. A Sikasa would talk to me because the Sikasa are very wise creatures. They speak a language which you can understand no matter what language you speak. If you speak English and a Sikasa speaks to you, the language that it speaks to you will be understood by your mind as English. They can speak to any human being.

One day I was walking in Nyasaland in the company of a number of friends. Amongst us there were three men and four women. All of a sudden one of the women said to us, "Look, there's a woman standing over there. But the men said, "That is not a woman, that's a man. But it's a strange man." Now, this is very interesting, in that when we saw this strange creature, which was about the size of an average human being, the women saw it as a woman, and the men saw it as a man. And the creature raised its hand to us and simply walked away and disappeared. All I know is that that creature looked like a colored person that is half white and half black, and it wore a kind of cloth clothing that was like an overall that covered its hands and feet, with only the head being visible. The head had very pale hair as if the creature were an albino and its eyes were dark, completely dark, without any white in them. For many hours we disagreed amongst ourselves, the women insisting that it had been a woman, and we men insisting that this being had been a man. Whatever it was, it excited this confusion in people about its gender. It seemed deeply mysterious and ambiguous.

There is another strange creature some people have seen. It is twelve or more feet high. It is a gaunt creature, with thin arms, thin legs and a very thin body topped by its pointed head. It is also a harmless creature but a very curious one. If a group of people are walking through the night, they may suddenly find themselves being followed by one of these creatures. We call them *Mmkungateka*. Another name for it is *Muncwi*. It is very cowardly. It shadows people and then when they show aggression and rush towards it, it runs away. In fact such a creature has been reported here in Bophutatswana. It is usually seen in conjunction with its craft, which is like a round basin, a very large shiny one. Tribespeople describe it as a bowl which is inverted, flat at the bottom and bulging at the top. The *Mmkungateka* likes to pass vehicles on somewhat dead roads as is the case here in a place called Madeboho. I have not seen this creature, but other people have seen it many times and have never been harmed by it.

There are creatures who are watching over us curiously, and whom I think are actually regulating human progress for some reason known to themselves. One of these beneficent creatures I should mention is a called a *Nafu*. This creature has got a round head with no features whatsoever that we can recognize. The creature's head is smooth and round without any nose, eyes, ears, or anything. The creature has got only three fingers on its hand, no thumb — just three fingers, and this creature communicates with people by touching them. Its hands are sort of clammy, slimy — the hands of the creature exude a kind of sticky stuff and the creature brings its hand towards you and you are supposed to bring your own hand towards the creature's hand. Then when your hands are touching palm to palm, communication takes place.

This strange creature, the Nafu, is much beloved by many tribes in Eastern Africa and Central Africa. It passes knowledge of medicine on to the people. It taught us how to speak to trees and all the voiceless things of nature. Now let me tell you something very strange. A scientist from America, Dr. Jim Hurtak, visited me and told me a strange thing. He said that there are white people who have seen this Nafu creature and have been touched by it, and been very very frightened by being touched by the creature. But these people should realize that this creature is not harmful — it's simply trying to pass on knowledge to human beings.

These are the creatures that are seen very often in Africa by people who can neither read nor write, by people whom one could not accuse of making up a lie about things like this. The descriptions that are given by the Pygmies in Zaire are similar to descriptions that you will receive from the people deep in the Namib Desert, if they dare to talk to you about such things.

You cannot accuse a Bushman who has lived all his life in the Kalahari Desert of lying when he tells you that he knows that there are creatures that come from the stars which look like men. You cannot tell a pygmy of the jungles of Zaire that he imagined it, when he tells you that he once saw a strange creature emerge from a glowing sphere or disk which had fallen in the bush. All over South Africa you find stories of these extra-terrestrial visitors.

Communion

Doesn't it strike you as odd that there have been certain incidents in this world, in various parts of this world, that have been deliberately hushed up? When I was in the United States, I learned from very reliable Americans who had once been in the American Army, that in the early 1950s a flying saucer actually crashed in the desert in the United States and the incident was covered up; and furthermore the President of the United States at that time, General Eisenhower, was actually forbidden from seeing the remains of the UFO, or talking about them.

Now again, in South Africa, way back during the Second World War, a strange craft crashed in the country now known as Zambia, and there were men and women who knew about that, but for some reason the whole thing was hushed up, and the material that was recovered by a black witch doctor from this crash site, a material like paper or parchment, a material that could not burn, a material that even if you heated it, refused to be heated, is identical to the material that the Americans told me had been recovered from the crash sight of the UFO in 1948.

Let me raise another issue. Whenever a certain space program reaches a certain stage, some kind of massive accident occurs which pushes back progress several years. I am thinking about the three astronauts who burned to death while their rocket was still sitting on the launching pad some years ago. I think they were one of the Apollo missions unless I am mistaken. And I am thinking about the incredible Apollo 13 which nearly came to grief. Western people have believed that the number 13 is unlucky. It is just too much of a coincidence that it was the Apollo 13 that nearly came to grief.

Isn't it just too much of a coincidence that astronauts have been killed just when certain space programs in Russia and the United

States seemed to have reached heights of perfection? Astronauts died on landing in Russia, all three of them. The Challenger space craft blew up while it was ascending, and the Challenger was the most perfect of those shuttle spacecraft. Don't you think that there is someone somewhere regulating human progress for certain reasons known only to himself or herself? Strange events have taken place in Russia and other Eastern European countries. Somewhere in the Soviet Union jet fighters shot down a flying saucer.[14] Then when some people, picking mushrooms, came across this wreckage and were curious, and handled it, all of them sickened and died of that sickness I have told you about, which we might call radiation poisoning. It was well publicized. Somehow these creatures are attracted to great events on Earth. Wherever there is a lot of human activity, whether negative or positive, these creatures make a beeline to have a look.

So sir, somebody is hiding something in this world. We are being watched, we are being explored and investigated, and we are being controlled, and yet there are those amongst us who refuse to accept this fact.

Outside Soweto, near Johannesburg, we have got a number of Sangomas who claim that they know very much about these space creatures. When they talk, I can identify the kinds of creatures and the kinds of things they do. Our wise people are expecting something very dramatic to happen during the 1990s. It will involve the United States, and there will be creatures from other worlds seen.

But what I find very amazing, sir, is that the Navajo people, like the African people, believe many of these same things. If ever a spacecraft from outside the Earth visits an area, the chief of that tribe must go forward and appeal to the people inside this craft not to harm his people and the people must desert the village in which they stay and seek safety in the bush. They must, under no circumstances, approach this landed thing. The reason for this is very interesting because of what happens when people get too close to a thing like this one. They get sick, they vomit, they become weak, their hair falls out. And this is why my necklace [the bronze ornament Credo Mutwa wears on ceremonial occasions] tells the

Sangoma to instruct ordinary people that they are under no circumstances to approach a landed spacecraft from the stars.

There is a whole language of signs and rituals by which we have been taught to communicate with alien creatures to show them that this is a friendly world and that they need have no fear.

Only the Sangoma or chief priest of whatever people experiences an alien visit should approach the craft. He should hold his hands as far away from his body as possible (the hands being empty, carrying no object) and then he should raise his hands high above his head and then join them, clasping them on either side of his head, revealing a shape with his body symbolizing "the Eye of God." Then, he must lower his hands keeping his palms open for the creatures to see and then he must repeat the gestures again and again until the creatures inside respond. Should one creature emerge, the high priest must speak to the strange one with gestures like that. In other words, "I see you, I smile with you, you are my friend, and this one is my friend."

But I must warn all people who are investigating flying saucers that, while they are actually investigating, they must try to avoid eating meat. If you want to have any peaceful dealings with them, you must be a vegetarian. They say that the eating of meat is the sign of an aggressive beast, and this is why, as they tell us, they don't like to come amongst us nowadays — because we eat too much meat. They prefer communities which feed mostly on grain.

Also, when you encounter a creature for the first time, don't go blabbing to people at the outset, because very often, if a creature greeted you, it means that it wants to see you again, but you must never tell people what has happened until you have seen the creature twice.

Also, if you are touched by a creature from the stars, try not to show fear. Wise people of Africa say that if you show fear, you give out a terrible smell which could make the more violent of the star creatures attack you. In fact a wise man, a gentleman called Lentswi, with whom I had seen the two creatures running away in the bush in Botswana, South Africa told me afterwards that the reason why the creatures ran away is that we were showing extreme excitement and anger, and they could sense this.

So what I have learned, and which enabled me at one time to study one creature very close up, was that I must disarm my mind; I must think peaceful and beautiful thoughts, I must project a smile towards the creature. I must open my hands with my palms outward to show the creature that I'm carrying nothing. It will do exactly the same. It's uncanny, Doctor. I once was facing a creature quite different from the others — it looked more like an ape, it had ape-like features and stood about five-feet something, almost as tall as myself. It is called *Mbemei*. I saw this creature in the country called Namibia today before the start of the war there.

I was with the Ovahimba people and they told me to go towards the creature. I had not noticed the creature standing under the tree. All I could see was something shining like tin foil. You see Doctor, these creatures wear a kind of attire which looks like tin foil, but this tin foil has got a golden color. I don't know why all of them favor this type of color.

Mbemei is a very friendly creature, but it's shy, it keeps away from human beings. When you come upon it by surprise, you must show your hands to be empty. But whereas a Sikasa will appreciate and understand when you kneel to it, the Mbemei might run away or attack you, because to it kneeling is a sign of aggression. With this creature you must try to stand as tall as you possibly can. So when I saw this Mbemei I tried to walk towards it on tiptoe and it stood there just looking at me and then the people behind me began to sing very softly a beautiful tune and then I approached this creature, showed it that my hands were empty, and then I showed it what I wore around my neck. For a long time we stood there looking at each other, nothing was said, nothing that I could hear. The creature made no sound whatsoever, and then it raised both its hands and then walked backwards away from me. It did not turn its back on me until it was some distance away. I think it was going towards its ship because afterwards we saw something rise out of the bush and disappear into the sky.

Another thing is that people must never carry any weapons of any kind when they are talking to a space creature. They must not handle a firearm or any sharp aggressive instrument like a sword. If you are doing an investigation about aliens, you should stay away from meat, weapons, and even garish clothes that might be surprising to them — the less color the better. This is why creatures like these are often most seen in shadowy places out in the country — because all space creatures seem to fear city lights. But they do seem to love the very long roads that in America are called Interstate Highways. Sometimes in Africa too, they land on long tarred roads in isolated places.

These things have got places in South Africa in which they are often most seen, and their coming is not just random. It occurs after a period of about four years. If you saw it in this place, four years will pass and then you will be called to a sighting in more or less the same place. It seems to me that these space creatures prefer certain parts of a country. I don't know whether this is true with other countries like the U.S., but in South African and Eastern Africa there are places where these creatures are seen more so than others. I'm wondering why they go to those specific places.

When one's country is in danger, one could become desperate. You have prayed to the gods and to the spirits, and they appear to be very slow in answering your prayers. Around you you see the violence go from bad to worse. Then you might enter into communion with other entities, whoever or whatever they may be, for the salvation of your people. There is a lady, Mrs. Clarer, who is known throughout the world as being a South African woman who not only communicated with, but mothered a child by a father from another world. There's nothing unusual or so unearthly about Madame Clarer's story. There have been many women throughout Africa in various centuries who have attested to the fact that they had been fertilized by strange creatures from somewhere. She's not alone. Last year I made a prayer with Elizabeth Clarer to the extraterrestrial beings, on behalf of the people of Africa.

It is a difficult thing to be the one who sees something like I have described, because it is very easy for others to accuse one of madness, or worse yet, of deliberate falsifying. Yet those people who have been in proximity to such a thing lose all their doubts when they have had the experience. There is such an enormous gap between those who have seen and those who have not. I suggest to those who have not to keep an open mind, and have sympathy for the ones who have. We are being watched, sir!

6

The Common Origin of All Humanity

Sometimes I have felt very angry because in my adult life I have seen men like Hitler. I have seen white men and black men who have used the so-called differences between the various languages of the world to stir up nation against nation and race against race. These people have kept human languages divided and labelled with tiny little labels like stolen goods in a thief's storeroom. And they ignore the fact that human languages have more in common than they are different, and that should we ever point out these similarities in language to the peoples of this world, the stirring up of people against people, using language as the goad, would immediately fall away.

Commonalities of Myth, Ritual, and Custom

Although Africa is regarded by many people as the cradle of humanity, where humanity began, there is another continent and people who are, I believe, candidates for that same honor — the Bushmen of Australia. There is in fact, let me tell you, a golden thread of continuity that runs from Australia to Africa, and I wonder if this is not the oldest thread we can find, that all the others spread out like filaments from it to the other cultures which derived from them.

I do believe that the Australian Bushmen are related to all the other races of the world, because they have some characteristics of all of them. This is also true of their mythology, and there are many astonishing parallels between their legends and ours. For example, the Aborigines of Australia believe, as do the Africans, that red ochre is a very sacred substance. They say that in olden times, in what they call the *Dreamtime*, there were women ancestors who went around the world and that their menstrual blood congealed into red ochre, which can be used for healing all sorts of problems, especially those of women.

And in Africa the Zulu people, the Shanga people, the Mashona, and the Swazi also say that red ochre is the congealed menstrual blood of the Great Earth Mother, Ma, or the blood of the Moon Goddess, *Tswedi*, whom we know is related to menstruation, and that the ochre was spread in the most ancient times as the world was being created. The Moon Goddess was sacred to lovers, and women would tie red ribbons around their waists as a symbolic way of asking Tswedi to restore their fertility.

Among the Zulus we also have the equivalent of the Dreamtime. We call it *Endelo-ntulo*, the most ancient of times. We also call it "the time when the rocks were too soft, the time when everything was being formed." Ancient people are believed to have made the rock engravings during that time and fashioned some images of gods and animals. Also some of the tracks of animals that were made when the rocks were soft still can be seen.

We believe that in the very ancient time, the pattern of dreaming was laid down that still affects our dreams today. And there are some dreams that make us crazy and some dreams that make us wise. For example, the sacred dream that we have when we are about to become sangomas, in which animals, usually four lions or leopards (sometimes crocodiles or serpents) come to pull us into parts and devour us, and afterwards may become our helpers.

There is a dream we call "the star dream," which I was amazed to find occurs to children all over the world. It is a dream in which they are falling, falling from a very great height. And they might be frightened, or they might spread their wings and fly through the dream landscape. And this comes from a time when the souls of all children flew like birds among the stars.[1]

And in that time they saw the great ostriches of light going among the stars. We have a legend that there are twelve of these birds, who carried the children on their backs from star to star. The Zulu word for ostrich is *Intshe*, which means, "the Renewer." It is held that once ostriches could fly, but they sacrificed their ability to fly in order serve the Great Earth Mother. They brought our ancestors out of a terrible congflagration, a great fire in the center of the universe. But the ostrich who did that died in sacrifice for humanity. Hence these birds are considered among the most sacred in Africa, and it is a great sacrilege to kill or harm an ostrich in any way.

In Australian mythology it is a very similar bird, the Emu, who is often shown emerging from a great spiral in the center of the universe. The Emu also is depicted as a savior of humankind, and so these stories are remarkably similar, if they were not in fact originally one.

In Nigeria, in many of the countries of Western Africa, in Mozambique, Namibia, and Natal, there is a story of a great serpent that brought the Earth Mother to this world, and how that snake was shooting rainbows out of its body. In Western Africa they say that the Goddess travelled through the world in the mouth of a great rainbow serpent, creating mountains and valleys and stars. The serpent is sometimes depicted as a great Python. The Vedaps of Northern Transvaal say that it was this python who first taught men and women how to make love.

You see, sir, it is very different from the book of *Genesis*, in Judeo-Christian culture, where the serpent is the principle of evil (and I think they don't like sex very much either, sir, if you will pardon my saying so). But in African Mythology, making love is one of the greatest of blessings, and so we say that the serpent is the source of blessings, not of evil. He is called *Nyoka*, "the instructor"; and so the serpent is identified as an "expert," the one who knows what is going on, what the truth is.

Likewise I know that for the Australian Aborigines, there is a great rainbow serpent who is often shown encircling the Earth or bringing the people special blessings, and I know also that their sangomas, who are called "clever men," ride on the back of this serpent, or climb up on rainbow serpents to enter the heavens or the upper realms.[2] So in the legends of the Australians too the serpent is a very benevolent creature, and not at all to be equated with anything evil.

I think that in general, sir, if you will examine the myths and legends of all people, you will find continuous parallels, and this speaks to me of the origins of all mankind. If you consider this, it could be a tremendous unifying force, because it means that we all are brothers and sisters, not only in our dreams, but in our mythologies and our very origins. There are the most profound similarities between the great and the oldest religions of the world. Now, let me say this, that when a human being is ignorant, that human being becomes afraid. Because of his fear, he can commit or be made to commit the foulest atrocities that the human being is capable of.

When the first Christian missionaries arrived in South Africa, they approached the tribespeople of South Africa with a great fear. It is an historical fact that men like Reverend Moffat and men like David Livingstone used to keep the flaps of their revolver holsters open whenever they preached to the tribespeople. Thus, the missionary had his Bible in one hand, while his six-shooter was ready in his holster. He was afraid of the people to whom he was talking, because in his eyes these dark-skinned people, wearing animal skins and birds' feathers, were the very epitome of what should be disliked, hated and feared. But had David Livingstone known the truth about these black people, he would not have feared them at all, and what was true of David Livingstone in those days, is still true of white and black people today. If you go to some of the greatest universities in South Africa, if you ask the white professors there what they think about men like me and women like my wife — namely traditional healers — they will either hem and haw politely, or they will reveal their utter contempt, calling us charlatans, fetish worshipers, and other uncomplimentary names.

Here are some examples, not only of mythologies, but of rituals that are common between peoples. There is a ritual amongst the Eskimo people in which the mother of a young boy deliberately frightens her young son. She makes a mask out of birds' flesh and feathers, and she uses this to scare her son into paying attention or being more obedient. This fear ritual is called *tukok* in Inuit, and in Zulu, where we do similar rituals, we call to be frightened: *ugutga*. Even the word seems similar to me.

Amongst the American Indian *Cheyella* people, who were sometimes known as the Cheyennes, and other war-like tribes of the past, there was a custom of "staking one's self out." This was where a warrior had sworn not to survive a battle but to die where he stood.

He would tie himself by thongs of leather to a stake driven firmly into the ground with a hammer or a stone. Among the Zulus we had an identical custom, where a brave warrior tied himself to a tree by the ankles with lengths of rawhide and he fought and died right where he stood.

There is another war custom also which I found among the AmerIndian people called "counting a coup"; that is, a very brave warrior will rush right in and touch an enemy with a weapon without injuring that enemy or killing him. We have an identical custom among the Zulu and Causa people of South Africa, where during a stick fight a man can just touch the other man against whom he's fighting, with his stick, and that is counted as a blow.

Now where shall we go from here? There is not a single nation among the Native American peoples whom I have visited in my journey to the United States that does not have cultural and linguistic links with Africa. Among the Hopi Indians of the American Southwest, I found a custom where masked people, who are called *Kachinas*, come at certain times during the year and conduct sacred ceremonies and bless the people. In the African country known as Zambia, there is a group of people who practice what is called *Mackishee*. People wearing elaborate masks, which refer to certain spirits, visit villages at times and listen to the confessions of the villager's sins. These "spirits" bless the people for the coming period of time and go on their way again. An identical custom exists in Nigeria where Masked people visit a village and hear confessions and reconcile quarrels. Then they bless the people.

In the Navajo language, *tse* means "stone," the bones of the Earthmother upon which we walk following the pollen path of beauty. The Zulu word for stone is *tshe*. Among the Cree people I found that a married man, who should not fool around with other women, is called *idoda*; in Zulu, he is called *indoda*, married man.

Sometimes, the customs are so similar, it seems funny, sir. Among one AmerIndian people there was a custom where a man paid nine horses for his bride. We have an identical custom, in which nine cows are paid for a girl by the prospective bridegroom. I could go on and on and on, but there are links of ritual that extend throughout the world, and the farther back into the past we go, the closer and more remarkable these links become.

Roots and Commonalities of Language

Were I to say to you in Zulu, *gosi yibaname,* would you under-stand what I mean? No? Let me explain it. "Gosi" means "lord," which is very close to the Greek word, *kyrios,* which also means "lord." "Yiba," "Yi" means "you," "ba," means "be," "name," means "with me." (The word "me" in Zulu means exactly the same as the English word, "me," which refers to myself.) The whole phrase thus means, "Lord, be with me." I am talking Zulu and yet I have linked the three languages: English, Greek, and Zulu. This sentence is in pure Zulu, but already I am leaping over boundaries customarily keeping languages and cultures apart.

Now that you are beginning to understand, I am going to give you another phrase in Zulu. *Uguba nogugaba umbosolowa.* This is Shakespeare's line from *Hamlet,* "To be or not to be," in pure Zulu, and you see again the Zulu verb, "ba," which is the same as the English word "be." I could go on and on, but maybe you are already understanding the fascination that drew me into these studies. When I went to mission schools, I showed an aptitude for English, because I heard these inner similarities.

My fascination with languages grew as I grew into adulthood. And when I started travelling through Africa, it did not diminish but grew still more, as I learned many of the African languages, and then went on to travel to many other parts of the world. I found connections linguistically between Africa and all the nations of the world; and even in the remotest of the remote corners of the world, I found people who spoke languages which are very close to mine.

I know that interest in such langauge parallels is often forbidden to your scholars of language, those people you call linguists, who must be very scientificially precise in studying languages, and they believe that only words and phrases of related language families are truly similar. But sometimes I have felt very angry, because in my adult life I have seen men like Hitler. I have seen white men and black men who have used the so-called differences between the various languages of the world to stir up nation against nation and race against race. These people have kept human languages divided and labelled with tiny little labels like stolen goods in a thief's storeroom. And they ignore the fact that human languages have more in common than they are different, and that should we ever point out these similarities in language to the peoples of this world, the stirring up of people against people by using language as the goad, would immediately fall away.

But I cannot hold back my mind, sir, and if you will bear with me for a while, I will show you just a few more of the remarkable similarities I have found in language and custom that argue for the common origins of all humankind.

It seems to me that at one time human beings — on this Earth or some other earth that we have long lost — used to speak one language. And in fact that same story is told in the Bible: that at one time all human beings spoke one language.

Let us travel on the wings of imagination first to the South American jungles of the Amazon basin where you will find the *Jivaro* Indians. The Jivaro used to practice, until recent times, a frightening, and some would say barbaric, custom which was once practiced by many tribes of Southern, Central, and Eastern Africa: namely, the custom of taking an enemy's head and then drying and shrinking it, and then carrying it around like a grisly talisman. The Jivaros call a head that has been taken from an enemy in battle, *insansa*, which means "that which has been gained, which brings power," and the Zulu word for "good fortune," or for gain, is *intanta*.

Now the Jivaro use a poison for their arrows which the Spaniards mispronounced "curare." The real Indian word for this poison, as I understand it, is *wurara*, which means "to paralyze, to cause to sleep and to make dead, to kill." It struck me that the Zulu word for killing a man is *bulala*, not exactly the same, but there is a similar rhythm in the vowel sounds, something I often look for in my search for the common roots of language, even if the words are superficially different.

Now, let us fly farther on these wings of imagination, to where the air freezes one's beard and hair, and where the sun is a tiny cold dot on the winter horizon, to the people of the most northern part of North America, the *Inuit*, or "Eskimos," as they are called. You would not imagine that these people were remotely connected with Africa, would you? But listen to this: In the language of the Inuit, a dwelling is called *igloo*. In the language of the Zulu people a dwelling, or a hut, is called *indlu*. But there is more. In the language of the Inuit, a man like me — a shaman, or a witch doctor — is called an *angakoq*. In Zulu we use the term, *inyanga*, "a moon person," because the moon plays a big part in our magic. At first this seems to be no similarity at all, but the Inuit often shorten angakoq to "anga" and we in Zulu shorten our word to "nyanga."

I am the only black South African member of a society in America called the Epigraphic Society which was at one time under the presidentship of Dr. Barry Fell, in Massachusetts. Dr. Fell and I have corresponded for many years regarding some of these similarities. He has opened my eyes to many of the ancient and modern languages of the Western world, the Middle East, and the Orient, and perhaps in some small way, I have been helpful to him with my knowledge of the languages of Africa.

For example, there used to exist a people in Europe and in the British Isles, called the Celts. The Celtic Iberian people were so adventurous that they travelled the sea in boats of reeds all over the world. It is this kind of adventuring, which was also practiced by the Phonecians and the peoples of the South Pacific, which could also explain these commonalities of language.

The languages and customs of the Celtic people have very many similarites to those all over Africa. The Celts had a form of writing with marks or notches, which they called *ogham*, which is very similar to our traditional writing, which also consists of notches, and which we call *coolu* or *igamm* in Zulu. Even to this day Zulus call a written letter, a letter like the letter "a" or the letter "b," "igam," and the word "igam" is very close to the Celtic-Iberian word "ogham." In the language of the Celts, the name for a home was *caer*, which today occurs in places in England such as "Cairnavon" and "Cairlewon" and in Zulu the name for a home is *kaya*.

But let me go a bit further. The Hebrew language and the ancient Egyptian language — I am told reliably — and the languages of other countries of the Middle East such as Mesopotamia and Anatolia, are related. Why? Because these were the languages of the so-called Sea People. And the Jewish people are part of this great family of Sea People. The figure called "Nommo" among many of the African tribes is depicted by the Sumerians and Babylonians: he is shown as a fish-tailed man, rising up from the sea and giving them knowledge. They call him *Oannes*.

Do you know of a very aggressive ancient people called the Hittites? If you were to write a line in Hittite and present it today to a modern Zulu-speaking African, he might understand it, because the language is so similar. Ancient Egyptian resembles the language that is spoken in modern Botswana. Here is one curious fact: The ancient Egyptians had a very important charm or symbol which was like a little cross with a loop on top, and they called that symbol an *ankh*. But the word "ankh" could also be used to mean "to smell, to feel, to be alive." And in the language of the Zwana people, the word to smell with your nose is *ngnkga*. Ankh and ngnkga, one and the same thing.

We also find very close resemblances between the languages of the tribes of South Africa and the Hebrew language. A father is called, *av* as in Avraham or Aava and in Zulu a father is called *baba*. In the language of the Zwana people of South Africa, to heal a man or any person is *alasa* or *arasa* and in Hebrew, healing is *raffa*, as in the angel Rafael. In Zwana the word for a lord or a master or a mister is *ra* or *rey*. For example, if I were to say "Mr. Hurtak" in Zwana, I would say, "Rahurtak." The Zwana word *ra* means exactly the same as the ancient Egyptian word *ra*, which meant lord or master. I understand this is also the word for king in Spanish, related to the Latin, *Rex*.

In Africa we have a tribe that has been in existence since the days of ancient Sumeria. They are the very remarkable people of Kenya called the Massai. These are the warrior people whom you see depicted in films and in books and novels with their colorful shells and lion-mane headresses. Now, the Massai told me a very strange story when I was living amongst them in Kenya many years ago. They told me that they worship God under the name of *Enki Enkay Urungai*. Now I understand that *Enki*, a god of the sky, was also worshipped in Sumeria, long before even Babylon was built.

The Massai were also given the task of looking after cattle many many centuries ago by a wise man from the stars called Uru-Wantayi, of whom I have spoken. But I must tell you that the word *Wontay* is ancient Egyptian, and *Ur*, the name of an ancient city of the Chaldeans, or Sumerians.

You know it is said that the city of Jerusalem is the mother of only three religions. I disagree. You see, behind the patriarch Abraham, who is usually cited as the father of the Israelites, scholars know of a shadowy king call *Ebere*. This Ebere according to legend was a member of the sea people. The people of Ebere were everywhere in the Middle East and they had a city called *Orsolim*. The word *ur* is very interesting to me because it has to do with light. Could perhaps the city Orsolim — which afterwards became Irushalim — have been "the city of light?"

It was in Orsolim, according to African legend, that the religion of *Baal*, or *Bel* was born, an ancient Middle-Eastern religion that incorporated a worship of light. It was in Orsolim that religions from Egypt were modified to suit the people of the Middle East. Orsolim mothered more religions than it's been given credit for. And it will not surprise me in the least that this city of light, this Orsolim, Irushalim, Jerusalem will one day again becomes the capital of a new nation in the Middle East. It is a joyous vision I like to entertain: The children of Ebere, of Abraham once more coming together in brotherhood, burying the sword in the desert sands, and facing together the joys and sorrows of existence, in peace.

As we travel east around the globe, the comparisons get more astonishing. One that has amazed me is that in India, a holy man is called *sannyasin*, and in my role as "uplifter of the people," I am called, *sanusi*. In India, when an Indian says "no," he makes a particular clicking sound. The same sound is made by Zulus when they are angry or denying somebody permission.

Now, let me conclude this discussion with something that happened to me when I was travelling in Japan with my wife, Cecilia. We were there as guests of the International Transpersonal Association and Dr. Cecil Burney who was its president. Because our funds were a bit tight, we decided not to eat the meals in the hotel, but find our own food elsewhere. Cecilia went out into the great city of Kyoto with our friend, Professor Len Holstock. After not too long, they returned loaded with all kinds of food. I said to my wife, "But how did you achieve this? I am told the Japanese are very hard to communicate with."

Cecilia said, "My husband, I simply spoke Zulu to these people and they understood me. Within less than two hours, my wife had solved a problem which I — in my stupidity — had thought insurmountable. She had simply used African languages to make herself understood to the Japanese and the Japanese had understood.

As I went deeper into this thing to find out how this was possible, I learned of many commonalities. I found that in Japanese a stone was called *ishi*. In Zulu it's called *iechay*. In Japan a fierce warrior is called a *samurai*. In Mashona, a warrior is called *shamwari*. The terrible curved sword of the samurai is called a *katana*, and among the Kasai of Zaire, a similar weapon is called a *katanga*. The Japanese call their great original religion of the nature spirits, *Shinto*, which means "the way of the gods." The African equivalent is *Sintu*, "the way of man." For the Japanese, *hie* means "fire," in the Shangane language of Mozambique, it is called *hisa*. These are just a few of the comparisons that I found.

On the Family

If humankind is to be a family, sir, the individual must come from a human family that has some sense of connectedness, some experience of human kindness and love. Then these positive feelings can gradually extend out to the local community, and then finally to the entirety of humankind.

I want to appeal to all thinking people, that if you want to see peace upon this planet, if you want to see mankind return slowly to sanity in this world, if you want to see mankind have a peaceful and stable future, for god's sake, stop mucking about with the family, please. Stop setting children against their parents and stop setting parents against their children. Stop all things that sour relationships between men and women, please. Let me point out that at no time in human history have people ever gone so all out to damage the human family as is now the case. We see many strange things taking place nowadays, things whose cumulative effect will be the total expiration of the family as we know it within the next hundred years or so.

Why can't the rulers of the world — if they don't have rocks in their heads, and if they don't fall asleep at critical periods of discussion of mankind's fate — do something about once more restoring to the family the stability, the glory, the togetherness, the beauty that it used to have? I'm not being sloshy or sentimentalist when I say this. Even the worst dictators on this planet — your Fidel Castros, your Stalins — even they honored the family. Hitler, for example, did his best to stabilize the German family, in spite of the hideous evil that he did afterwards. Why should we try to destroy that which we don't really even understand?

Nowadays in many parts of the world we see terrible acts of senseless violence, violence which has no cause, and which appears to be committed for the sheer sake of violence. We have got people letting off bombs and mutilating other people for the flimsiest of excuses. We have got massive destruction of the spiritual life of whole communities, and this is not only in Africa, but also in America, Europe, the Middle East, and many other places. I believe that the senseless violence starts with the disruption of the most vital unit of human existence upon this planet: the family!

In Africa in traditional times, the extended family wasn't just a thing, it was a very efficient organization whose purpose was to bring up children according to the ideals of the tribe. But, with the coming of Western Civilization, if you wish to call it that, changes of an extremely destructive nature took place. In the modern townships no longer is the extended family allowed to live together. For example, only a certain number of people are allowed to live in a four-room Soweto house. So whether he likes it or not, a man or a woman has to discard other members of his or her family and thus be without the important members of this beautiful organization which should assist him or her in the bringing up of children. Thus, the extended family has been destroyed.

Today throughout southern Africa, we see youth in bloody revolt. Today in southern Africa we see the rising of young men and women who think nothing of burning a human being alive — a thing that was unknown in old Africa, even in the most barbaric eras of my country's history. And you will find, if you examine each one of the participants in such ugly deeds, that they all come from weakened or completely broken families. This is the harvest that Africa is reaping as a direct result of the deliberate destruction of African families. It is a well-known fact that the scheme under which black men left their families in the homelands and came to work in the towns, destroyed many many many black families and today, the living shards of those destroyed families — the living fragments in the form of misguided and ill-guided young people — are running rampage in many townships and causing incredible havoc.

In tribal society, marriage was a beautiful partnership between the man and the woman, where both partners were really equal. Now, with the coming of Western Civilization, our people were fed the very wrong Victorian notion that the woman is the man's inferior or the woman should be the man's ward with the man being the woman's guardian. Now this notion did not exist in traditional Africa.

Here is how our psychology of the family worked in the older days: We know that children have to be entertained, and entertaining the children with ancient fairytales and myths, including some of the stories that you have learned in this book, was the duty of the grandmother. Along with this, children were instructed about the history of the tribe and the history of the family and that duty fell to the uncle — the brother of the children's mother — which is why an uncle in Zulu is called *malumey*, which really means "a teacher." So it is the duty of the teaching uncle to teach children about the history of the nation, the history of the family, and the history of the tribe.

It is the duty of the uncle, and not the father or the mother, to teach children about sexual matters in Africa. I think this is because their parents have often hidden sexual matters from the children when they were little, and told them that babies arrive on the backs of great white eagles, and so on. (So, now it would cause the parent to lose face if he or she started telling them the facts of life.) So, instructing the children about these things is left to the uncles, and they do it very very efficiently, I assure you. This may raise some eyebrows in modern Europe and America, but even today in Zululand, a young Zulu girl who is about to be married first pays a ritual visit to the home of her uncle. There she is instructed in the finer ways of lovemaking and of caring for the husband, the children who will come, and of caring for herself.

When I hear of the terrible widespread sexual abuse in modern societies, of young girls by their fathers or grandfathers or stepfathers or others, I wonder if this is because the practice of sexual initiation is not formalized as we formalized it traditionally. In our traditional way, sexual initiation is performed at a definite time of life, when the young woman is ready, and the whole focus is on what is beneficial for *her*, not on the pleasure of the uncle or whomever.

The nuclear family by itself now often seems helpless in confronting misbehavior, but in the African tradition, a naughty child was confronted by many relatives. He was confronted by uncles, by aunts, by grandmothers and so on; and each one of these relatives had the same power over that child that the child's natural parents had. Thus, for example, if my son was very very naughty and I felt that he no longer obeyed me at all, I would send my son for a few months to my brother's village to learn the law under new surroundings. Because he would be startled. You see, an unfamiliar person is easier to obey than an all-too-familiar person. Also, when a child who was wayward and naughty found the entire family against him, he used to tow the line immediately. This is why in Africa you found many relatives coming together to rebuke a naughty child.

There are wise and unwise ways to use discipline. For example, some years ago I found two of my little boys really having a go at smoking behind our house. I realized that if I took my belt and started tanning these young people's hides it would only make them worse. So I went to my brother, who works in a chest clinic, and my brother advised me to take these children on a visit to the hospital near Soweto where there are people who suffer from chest diseases such as tuberculosis and others. And I showed my sons these people, some of whom were suffering from cancer of the lungs. And I said to my sons, "Well, have you seen what's in that hospital?" and they said, "Yes!" And I said to them, "Do you know that some of those people are suffering now because of indulging in smoking?"

And my sons said, "My father, we had not known about this."

I said, "Look, from now on you have to learn! And I sent my two sons to my brother for six months, and in those six months, they learned about the lungs, and my brother taught them very skillfully. To this day, not one of my sons smokes. Not one.

We recognize that it is very good in the earlier stages of life to raise children to be fearless as well as obedient, and there are some interesting rituals of birth that were developed in Africa. I could describe five or six different methods of giving birth to a child, but I will let this one suffice: In those tribes that dwell by bodies of water — rivers or lakes — or ones where the children used to grow up to be professional boatmen and boatwomen whose profession it was to carry people across the great rivers of our country, it was especially important to be without fear of water from an early age.

They made sure that their children were born inside huge clay pots. The mother crouched inside the clay pot waist deep in the water, or even water up to her armpits, and then she gave birth to the baby in this position, sometimes held by the shoulders by midwifes as well. You must know that the pot was dug into the ground to prevent it from cracking through the struggles of the woman, and that it was filled with pleasantly warm water.

Now, the miracle is this: One would expect the child to drown or to sink under these circumstances but it never happens. The child floats, even with the umbilical cord still attached to the placenta. The child floats gently in the water and then the midwife cuts the cord and the child is free. But after that, as the baby grows, it will be put into this large clay pot of nicely warm water again and again — say about two or three times a month — so that the child develops a love for water. It learns to swim even before it has learned to think properly. And this was the thing. In fact, this form of birth was once quite common amongst the tribal people of Africa including my people, the Zulus, but as recently as some 40 years ago, it was confined to that part of Botswana where we find the Okovango Swamps. Also, in Malao this form of birthing was practiced widely.

When two people meet, a male and a female, or even two females, or even two males, meeting and deciding to live together, why should we interfere with them so long as they don't by so doing destabilize or harm others in the process? Why should we interfere with the private lives of people? If we insist that relationships have to be one way only, aren't we leading to a tyranny of the type that George Orwell prophesied so many years ago in his book, *1984*? I say, look at the quality of life that people find when they are left to their own devices, without prejucice, and without persecution. I say, give children the best possible start you can in life, in the bosom of an extended family of people who care for them, and then let them find their own way through life as adults.

I want to point out to you that there are animals on this Earth which form lasting family units. I have seen lions in the African forest that marry for many years and if the male lion is struck down by poachers, the female also looks for those poachers and deliberately seeks death at their hands. If you look in the bush, you will find that these married lions bring up their children in very, very loving ways. They punish them, but they also show them much love, love of a kind which we modern human beings rarely show our offspring now.

And I want to say this in conclusion: Do not destroy something that you do not understand. Stop tampering with the way human beings are made. We should concentrate upon fighting disease, fighting hunger, fighting madness, instead of trying to mess up things that were already ancient before man evolved from whatever ape that was his ancestor. I say to you, strengthen the family and gain a peaceful world; destroy it and gain hell, believe me!

On Banishing Fear

You see sir, the black people of South Africa — all tribes — tried their uttermost to banish certain fears from their children. For example, in the Transkei, after a Pausa child is born, a few days are allowed to go by, and then the child goes through a naming ritual in which he or she is given a name. At that ritual, one grandparent sits on one side of the fire, and the other grandparent sits on the opposite side facing this one across the fire. Then the little baby is thrown from the hands of this old person to the hands of that one so that the child passes over the flames. This is intended to make the young child to grow up not afraid of fire, not having a phobia about fire, and indeed it seems to do that.

Much of the violent or foolish behavior of the world relates to fear, to people who have never broken free of the cocoon of this thing known as fear. As a traditional healer, much of my practice has to do with overcoming fear. And you know, in a strange way, the more unfounded, the more irrational a fear is in the mind of a human being, the more deep-rooted that fear happens to be.

I want you to imagine a case I've witnessed many times with different variations. A young, black sportsman gets injured in a car accident. Let's say he has been a football player — a man used to running and scoring to the adulation of the crowd — a man used to being worshipped like a god up on this Earth. All of a sudden this man loses his leg in that car accident. The doctors in the white man's hospital with their modern medicines and also their modern surgical techniques will save the life of this man.

They can save his life, but there is one thing that they cannot save him from. After that operation, this man's mind, his soul, becomes filled with fear for his future and with self-loathing and self-pity. It is the job of the sangoma, the soul-doctor, to help that young man to find a new relationship to life. Even with that terrible impairment, if his soul is right, then he can go on to a happy and even a fulfilled life.

One day while I was a young guardsman in Kenya who looked after people on safaris, I was putting up a tent — what they call a bell tent, with canvas walls — when all of a sudden the tent collapsed on top of me and something heavy pinned me to the ground under the canvas. It wasn't until a few moments later — because the dust was so thick all around — that I managed to peer from under the canvas, and as I did I looked into the most fearsome face that I have ever beheld in my life.

You know a lion is a beautiful animal when seen from a distance, but when seen from about six or four inches away, it is utterly terrifying!

The lion was big and it was staring right at me. In fact, some of its saliva was falling on my face. Well doctor, I wet my pants, I was stiff with terror, and the lion was doing its best to tear the canvas that separated me from it. It wanted to get at the food under the canvas. It went on for about — I don't know how many minutes — when all of a sudden I realized that somehow I must stay calm; I realized that my fear was actually making the lion extremely aggressive. The more scared I became, the more I trembled or tried to scream, the more the lion redoubled its efforts to get at me from under the canvas. Now, try staying calm with a lion pressing down upon you with its four paws and looking into your eyes as you lie terrified under a tangle of canvas. A long time passed, and I sweated, but I gritted my teeth and struggled to find calm within myself. And when I thought I had achieved it — to my amazement the lion just walked off and stood some distance away watching me.

Then it was that I began to realize that ferocious animals are actually driven on by the smell of fear. But my fear returned again, and I tried to struggle from under the canvas; but unfortunately the lion had broken my left leg when it sprang upon me. My left leg was useless and a mass of pain. I struggled, and the lion came back. It tried to use its front paws to get at me from under the canvas. I could feel the terrible scratching as the lion's claws tore it. Then once more I fought for calm. And then I tried to talk to the lion as my grandfather had taught me. I talked with my mind. I said, "Please, I am not food! Please, I am not to be eaten. I smile with you. I have no sharp teeth, please go." Was it that which made the lion go away? I don't know, but go away the lion did. And some time later I was found unconscious, and I was taken to the hospital.

It turned out that this same lion was an old man-eater whose teeth were broken, as I had seen when it had snarled trying to get at me. This lion had accounted for the deaths of about eight women and a number of children in that district. For me, this experience showed that if you can conquer fear, you will not receive aggression in return.

Today there are people who walk about in this world fearing other people; a man of one race is conditioned to fear people of another race. In fact this is the deadliest, most devastating fear that we human beings have got to face: Our fear of our own brothers, our fear of our own sisters. How can one overcome this fear? As I have said to you, the more unfounded a fear is, the deeper the roots and the deeper its intensity often is.

First you must ask yourself, why do I fear those people? What do I know about them that I have got to fear? Face your fear, look at it in the face as a lover looks into the face of a lover. What have I got to fear? If I am black, what have I got to fear from the whites? If I am white, what have I got to fear from the blacks? If I am Caucasian or

Aryan, what do I have to fear from the Jews? or if I am Jew, what do I have to fear from the Gentiles? You will find on facing your fear squarely that your fear is based not on what you know about those people, but on what you do not know about those people. And once you make it a point to know more about those people, then you will overcome your fear.

When I came to the United States of America, I was apprehensive about meeting the people known as the red Indians. I had come with preconceived ideas about how these people look. I was expecting tall, wild savages, with blood redskins and long hair, perhaps the sort of rubbish that we are shown in comics about them. I was very surprised to find not only that these people were not red, but that they were like our own Hottentots in appearance. I found that they were my brothers. I found that red Indian hieroglyphs and African traditional hieroglyphs are not only similar, but I felt their meaning to be the same. For example, if you were to write a message using Zulu traditional hieroglyphs, I think the Amer-Indian would understand that message because his hieroglyphs resemble them. I found that these people instead of being people to be feared, are really people to be loved.

I always have had a liking for people, white people and black people. I felt that I loved them, that I wanted to talk to them, but I have seen much conflict in Africa — for example I was in Kenya when the Mau-Maus started their ferocious attacks, I was in South Rhodesia when the trouble started in 1959 which led to the long bush war there. At first I was afraid that I had run across so much violence because I had broken my oath about telling traditional lore to non-Zulus. I imagined that not only these, but other calamities would come my way. I had to ponder very deeply to overcome this fear, and to understand the nature of the things that were happening around me.

*Ceremonial hut at Crafts Village, Bophutatswana, built by Credo with bull
(lunar) and lion (solar) guardian figures*

7
Dreams, Prophecies, and Mysteries

Today, human beings are inter-connected like grapes in a bunch — connected by the mothering vines. If you destroy one nation, you destroy the others. If disease invades one grape, soon the whole bunch of grapes becomes rotten and diseased. Men have come together as never before. Communication has made the world smaller. What happens in one country will reverberate in another. The wars of the Middle East are fought not only in the sands of the Sinai Peninsula and in the sands of the land of Israel. They are fought in Lebanon, and they are fought right in the streets of Europe and in avenues in cities of the United States. Doubt me if you dare.

There are many mysteries in life and one thing I do not accept is that death as we know it is the end of life. It cannot be, otherwise it would be the greatest waste of all time.

On Sleep and Dreaming

The Zulu word for Sleep is *butongo*, "the state of being one with the star gods." The word for dreams is *ipupo*. The verb "pupa" refers to flight, therefore to say "I dreamt" means "I flew."

We believe in Africa that if you dream of something, that thing should be enacted in the light of day — that you should try to do the thing of which you have dreamt. If you dream of shaking hands with a man, you should go to that man and shake his hand and then see what comes of it. People in Africa spend a lot of money acting out the things that appear in their dreams, because if you dream you must visit a distant relative, then you must find the money to go and visit that relative. There are people who spend many days on buses or trains and doing all kinds of odd things because their dreams have counselled them to do so.

It is very good for a person to take dreams seriously, because we believe that if you do act out the dream, the creative force of the soul that makes dreams recognizes this, and brings you more dreams that guide you and make your life richer and more interesting. We believe that dreams notice the fact you notice them. It is not a good thing to ignore your dreams or treat them as if they were inconsequential or silly. I must show the dream spirit that I have received his message and am prepared to act on it.

Many people, when they reach a crisis in their lives, watch their dreams very very closely. I remember a young man who had run away from his wife many years before. One day he was in a hospital after an accident. In a dream he saw that he was kissing his wife near a rubbish dump. When he got better, he went to find his wife. He actually persuaded her to come with him to a nearby dump, and there, amidst heaps of garbage, he kissed her, to give life to the dream. Though we do not know what she thought or felt on the occasion, after that they were reconciled.

In Africa many people not only respect the dream, they feel they must obey its message to the letter. But sometimes, I must say, this has very disastrous results.

One day when I was working in the Witwatersrand mines, a very peaceful man from Transkei suddenly attacked another one and stabbed him to death for no reason. And when he was asked why, after being arrested, he said because he had dreamt of himself killing that man, and felt he must act it out, as if that were what the dream required. The man he killed was a boss boy, a kind of overseer. They had never fought before, and did not even belong to the same team of miners.[1] This all has to do with the notion that the dream must be brought to this world and made alive; but maybe in this case he could have tried another way to realize what it meant!

When you find yourself confronted by a problem on which your very existence may depend, sometimes you can go to sleep and in the morning there is the answer to your problem. Where was it hiding all this time? How does it happen that a man who has never seen a certain thing can find himself building that very thing guided by no more than a dream? It is thus that dreams show us their miraculous nature.

During the time that I was living in a very very rough township called Zolaensoweto, on several occasions I was attacked by robbers who waylayed me, roughed me up, and took my money. Each Friday I could look forward to something like this. Then one day I decided that I'd had enough of this nonsense and that I had to do something about it. I longed to build myself some form of protection, and then one night I had a dream of a suit of clothes made entirely out of metal. I had never seen such a thing in real life, only in pictures. I had never seen how a suit of armor looks on the inside or what holds it together, but I was guided by a man in a series of dreams.

I was able to build a heavy but highly effective suit of armor which I wore on several occasions and which gave my would-be robbers a very great surprise. On the Friday night after my armor was completed, I wore it to town. As I was walking through the darkened streets, I closed the visor of the helmet, and then the gang that loved to attack me and other people in this place threw a stone at me, and surrounded me raining blows with axes and sticks upon my head and shoulders — but to no effect! I tore the stick from the hand of one of them and gave them the biggest thrashing of their lives. They could not injure me but I definitely injured them. Never having seen a man wearing iron clothes before, the eight robbers took off and never robbed people again in that part of Zolaensoweto.

Even today if you go to Zola, you will hear the story of how a witch doctor dreamed himself into a person of iron and beat up a gang of robbers on that street corner. I had never done anything like this thing before.

On a later occasion I wanted to build a telescope, to see for myself the mountains of the Moon. A dream guided me in grinding the lenses, and in how to make the telescope. I'm good at welding but I had never made a telescope before. Each time I made a mistake, the dream would come and correct me. Eventually I was able to complete a 4-inch telescope which still stands in my house today. Now, I ask myself, how do such things happen? Who were the people who appeared in my dreams to guide me? I don't know. All I do know is that they were definitely not people of Africa.

Dreams often try to tell us something, to give us warning of something which is coming — it may be a danger or something else. On many occasions I have had dreams which I have ignored, only to find the dream coming true within the space of one day. But on other occasions I have paid attention and actually been saved from something terrible.

I always used to commute by train between Soweto and Johannesburg. One day I had a very strange dream that a train was on fire and that I could not get out. I was trapped by the flames.

Late in the afternoon on the return journey to Johannesburg something forced me not to take the train that I usually took, namely the 6:30 train to Nalady. The train came to the platform and I felt glued to my seat at the platform, unable to move, refusing to move. The train was quickly filled with people and then roared away, leaving me on the platform.

The logical part of my mind was wondering why, but I was becoming increasingly familiar with this sort of thing; and so I just waited patiently for the next train.

I took that following train, and just when we reached a station called Jaboulani in Soweto, our train stopped. A hideous scene of carnage greeted our eyes. Ahead of us there had a been a terrible accident involving the train which I should have boarded, the 6:30 train.

The train was on fire and many people were lying dead, some horribly mangled, along the stretch of railway that ran next to the burning train. The train I would have been on had caught fire and people had panicked and jumped out of the windows; and as they ran across the rails, an express train coming in the opposite direction plowed into these people and killed many of them.

Some dreams, then, are secret messages which bring warnings of things to come to a person; but I think also some bad dreams could be caused by drinking too much or eating too many McDonald's hamburgers! Sometimes you can dream a silly dream such as moving furniture from one part of your house to another; and then on the following day you find yourself having reason to do exactly that, and thus is your dream fulfilled.

One thing our people know is that dreams with a really serious message behind them have a very strange characteristic: they are almost always in brilliant color, and they come just before the dawn is about to break. You dream them and then you wake up and forget them; and then later in the day something happens, and you suddenly say, "This is what I dreamt last night." This has happened to me and to members of my family many times. Also, dreams that occur two or three times during the course of one night are dreams that have something behind them.

Dreams like my warning dream with the train prove that there is something in the human being that actually travels through time. We believe that the human being has three souls if one is a female, and two souls if one is male. One of these souls, carrying an essence of you, can go into tomorrow, or the next month, or far away, and actually experience things before your physical body does. This is what we believe in Africa.

Prophecies

There is something in this world that I dislike discussing. It is the subject of the prediction of the future; because once you get deeply into a profession like mine, once you start dealing with things that are beyond the so-called normal, then you develop a reverence for discussing things like this. Prediction is a thing that we should not at all treat lightly. First, why are human beings capable of predicting things? Because prediction is a very vital human power. It is an "early warning device" that the gods placed within the human soul so that one can recognize future dangers, which is why no prophet has ever been able, for example, to predict a delightful happening such as a soccer match, or to predict the result of a race.

But a prophet can and often does predict with remarkable accuracy the coming of something which could endanger the well-being of people and their safety, or change their lives. One of the reasons why I have abandoned my practice of healing people full-time and have taken to going through South Africa trying to build places where the culture and religion of our people might be preserved, is that I am frightened by a number of predictions that have been made, by other healers, as well as myself.

There have been many great prophets in Africa. One was Nsikane, the great prophet of what is today Transkei, who foresaw not only the coming of the white people, but also the coming of Christianity to South Africa. He also foresaw things like the telephone. He said that one day people would communicate with each other through a wire such as the wives of the chief wear around their necks for an ornament. He foresaw the coming of airplanes. He said that birds made out of steel would fly from land to land. Even more astonishingly, he foresaw television. He said that one day men will sit and look at and talk with an image of a man who had died many generations before. (May I say that he could have foreseen the hologram because that is just what it will do. It will preserve the three dimensional images of people, and a person might be able to sit with the image of a parent or grandparent, even after death, in this manner.)

There was a great prophet named Pindamulili of the Bachioko nation of Angola. Pindamulili foretold the pollution of the world. He said that a thousand years after his death, men would practice what is called forbidden knowledge, and as a result of this forbidden knowledge, the skies would become dark, the vegetation die, the animals vanish, leaving only a few survivors. And then the people, out of fear and shame for what they had done, would tunnel into the underground regions of the Earth and there build their cities and villages as refugees from the terrible catastrophe they caused on the surface of the Earth.

The prophecy says that a beautiful girl shall appear who will be accompanied by a gryphon, a creature half-lion and half-eagle. This girl shall make use of an iron god to build a city in the center of Africa, where she shall keep the last remaining wild animals, the few surviving domestic animals, and the few surviving people, because, by that time there would be no rivers in Africa at all, but a huge desert where nothing lives.

What I find most amazing first about the prophesy of Pindamulili is that there is now a massive pollution of the environment in all countries of the world. The Chernobyl disaster and similar disasters are but part of this gigantic destruction of the world. The pollution of the Rhine, with the death of millions of fishes and the pollution of many rivers in Africa, are part of the fulfillment of Pindamulili's prophecy.

All African prophets say that a woman will sit as chieftain over the great nation of the West — which is America. What we know is that one of the women will reverse many things that are at present destabilizing the American nation. That woman will really be like a new broom, sweeping clean all that which is not good, and she shall bring the American nation to new heights of greatness.

Nsikane foresaw that there would come a time when women would rule the nations of the world. And this was also foretold by another prophet, a man called Leembah, who lived in the land today known as Zambia. Leembah prophesied that 40 years before the coming of the greatest war of all time there would come the age of the flower — because a woman is sometimes symbolized as a flower or a flowering plant. He said that during this "Age of the Flower," great women would arise and rule some of the strongest nations in the world; and that this would be an attempt by God to give mankind a new direction, a new feeling of responsibility and a new caring about mankind itself and the world. And sir, this time has begun to arrive: Madame Ghandi, Madame Thatcher, and in Argentina, Madame Perone, and in the Phillipines, Corey Aquino. They are ruling the nations of the world. All this has happened exactly as the prophets of Africa have prophesied.[2]

Murire (or Muwari) was a wise man who lived in a cave in the land now known as Zimbabwe, formerly Rhodesia, at the time when English adventurers and colonists were streaming into that part of Africa. Murire was the last of the god-kings. He was the High Sanusi, and he made many prophesies. One was that dragons made out of wood and iron would carry people from place to place; another was that one day eagles of steel and vultures of iron would fly through the air.

He went on to say that at that time people would be able to talk with people long dead out of strange contraptions [tape recorders?]. And he also said that at that time people would talk to each other through a very fine wire, such as the women of the king in old Africa wore around their necks. You can recognize the telephone in that prophesy.

And then Murire prophesied that there would be four great wars. He prophesied the Anglo-Boer War of 1899-1902. He prophesied with great accuracy the first World War, 1914-1918, and with un-canny accuracy he prophesied the World War of 1939-1945; and he actually named the ruler "Massolina" who would be one of the rulers involved in that great conflict; but he did not name Hitler, only "Massolina."

Now, he said that after those great wars there would come a gigantic war in Africa lasting several decades, which would be the first of seven wars involving Africa directly. And then Murire went on to prophesy the coming of his own death. He told his followers that he would die as a result of being shot at by a white man with a pipe out of which fire came.

The people around Murire did not believe what he was saying; but he went on to describe his own death in great detail. And then, when Murire was a very old man, there arrived in the country Zim-babwe, an American adventurer called Barnum. The man was going through Africa in search of unusual creatures to put in his show. Barnum had heard that some black tribes had gold hidden away in caves and he demanded that Murire should give him some of this gold.

Murire said, "But white man, I have no gold that I've hidden away. I've got only the gold of wisdom that I can give you."

The white man then threatened Murire with a gun and still Murire refused to show him any gold because he really didn't have any; and the white man pulled the trigger, and the greatest prophet of all in South Africa was no more. He died from a tube out of which fire came.

Everybody has heard of King Shaka of the Zulus and that he was a great warrior. But what people don't know is that Shaka — about whom the film *Shaka Zulu* has been made in South Africa — was also a great prophet. On several occasions during his life, he made astonishing prophesies that have since come true.

He said that after his death, the descendants of the Zulu Nation would be awakened by the ringing of a gong and that there would be great animals with burning eyes that would travel at great speed along strange roads.

With his dying breath he asked his brothers, after they had stabbed him, "Why are you killing me, my brothers? Do you think that by killing me you shall take this country of the Zulus and rule it? Oh no! The white swallows, the white men who build their huts out of wood shall take the country and rule it and you shall be as nothing in the lands of your forefathers!"

There are those who will bear witness to this fact — that when I was a child, back in the early 1930s, I told my father that there would come a time when airplanes would fly through the air with wide-open mouths like fishes drinking in air through one end and expelling it through the other. I told him this because in a dream I had seen an airplane like this, and it was diving at me with its open snout. Now there are jet planes everywhere.

Way back in 1964 I first tried to put one of my predictions into writing. I had predicted great conflict in South Africa and that this conflict would go on for several decades, going on well beyond the year 1989. Not only I alone, but others of my sangomas such as Mrs. Danisa and Mrs. Simube to name but two, have seen these things. And I know that in the early 1990s, there will be a great war in the Middle East.[3]

I have predicted that very very soon the nation of Israel, which is in the process of losing the battle for its survival against the Arab nations around it, will come to some kind of agreement with the more moderate nations to form a loose federation of states in the Middle East. [This prophecy was made in 1989 — Ed.] In the year 1998 there will come to power briefly a ruler in the region of India and this ruler will be assassinated and it is this assassination which will cause a short, sharp conflict between East and West in the year 1999. This conflict will last less than 72 hours but it could destroy many millions of people. It will be concentrated not so much in Europe as in the Middle East and in areas around about Greece, [the former] Yugoslavia and thereabouts, and I foresee that this conflict will be brought to a sudden halt by an event that will take place high in the sky. Something will fall out of the sky which will make people so afraid that war will stop immediately. I don't know what will happen here, but I do know that all the major nations of the world will be involved in it. At the end of that conflict several nations in North and South America, which at present are not united, will merge into one super nation to try and counter the Eastern nations, but after that there will be a period of about 30 years of complete peace on this Earth, before another conflict takes place, but this time between people settled on the Moon and people on Earth.

Over a hundred seers in different parts of Southern Africa have foreseen some of these things; and one of these men who foresaw what I have just described was a man called Parangeta. Parangeta lived in the country formerly known as Rhodesia. He foresaw that by the year 1999 a dramatic happening would come upon this world, and he thought he might survive long enough to help avert that catastrophe; but he had also foreseen his own death at the hands of Joshua Nkomo's guerrillas. Unfortunately he was murdered by them exactly as he himself had predicted.

You know, it is sometimes very silly and useless for a man to stand alone prophesying to the trees and to the passing wind like a lunatic. There are many things I have been shown which I would rather not talk about, but one thing that makes me very happy is that side by side with the great dramas that will happen in this world, great dramas whose purpose is really to purify mankind and to put us on the right track again, there are also many beautiful things that are going to happen.

In the near future, [This prophecy was made around 1987 — Ed.] you are going to get a very big surprise in the United States, because a new leader will appear there who will surprise you very very much. This leader will have the distinction of being the last male President of the United States, because after him there shall rule a flower in the land of the West. In other words a woman shall rule the United States after that president. The man who is going to rule before the coming of the great woman will suffer a serious illness or injury towards the ending of his term.

About two months after Mr. Ronald Reagan had been chosen as President of the United States of America with Mr. George Bush elected as his Vice-President (1984), there arrived at our traditional museum village in Soweto a very friendly gentleman, a Mr. Rommelfanger. This American told me that he knew President Reagan and Mr. Bush personally and that he had supported them during the Presidential elections. It was during our talk that I told this gentleman that Mr. Bush is destined to lead the United States as full President during four extremely critical years in world history, and that great dangers would hover close to the face of humanity.

Now, the events that are in process will have great and beneficial results for my people in Africa. They will have the result of stabilizing many decades of conflict and bring peace to the continent of Africa which will enable my people to pick up threads that were dropped many decades ago. [This prediction was made about 1987, when an end to apartheid in Africa seemed very far away.]

The one flag that I see no longer flying will be the flag of the United Nations. This organization will be replaced by two great alliances of nations, one oriented East and one oriented West.

We all know what is going to happen to the world very soon. We are aware of the fact that in one of the dramatic happenings that will happen to mankind in the very near future many many people are going to take to the sea in ships and flee their countries because of the upheavals.[4]

I do not want my people to perish. I do not want my part of Africa to be plunged into a new dark age from which it will never emerge. Africa is beset by problems, by drought, by starvation. The Sahara is coming down the map of Africa. It will drive more and more people southwards. It is a guess of mine that if this phenomenon does not stop, you will find Ethiopians living in Kenya very soon. You will find Ethiopians living in Tanga-Nyika and you might even find Ethiopians living next door to us in Botswanaland. Because Africa is drying up. It dried up before, and this is what forced many tribes to migrate to the South, which is how my people the Zulus originated.

But what must a man like me do? To whom should I go? Even Moses went to Pharoah. Who shall be my Pharoah? Even Samuel went to Saul and also to David. Who shall be my David? A prophet has got to go to someone. Prophets went to Achab to warn him. Jonah was sent to Niniveh to warn whomever the king was there, at that time. Now who shall be the one I shall go to? You cannot be a prophet and simply talk to the mountains and the trees on your own. You cannot be a prophet and not communicate with someone whose eyes you will open as to what you are talking about. Now, to whom shall I go?

You know that one chilling discovery that I have made — a discovery that has weakened my knees — is this: that there are many white people and many black people in South Africa who foresee that we are headed for troubled times. These people not only foresee this, but they accept it; and some of them — in fact many — welcome it. There are people who say that violence will be good in South Africa in that it will remove "certain systems." But these people don't realize that if violence is allowed in this part of southern Africa, it will plunge the whole of Africa into a new dark age from which Africa will not emerge for the next 50 years, if not the next 100 years. You cannot win a fight between races.

After this, for the next 10 years or more, there will be violent conflict in Southern Africa, a conflict which even now is going steadily from bad to worse. [This prediction was made in about 1985 — Ed.] But beyond that conflict there shall be a period of peace in which people will actually seek to shake each other's hands; and my greatest wish would have been to be alive when that hour of forgiveness does come — but unfortunately I doubt it. (Sometimes I see my own death coming, and frankly sir, it leaves me cold!)[5]

I see a dramatic discovery that will put an end to some major diseases for mankind. The disease called AIDS will be destroyed within the next few years. The cure for this disease is already here but the great scientists don't recognize it yet. Also destroyed will be the disease called tuberculosis, once and for all. All these diseases will be destroyed by one vaccine which already exists, but which will be developed much more powerfully.

I see harmony developing between many nations and many different peoples. In short, I see an end to crude race discrimination, not only in Africa, but also in Europe and in the Americas. But strangely enough, I see a completely new nation which will come into existence in Southeast Asia, a nation which will occupy territory at present occupied by eight different nations there. What it will be called, I don't know.

My message is this: When God reveals to you something that is going to happen, when God reveals to you dangerous things that are yet to come, it is because he has also given you the power the avoid those things; and I say that urgent steps must be taken now by all people throughout the world to avoid what is coming. Because in this conflict which I and many other seers have been shown, nuclear devices will not be used so much as bombs carrying diseases; and this will be the most horrible thing the world has ever seen. It must be stopped now. Also, the devastation of West, Central, Eastern, and parts of Southern Africa which will happen within the next five years must be stopped immediately.

We are capable of changing our future, but the people with the positive aspects in their minds are too few and far between. The eyes that are blind are many, and the eyes that see are so few. If all gifted people, if all spiritual people, could forget their selfishness and come to one great place at one time to pray, we could avoid many things.

Now sir, what must we do? Today human beings are inter-connected like grapes in a bunch — connected by the mothering vines. If you destroy one nation, you destroy the others. If disease invades one grape, soon the whole bunch of grapes becomes rotten and diseased. Men have come together as never before. Communication has made the world smaller. What happens in one country will reverberate in another. The wars of the Middle East are fought not only in the sands of the Sinai Peninsula and in the sands of the land of Israel. They are fought in Lebanon, and they are fought right in the streets of Europe and in avenues in cities of the United States. Doubt me if you dare.

The following prophecies were added
during the fall of 1994

We must return to women the dignity that used to be held by them. Many, many centuries ago, women used to be worshipped. We must return to that attitude; and we must return once more to respecting the child. In fact we must venerate our own souls — so that the people will no longer take drugs or inject themselves with funny things. We must return to the spiritual side of life.[6]

I don't want to offend people who eat meat, but I wish a new kind of meat substitute could be produced, because the greatest destruction that is happening on earth is due to people eating excessive amounts of meat. These foods also make human beings very aggressive, and by being aggressive, they become prone to certain diseases. More land is being destroyed to make room for the cattle and the sheep and the goats than land which is allocated for cultivating the crops. I do not know why this is so; but I think we must return to the pure, simple life. People throughout the world should return to natural ways of eating. Those who do that will survive. There will be a new disease among human beings which needs to be preventively fought right now.

And we must get rid of gold in our lives. How, I don't know. Because gold is a curse. I am told in visions that the many mines that are mined all over the world are creating worse pollution of the earth than anything we imagine. Men have enough minerals now on the surface of the earth in the form of scrap metal and other metals. It doesn't require more. That is what the dreams say, that you have taken from the stomach of the Earth Mother all the metals you need. Stop now. Otherwise the planet herself will sicken.[7]

The things that are called "nuclear," which were made to fight the Third World War, will be grossly misused in the next few years or so; and some terrible things could happen. But that too will end, and peace will prevail.

As a result of physically transmitted diseases like AIDS, new machines will be created which will allow people to make love to each other over unbelievable distances. How could this be, I thought? Electronic love, made through the mind, and machines! This could happen within 5 or 6 years.[8]

There will be many amazing things that will happen very soon. There will come on the market new cosmetics which will allow people to alter their color, their race. This will be very much in fashion, to be black if you are white, or wish in some other way to change your complexion. And this might lead people to understand what it is like to be in a skin of a different color! And with regard to the differences between people, I wish to say this: That the voice of love must be heard throughout the world. Between men and women. Between young and old. Between white and black and red and yellow. Between the living and the non-living. Let there be peace.

Because we are headed for great events in the next thirty years or so. And all who heal must join hands. And pray together and love together.

A certain machine will be invented by the Japanese very soon that will change forever our way of dressing, because people will just put a little shining object, a square object, into this machine, and the machine will use a liquid like material to squeeze new clothes. You will be able to buy a liquid and you will put this liquid into the machine, and you will tell this machine what kind of clothes you want for that day, and the machine will make and exude clothes. I saw this in a vision. It will pour out clothes. Not sewn clothes, but cast clothes, like sheets of plastic, but they will be clothes. And you will be able, if you are wearing a jacket made from this machine, to press a little button if the weather is too cold, and the jacket will warm you nicely, and you will switch it off if it is a hot day and the jacket will cool you very nicely. This is seven or eight years in the future. The material will also be edible. You will be able to recycle your clothes into a jelly-like food substance which you can eat. You just flavor it. A person uses the machine to produce a suit of clothes; then in the afternoon, he becomes angry with those clothes, puts them back in the machine, and the machine will squeeze out a liquid food which the person will eat with a spoon.[9]

The present President of the United States could be brought down by a woman. She won't rule America, but she could cause great trouble in the year 1996. There is a shadow of a woman standing very tall over him. A woman who is frustrated, a woman who needs help. She will bring much sorrow to the people of America. I don't know why, because President Clinton strikes me as a very good young man.

In the year 1997, the country called South Africa, and other countries near it, will be taken over by the people of Islam. Islamic Fundamentalism, even now is on the rise in Africa, and this will expand even more. I see that several of the states in Africa will unite and form a federation. And this federation will be under a man who comes from the land now known as Zimbabwe. This man will form an alliance, a powerful alliance, with a ruler in the Middle East, and they will become a big power in Africa and in the Middle East.

I also see that the nation of China will fall to pieces, as the Soviet Union has fallen to pieces. I saw when the Soviet Union would fall to pieces, I saw and was astonished, but I wrote it down, and now it has come to pass. When China falls to pieces, Japan will become the biggest ruling nation in the East. She will rule China, she will rule southeat Asia, not with politics, but with money and much knowledge. And the Pacific Union, as it will be called, will come and the only country which will not be a part of the Union will be Australia. But Australia, too, after a few years, will stop being an all-white-people country, and will become a very Asiatic country.

There is a man who will rule Southern and Central Africa and parts of East Africa, and who will be a very amusing dictator. He will be called the "The Shepherd of the People." And he will form a friendship with the Sword of Allah, the new ruler who will arise in the Middle East. I think the country called Iran will become supreme in the Middle East, together with Afghanistan. But Saudi Arabia will lose its king, I don't know how or why, very soon, maybe three or four years; it will no longer be a country with a king.

In the year 1999, even beginning perhaps as early as 1997 — many people will laugh at this, but please they must hear — this world will be visited by some of the gods from the stars, the so-called "aliens." They have been secretly visiting, but I think now they will become visible. Because a great decision is going to be made, in the stars, about the fate of the Earth. The Earth is a very special planet to these people of the stars. It was an artificially created world whose purpose was to breed living beings. This is why the star people are so interested in our Earth. It is a womb world. Now we are going to see many strange things coming from the stars into our world.

We are going to see a great spiritual revival in the world, and it will be led by two people. A man in India, and a woman in the United States. There in the United States, sometime in the year 2000-something, the United States will have a woman president, who is already alive today as a young girl, and she will be a former actress from Hollywood. She will rule America, a greater America which will be a combination of Canada, United States, Mexico, and other Central American countries. But the forests of the Amazon will be eaten more and more, for the next six years. And then this woman president will make a very strong law which the world will follow, that no more trees will be cut down. She, this red woman — she will have reddish hair, or coppery hair — was also prophesied by other prophets in Southern Africa, many years ago. She is going to be called "The Red Savior." She is one of the four great people, one yellow, one black, one white, who will save the world in the very near future.

In these coming times the world's nations face a great task: to reverse the effects of pollution, and to try and save the big cities like Capetown, like London, like Delhi, and others, from being flooded by the big waters which will be coming. Because the big waters are coming; I don't know where and why, but they are coming. Even my wife, Cecilia, and even our student, Nobela, have foreseen the world being eaten by very big water. These will not be waters of the rain. They will be salty waters which you can't drink, so why they would come and eat the cities of the world, I don't know. I was shown many cities coming under water, in Africa as well as in Europe and the US. Many cities, London, in the near future, London will become like Venice, with many of its streets turned into water, no longer streets like they have been.

We human beings have for centuries been like an egg which is unhatched. Now we are hatching into gods. But we have already done so much damage to our nest that our hatching is going to be in water. In fact, I see that around about maybe 2005 or 2007 or so many people will take to living underwater instead of on the land. Already I am shown that there are nations in the Far East which are secretly experimenting with bridging a new people. And what they do is what is making the visions angry. There are people who are using dolphins to carry human babies. I have been shown this again and again. They are trying to create a new type of human being who will be able to live in very deep water. I don't know where this thing is being done, but it is being done by yellow people in one of the far away Eastern countries. The visions say that this is wrong. You see, we in Africa believe that dolphins are gods, and they should not be humiliated and treated in this way. Why should they be made mothers of human children? The babies that they produce do not survive for long.

I cannot dictate to people what and what not to do; but please, your society can start by checking out how many of my prophecies have also been seen by white people in America. I don't know what these waters are going to do. I don't know why it is that there will be a mirror in the sky. The whole sky will turn into a mirror, and we are not going to see the Sun except as a shining blob-like thing through wet tissue paper. Because in many parts of the world, a big mist will cover the world, and people will not see the sky anymore. It will be for a long, long, too many years-long time. Now, what must happen is that several wise people must come together and make a meeting. And they must ask the gods why they are so angry with us that they should do such a thing. Also, many people will lose their eyesight.

I see water, ordinary water, being sold in the streets; and if you are caught by the police with a bottle of water, you will be arrested if you don't have a permit to carry that water. And that law is coming soon, maybe fifteen or twenty years from now. Water is going to become so precious that people will buy it from special shops with a lot of engines, a lot of funny machines in the shop. People will no longer be allowed to urinate except in special places where the urine will be turned back into drinkiing water. All I know is that people in South Africa will go to the south of the world, and there they will pull much big ice and bring it to South Africa to irrigate the country. But why people will be irrigating with ice, I don't know, because I don't know what will be happening then.

After the great flood, the human race will rise again. But before that civilization will return to a barbaric state, where many wars will be fought, and much upheaval occur, until the continents of the world no longer have connection with each other. Then civilization will be born again in Egypt. And the person who will do the organizing of this new civilization, will neither be a man nor a woman, but a person with part man and part woman. And this person will do miracles. He/she will use great knowledge to move the planet Mars into the same orbit as the Earth. And She/he will give the planet Mars an atmosphere and greenery like Earth. So these two planets, Mars and Earth, will orbit the sun together, but not interfering with each other. If one is on one side of the Sun, the other will be on the other side. And the world's population will settle on the three worlds: the Moon, which will also be made green and full of water, the Earth, and Mars. And the water which they will use to make these worlds green will not come from Earth, but will come from the big planet, which white people call Jupiter.

And when the three worlds are full of people, living in peace and happiness, the gods of the stars will come down and welcome us to the great gathering of the stars. Because human beings will have proven their ability, not only to have messed up the Earth, but also to have reconstructed and renewed it. He who destroys must also be able to create. At this moment, we human beings are destroying the Earth. Only with great hardship, much pain, and work, will we be able to restore the Earth. But when the great prophecies are fulfilled it is very very good. The Zulus say that where a lion goes, there shall the bush be green. In other words, where a great person of peace goes, there shall great peace flow about him or her.

And the new city of the world, the City of Eternal Peace, will be built not in America, not in Africa or Russia, but in the land known as Tibet. There, the City of the Stars will be established; and a great holiness shall fall upon the Earth.

On the Sacred Rock Carvings

There is an English proverb that says that there are none so blind as those who will not see. The meaning of this proverb is quite obvious: that when people refuse to see things, no one can ever open their eyes. I'm sitting here next to a rock which is the exact twin of a rock I once saw in the United States of America. Engravings identical to the ones I see here before me were clearly visible on that rock near the Colorado River.

The owner of this farm [where the African rock carvings are] told us that these engravings had been made by the people called the Bushmen; and this is the opinion of many in the scientific establishment of South Africa. But let me ask you, do Bushmen build structures like this one? It is now very clear that this stone enclosure was built many thousands and thousands of years ago. Do Bushmen build such square structures? Do Bushmen possess a form of writing of the type that we call *igam* or *polu* in the language of the Zulus and which was called "ogham" in Europe?

This sir, is a rock of sacrifice upon which human sacrifices were performed in honor of this god whose name is *Bel* or *Baal*. This god was worshipped both by the Phoenicians and by the ancient Babyonian people. On the head of this figure you can see the three rays that spell the name of Bel or Baal, and you can see that the figure has been given three legs again to spell the name Bel, and on this rock the person to be sacrificed has had his or her heart torn out of his or her body and these here are the representations of the hearts of three people who were sacrificed upon this rock at different times.[10]

Now what I find very interesting is that this rock exhibits a very dark surface in comparison to the other rocks around it. This is due to the blood of the many victims that were slaughtered upon this rock. The victims could have been anything — animals, domestic and wild, bulls, lions and even human beings, all sacrificed to this strange god; and here you can see the detail of an animal skin.

In South America, North America, and the Pacific Islands you find rocks like this one, and also in the United States of America in the Virginia area and along the Colorado River. And it is accepted by many scientists that these rocks were engraved by ancient people who travelled throughout the world in ships in a search of copper, gold, and tin. It is also recorded in the Bible that the king Solomon acquired most of his gold from a place called "Offere." There used to be a community along the East African Seaboard called "Luferi," the place of bronze, by our people. This is what I think this Offere was.

Now, the people who made this inscription that I see here were not Bushmen as the owner of this farm and other people in the scientific world in South Africa love to believe. These people were a highly civilized, literate people who possessed a number of kinds of writing which they used freely upon rocks that they used as shrines or as places of sacrifice and of worship. This one here reads — and the language used here is the same as Phoenician — "Baal is great, his eye is the sun."

This form of writing was preserved by the black sanusis of Southern Africa exactly as it was used in ancient times. When we make incisions upon the bodies of people to cure them of illnesses such as rheumatism and so on, we do not simply make incisions at random; we use incisions exactly as these ancient people used the lines upon such rocks: to form letters. A number of rocks in addition to the one that we have seen show remarkable things of a non-African origin. We see a rock here which carries an abacus, which was an instrument of counting used by ancient people. This shows that here in this place, not only was there a temple, but there was also a school where children of priests and merchants and traders of all kinds could learn the basics of counting, using the abacus. I have seen identical abaci in America engraved on rocks — identical to this one here — and I've also seen identical abaci on rocks in other parts of the world.

This proves beyond all doubt that this was all part of a gigantic world-spanning culture of sea voyagers and adventurers to whom the oceans of the world were no barrier whatsoever. In the next rock we see a long message again in praise of the god Bel and also we see on the next rock the signs of the zodiac and written instructions on holding an important festival at the solar equinox. Around this ancient rock temple we see also signs — clearly recognizable signs of the zodiac. We see the Virgo sign, we see the Leo sign, we see a clearly recognizable and beautifully executed engraving showing Gemini, the heavenly twins; and we see also a sign that could be Capricorn, the sea goat, and one that is definitely Aquarius, the water-carrier. And anyone who persists in telling me that these signs were engraved by Bushmen does not know what he is saying because at no time in their history did the Bushmen ever engrave signs of the zodiac this way. The only people who did were the Coison people and the Bantu speaking peoples of Southern Africa, and they had inherited the concept of the zodiac from these ancient and half-forgotten seafarers who came to Africa in large numbers to mine gold, copper and tin for selling to nations far beyond the seas.

[Credo here begins to interpret rock-carved engravings.]

We have here an engraving of two suns and an inscription, this time in ancient Egyptian, dedicating this rock to Bel. Shown amongst other things in this engraving is a figure with a very large head

Credo Mutwa points to "Bel" or Baal in the sacred rock engravings

with rays shooting out of it which represents the god Bel with the disc of the sun forming his head and the rays around the halo spelling the name "Bel, Lord of the Sun," several times.

Engraved upon this rock is a charging rhinoceros with breathtaking detail and the three strokes on the flank of the rhinoceros spell again the name of Bel, the God of Light. Here we see an African animal being used in lieu of a bull as a symbol for a foreign god; and we also see two leopards, one above the other, which were sacrificed or hunted down in honor of this foreign god.[11]

There should be absolutely no doubt whatsoever that voyaging the great oceans of the world was a very commonplace thing in remotest antiquity. Those ancient seafarers from wherever they came possessed something that we of this day and age no longer possess: immense courage and an unshakable faith in the Almighty, whether he was called Bel or whatever.

There was a script which was invented in remote antiquity (example here). Some say it was invented by the Phoenicians, some say it was invented by the Celts. But I believe it is much more ancient than either of these two peoples. It is a script in the form of slashes or lines (Ogham) and it consists of what we call a center line or stemline above and below each different letter.

This stone here is engraved with the ten great laws of the Al-

mighty and the serpent symbolizes one of the pillars of the traditional black religion, that is, a belief in reincarnation — that which
lives now shall travel along the road of life, shall die only to resume
the journey of life in another shape. This is the symbolism of the
double spiral serpent. It's a symbol of rebirth. Also it is a symbol of
the secret road that, according to ancient tradition, was taken by
people between this star system of ours, the solar system, and other
solar systems. We are told there was a secret spiral road which you
could travel from this Earth of ours to other planets, but when man
became aggressive and sinful, the gods closed "the Path of the Many
Returns" as it was called.

The engravings reveal not only a symbolism of rebirth, but also a
symbolism of the mysterious path, which, if you were to find it,
enter it, and travel along it, would lead you to worlds other than
our own.

This stone, is one of the sacred "talking stones." On the back of
this one there is a depiction of the traditional African zodiac, and
then here on the front, we are shown another spiral, but this time
the spiral represents not the secret pathway between the stars, but
the heat and force which can be harnessed by a sanusi for the healing of people.

We are told in the sacred writing on this stone that if you come to
a stretch of ground where you are seeking the heat and spiral forces
underground, you must have a goat, an epileptic person, and what
we call a "silver water woman." First you must bring the goat to
this place and start chasing it around and then wait and watch to
see where the goat will rest. This is where the secret power is to be
found. When animals, whether wild or domestic, want to rest, they
do so only in those places where they feel the heat and energy of the
earth flowing from the earth through their body so that it relaxes
them. Especially domestic animals, who realize that they are going
to be slaughtered sooner or later and thus live in a state of tension,
find these places.

At first, where the goat lies down, you must mark that spot, and
then you must bring to the same area an epileptic person. You see,
when people suffer from epileptic fits, they try to save themselves
by falling in those places where they will find some kind of benefit.

So an epileptic person will always try and fall where the energies of the earth are to be found. Also, the silver water woman — I'm sorry I have to tell you this, but a silver water woman is what is called a "sexy broad" in America — will have a double orgasm in a place where the heat and energies of the earth are to be found. Thus, once you have confirmed it this way, then you know you must set up a standing stone in that place. This is why we have got here the likeness of the Earth Mother to tell us that we are seeking the serpent underground and we must use the knowledge of the Earth Mother to locate the hidden river under the Earth.

When you visit one of our sacred sites here in South Africa, you will see that some of the stones have been brightly polished. So-called experts tell you that those stones were polished by many generations of rhinos and elephants scratching themselves — but wait a minute! No rhino or elephant can scratch itself against a standing stone without after some time causing that stone to topple over. And these stones are standing fast and they are polished from bottom right up to the very top. And furthermore, we have stones that rise only a few inches above ground and which are also polished. Tell me, how could a rhinoceros scratch against a stone that is so close to the ground? No. The polishing is done by people who are trying to draw up the secret energy of the earth through these stones. The polishing of the sacred stones is done with hands or with pieces of animal hide; and during a thunderstorm some of the polished stones can actually attract electrical force, because if you touch the stone, you feel this electrical power coursing through you.

There was a time in remote antiquity when people tried to use the energies of the Earth to heal illness and also to extend the human life span. The stones were first polished vigorously and then the women danced in a clockwise fashion and later in a counterclockwise fashion around the sacred stone. And these things were done by hundreds of people simultaneously, whose aim was to arouse the crackling energies of the Earth. In other words, the people, by various actions, by dances, by jumpings and even by fights and other activities, tried to arouse the energies of the Earth to full flame — and very very often the Earth responded. Once the stones began to give out a faint electrical feeling to the fingers touching them, then the sick people were led towards the stones and were leaned against the stone.[12]

The hidden earth power can also be directed by a crystal. This was an attempt by Africans to make a kind of device whose purpose was to enhance human telepathic communication. They imprisoned a lump of this crystal inside a receptacle of copper and then, with a length of copper links and a bronze ring, they chained a lump of iron which had been poorly fused. The idea was that if you wanted to send a spiritual message from your mind to another, you had to wet this stone — in fact the entire device, and then take it off from the sacred necklace and tie it around your head, with this between your eyes. Then you had to relax and breathe very steadily and send the sacred message you wanted to send to whomever that you wished to send it.[13] So you see, something unthinkable from before this century, radio, was preceded by these kinds of rituals.

It seems to me that when your scholars, your anthropologists or whoever, come to decode the writings and diagrams on these stones and determine what their uses were, they should understand; not only the objects themselves, but the whole way of understanding the world that lies behind them — otherwise they understand little or nothing.

Science and Religion

For many years science and religion went hand in hand. Science and religion were like lovers in the night, walking together; but today, science is trying to go it alone — with disastrous results, not only for man himself, but also for the planet as a whole.

We thought long ago that humanity might have come from Africa, and that "Eve" was probably an African woman. Sophisticated people laughed at that old myth. Now scientists believe that human beings really did originate in Africa and that all people presently living in the world are descendants of one African woman. Is it not amazing that the thing we in Africa have always thought is shown to be valid by science?

Represented in my sculpture [see page 199] is the great Earth Mother, and the python of the universe, *Nkanyamba*. It is the serpent that sleeps in the underworld and has got its tail in its mouth.[14] It is also the serpent that taught the first people on earth how to make love. The serpent shows the cyclical round of time in the universe.

Now we must leave Africa for a while and go to Europe. There was a time in Europe when great Greek philosophers actually believed that the human brain was a sponge that culled the blood in the body, that kept the blood at a reasonable temperature. There was also a time in Europe when people used to believe that a human being remembered things by heart, and to this very day we have got a phrase in English that says that to remember is to know "by heart." But even in those remotest of remote times, there were people in southern, central, and eastern Africa — the so-called primitive or savage peoples of Africa — who possessed a remarkable knowledge about the workings of the various organs in the human body, real knowledge about the functions of these things.

My people, the Zulus, call the human brain *ingqondo*. This word comes from the verb, *qonda*, which means "to understand." Thus, the word ingqondo means the seat of understanding, the place where understanding takes place. Not only did the people of Africa possess remarkable knowledge about the functioning of the human brain, but they also attempted, very often with a remarkable success, several operations of a nature which, even today, are conducted with extreme caution by modern doctors. For example, take the trephining brain operation. We have proof in the form of skulls which bear scars and marks of this operation that in ancient Africa this extremely delicate operation was in fact quite commonplace.

I have myself seen skulls of long dead black men and women with holes in them, showing that such operations were carried out on this person, sometimes a number of times, and that the person had actually lived for many years after the operations had been performed.

Now we come to the heart. Our people knew that the heart was deeply connected with, but not the actual seat of the human memory. The Zulu people called the heart *inizeo*. This word comes from the verb, *bushaazeea*, which means to refine, to purify, or to keep alive and moving. Thus, you can see that they believed that the heart

The Great Earth Mother (Ninavanhu-Ma) with the Tree of Life (Sima-Kade) and the Serpent of Eternity

had something to do with the continuous movement and the re-peated purification of the blood.

My people the Zulus and the Sotho-speaking and Tsonga-speaking tribes of South Africa possess knowledge about germs and bacteria that is astonishing, and they had names in their languages long before the white men came to South Africa, names that often described the shape of the organisms. In Zulu germs are known as the "*amagciwane*," a name which means "the tiniest living creatures." In Tsonga germs are known as "*ntsonga-ntsongana*" — an amazing word that means "spiral-spiral creatures," which is the shape of germs that cause venereal disease.

Sotho speakers call germs by another amazing name which is "*dinonokana*," a name which means "tiny, treacherous tormentors." Black people throughout Southern Africa made crude antibiotics, which they used in treating infection. They made these antibiotics by mashing fresh maize-break into clay pots and then placing the pots in a dark place until a furry mould formed over the mess, and this cobweb-like mould was the antibiotic.

All tribes throughout the parts of Africa that I have visited possess an uncanny knowledge of stars, worlds, and planets other than our own; and even the Bushmen in the Kalahari and in Namibia know — please do not ask me how — that the moon has plains, valleys, and mountains. Furthermore, the Bushmen tell me their eyes are sharp enough to *see* the great mountains on the surface of the moon and to see that there are no rivers or life up there.[15]

Now, our people also knew things which today have been confirmed by the greatest scientists and for which our people suffered ridicule and contempt at the hands of people from Europe and other continents of the world in the past. I am going to repeat a sad story which I mentioned earlier and which happened to my grandfather in the year 1925 when I was a child of some four and a half years. My grandfather had a tussle with a Reverend Lee, our local missionary, because my grandfather insisted on performing a ceremony which was known by the Zulus as *Inkulisela*, which means "the corn grower's ceremony."

Under this ceremony, a group of young men and young women were taken by my grandfather to the cornfields of the tribe and there they sang to each growing corn plant, they praised the corn, they gave it names and they caressed some of the growing plants to make them grow faster and more fruitful.

The missionary thought this was superstitious rubbish. But now scientists believe that if you pray or play sweet music around plants they grow better. And it is cruel to deprive a people of something they have been doing for a long time that does no harm, only good. The missionaries did not know that there are many kinds of prayers.

We in Africa believe that the soul goes through a number of incarnations in its development — toward reaching the goal of maturity. We believe that our present human stage is but one of several stages through which the soul must pass, and we use the symbolism of the butterfly's development from egg to caterpillar, to pupa, and then to adult, as a symbol for the upward movement of the soul through various incarnations.

What amazing creatures surround us with their lessons. Look at the ordinary mosquito. The mosquito goes through an aquatic stage in the form of an egg laid in water, then an aquatic larva, then a pupa, which tumbles about in the water; and then it reaches the aerial stage as an adult mosquito, which no longer dwells in water but flies above it. Now, if you look at these two you will find that the pupa lives a completely different lifestyle from that which an adult mosquito lives. In other words, if you were to talk to a mosquito pupa, it would know absolutely nothing about flying, and it would not even remotely imagine that it could ever fly in the future. But it eventually does, as it develops from pupa to mosquito. Could there be some symbolism in this for human spiritual development? Could we have as little an idea of the fully developed soul as the pupa does of the mosquito?

I think God could be the Source from which all living things come. There is a Source of all order and logic in creation. When one looks at a tree, for example, one can see the artistry and the logic behind each leaf, each branch and each layer of bark upon the tree. A tree is a highly advanced sort of living machine and that living machine could only have been created by something that was just as alive and just as wonderful. That is God, I think.

I don't know much about these things, but I do know that behind life there is something fantastic. There are things that we cannot see, things that are just as wonderful — if not more so — than those things that we do see. We live and we delude ourselves, for example, that we are masters of our own fate, our own destiny. But that is not the case. If we were masters of our own destiny, every one of us would be a millionaire and every one of us would be President of the United States or whatever. The truth is, whether we believe this or not, there are forces guiding us about which we know nothing. There are forces guiding the fate of nations, the fate of whole continents, and there may be forces even guiding the fate of whole worlds and universes. There is so much that we don't know and yet there is so much that waits to be revealed to us, if only we could knock at the right door.

In order that science break away from religion, both in Africa and in other parts of the world, it tried to go it alone; and breaking away from the hand of God is what has brought our mankind to the brink of disaster today because for many, many years religion and science had gone hand and hand like lovers, as I have said. But science has faithlessly torn itself away from religion with the results that we see in polluted rivers, destroyed environments, and poisoned human bodies. I think it's high time that science was brought back into the realm of the spiritual so that it would wear the blanket and feel the caress of spirituality and have a reverence for the world and all that dwell in it.[16]

A Path to Wisdom

I am just an ordinary man, trying to do some kind of job; hopefully to try to bring peace to my country and to show my people the way. It seems to me today that people are divided into two groups: there are those who want to create and those who want to destroy. These people represent the modern poles of good and evil. I try to be one of those who seek to create, to show our people the way to rebuild that which was lost and perhaps to make other lives happier, to leave the world a better place than it was when I came into it. I don't know what else to do.

I feel that people should communicate, people should tell each other the truth about themselves. I believe — rightly or wrongly, I don't know — that the basic cause of all conflict in this world is that people of different factions, people of different nations, people of different races, are being deliberately kept in ignorance of the truth about each other by self-seeking and conflict-loving people.

I believe that if ignorance can be banished from this world, if people can communicate with each other fully, frankly, and in depth, then all wars will cease because the cause of war is fear and hatred and hatred is the ugly little daughter of the evil witch of ignorance. People fight when they do not know each other. I have seen leaders in this world who deliberately made the people of their nations ignorant of things they needed for their own health and prosperity. I believe that once ignorance is eliminated from this world, peace will come to our troubled planet because there are people in this world who gain profit from every bullet that is fired into a human heart and every shell that obliterates a human body and these people find it in their interests, not only for strife between faction and faction, nation and nation, race and race, but also they find it in their interests to keep people of these different races, factions and nations ignorant of each other. They inflict ignorance on people in order to achieve what they seek.[17]

You are walking in the street and you come to a strange man. This man does not speak your language. You greet him, he does not respond. Perhaps then your mind begins to twist fearfully. In the eye of your twisted mind, this man now looks hideously ugly. Also, in the nostrils of your fear-ridden soul, this man smells strange, offensively strange. Your soul creates an enemy. How to remedy this?

First you must find points of resemblance between you and this man or this woman. First look at yourself and then at this person. The first thing you will find is that this is another human being; and the longer you contemplate, the more you will find that you have much in common. Now this is what mischievous people, self-serving people, don't want us to find: a commonality among different peoples of the world, a common ancestry, a common original culture, and a common original language. There are barriers in our mind and in our culture that ought to be broken so that we can take a closer interest in each other.

People get hypnotized by the outward appearance of a thing. We are so conditioned to accepting that which is strange as perhaps bizarre, outlandish or ugly, that we often forget that lying behind that strange exterior is a mind like our own. I may imagine the strange person's mind to be just as ugly as I think his or her exterior to be. But if I could reach into the mind of that creature, into the mind of that strange human being, and if that human being could reach into my own mind, we could somehow put an end to each other's fears.

After my stay in Japan, which lasted several weeks, I began to love and admire the Japanese so much because there was no custom that they practiced which failed to ring bells in my African mind — so great were the similarities. I began to love the Japanese people. I began to feel that I was one with them and they were one with me.

Then I was taken on a visit to Hiroshima, and when I took one look at the hideous exhibits in that museum in Hiroshima, I wept. For an hour I was in deep grief because I could see the hideous destruction that the people of Hiroshima had undergone; and I would never have wept this way, nor had such an intensity of feeling for the Japanese, had I not been lucky enough to reach a state where I could understand them and love them first.[18]

So long as man is divided by fear, so long as man is divided by hatred, so long shall he never know real progress. For example, it hurts me very much to see that although we have progressed today to the extent that we have been able to put men on the moon, still, the human life span, the average human life span, is a miserable three score years and ten as described in the Bible of many thousands of years ago. Logically, men should be living now to be one hundred years and more, but because man has only made progress in weapons of destruction, in missiles and airplanes and battleships, he has not yet made any progress in those things that will keep him alive. And if we are to roam the spaces between the stars, we cannot do that roaming with the pathetically short lives that we are leading today.

In fact, the human life span has grown shorter instead of longer. Many men today die in their 45th and 52nd years. Why? Because we live in fear, we live in anxiety, and we stress too much the aggressive and the negative in our lives. But who am I to preach? I too have been a candidate for all of this.

Why didn't I just lead a life of the type I wanted, a peaceful ordinary African life with many cattle, many wives, a village of my own, and perhaps a pick-up truck or two? I am not always sure I want to lead this life that I am leading. I didn't choose this life and quite frankly if there was somebody with whom I could exchange it, I might do so. What am I doing here? Is there something in life or behind life that is pushing us or guiding us?

I was born on the 21st day of the seventh month in the year 1921. I didn't choose the day of my birth nor did I choose the fact that I was my father's seventh child. I have not chosen this very interesting fact that has appeared in the course of my life again and again. But all people who play an important part in my existence, just happen to have seven letters to their names. All my greatest friends and my worst enemies have just seven letters to their names.

There was a time when doctors gave me exactly three months to live. When they told me that I had a very bad disease consuming both my pancreas and my lungs, the doctors were pitying. They were also were very very condescending. They were so sorry for me they even said that I would have to have operations to remove my right lung. It was then that I remembered the incident in Kenya with the lion. I decided to fight against this disease. I decided not to be afraid of this disease because we are taught in African tradition that certain diseases like cancer and others are not diseases but rather living entities which, if you show fear of them, get out of hand and devour you.

So what did I do? I began to imagine my disease as a living entity, an ugly old woman who was always trying to get in my way. I pictured my disease as a gray, wrinkled, old nuisance who cackled at me but who was really not something from which I should run.

I went out and I built in Soweto what is said to be the largest statue ever created by a black man anywhere in Africa. When I built the statue, I was fighting against this disease. I was coughing and falling unconscious, but in my fight against the disease I even went so far as to ask my friends to lash me with ropes to a ladder which I was using to work on the face of this tall statue of the Earth Mother.

And then the more I drowned myself in my work, forgetting my fear of this disease which the doctors had said would kill me within a few months, the more I began to feel I was getting better. The coughing fits began to subside, the terrible breathlessness, the bouts of unconsciousness began to go away, and when the statue was finished, the doctors asked to see me, and they took an x-ray of me and they were astonished because my lungs were clear, and only a few cavities remained where the ugly thing had been before. So, there is truth in the African belief that certain diseases are alive and that if you show fear of them, then these diseases will devour you.

I have learned that there is somewhere in America a man who wrote a book called *Clockwork Orange* and that this man wrote this book when he was under threat from the disease known as cancer and that he so lost himself in his book, so drowned himself and forgot his fear, that the disease actually turned tail and ran away.[19]

I also feel that we of this modern day and age tend to talk too much and do too little, and I feel that if man is to survive, somebody must have the guts to grab the entire human race by the scruff of the neck and show it a positive direction, a direction away from the slow drift to annihilation that we are at present witnessing. And I feel that instead of sitting here talking while great events are taking place beyond our immediate sphere, while people are dying, while there is disease and hunger and hatred, we should get up and be doing something. Let us do something.

Our forefathers did not wait for history to catch up with them. They went up to the elephant of history and brought it down. They created, they *were* history. Take for example the pioneers, the settlers who took their wagons to unknown places both in South Africa and America to establish history. Those men and those women were doers and not talkers and I would prefer that we should also be a people of doers instead of people wasting so much vocal energy in the empty air around us.

The sacred stones of the Zulu people are the touchstones of the stars and hopefully, seeing this and some of the other tremendous evidence, we will see that we are part of a much greater family in the universe. We can begin to take more serious our responsibilities of being citizens here as well as citizens preparing for a greater future.

A song that I sing with the sangomas says, "There shall arise out of the ashes of man, a newer man who shall rule the far stars, carrying with him the seven laws of love; and that the first and the greatest law of God — doing unto others as you would have them do to you — will be the law of that time." This, too, is the "Song of the Stars" — that humanity can stand fearlessly and joyfully before the Universe, with love in his heart, and be welcomed home as a long-lost child.

I have no message more important than this: All people, all nations, must seriously work for peace on this Earth. There are so many challenges facing humankind. There are so many things that call to us from far away that I do not see any need for hatred, for fear, and war in this world. I know that many have made this futile call, but I shall also make it: That there should be an end to all war and all conflict on Earth. More than that I cannot say.

Ultimately I saw that the lore of my people was destined to die with those of us who knew it, and that it would then die forever. I felt I gradually recognized that by breaking my oath — something originally made to protect the sacred lore in times that were very different from these times — I was doing something for my own people, preserving the eternal wisdom that had been carried on for centuries, and also doing something for mankind as a whole. For there are people of many lands and many races who should share in this wisdom, and learn the wonder of these stories — they existed for the good of our people, but also now for all people. This realization helped me to overcome my fear. May you receive it in the spirit that it is given! Indaba!

The Boundaries of Human Life

Our people believe that people die and are reborn again either as animals or as trees, even as bushes, or even as various types of insects, and sometimes one can be lucky enough to be reborn as a human being once again — albeit in a different part of the world and at a different time. In the course of my life I have had many reasons to believe that this could be a true thing, because many people appear to possess knowledge of their previous lives. They seem to possess memories of incidents which don't belong to this lifetime; and then there are those incidents where sometimes you will find two strangers meeting each other and finding that at some time they must have known each other. They know intimate things about each other's lives which they could not have known had they not at some time somewhere lived together. Such a thing has happened to me on several occasions.

There was a terrible day in my life in 1976 during the Soweto riots, a terrible day when I lost someone whom I loved very much. But I'm telling you there's more to life than meets these eyes of yours. So next time you decide to murder someone be careful that you don't get reborn in the same area as your victim lest he or she should murder you in his or her own turn. Shakespeare had his character Hamlet say, "There are more things in heaven and Earth than are dreamt of in your philosophy, Horatio." We must sometimes think very deeply about these mysteries. I accept as a fact that there is such a thing as reincarnation. I also accept as a fact that there is something that guides your life and mine. I accept that we were born when this power decided and that we shall die only when that unknown power decides we should.

The soul can go voluntarily into the future through the performance of certain rituals, or the soul can go into the future through the medium of death, the death of the body in this world. It is quite possible for a person to send his or her soul into their future to learn of something that is yet to happen and then to bring back that knowledge to the present and use it as a basis for taking action to avoid that occurrence which has been seen in the future. Because the future can be changed — it is not static any more than the present is. With one action taken today you can initiate a whole series of actions in the future and with one action avoided today, you can stop many actions in the future.

According to the traditions of Africa, it was a woman, *Iyaya*, the beautiful one, who discovered the existence of the Great Spirit. It was while people were still on the Red World where they had been created before. When people discovered God, they discovered a shapeless, featureless, endless entity with which no-one could cope, and so in order to handle the mystery of God, man reduced that mystery to a shape that he could recognize and therefore understand. People reduced their idea of God to the image of a human-like family, a family of God the Father, known by my people, the Zulus, as *Unkunkulu*, which means "the Greatest of the Great Ones," and God, the Great Mother, known by the Zulus as *Nomkumbulwana*, which means "The Flower of the Many Fields, the Lady of Many Plowshares," and God the Son, known by the Zulus as *Umvelinangey*, which means "The First Born of the Almighty." Thus, the idea of a trinity of a Godhead is universal, not only throughout Africa but also throughout many countries of the world. You always find this. You find most commonly a father, mother, and child trinity, but sometimes, with some tribes such as the Nigerian tribes, you find a trinity consisting of three main gods or three female gods.[20]

Take a lump of clay from near a river and put that heavy lump of clay into the hands of a child of about five years. The child will not know what to do with that lump of clay — it will be too heavy, it will be too clumsy to handle. But if you show the child how to form that lump of clay into the likeness of an ox, or any animal, or a human being, then you have given that child something with which he can cope, something which is within his control. Again and again in the Bible we learn how the people of Israel very often turned their backs upon the Lord of Abraham and started worshipping false gods. It was because these people were not capable of dealing with the concept of a God without shape. They could not conceive such a deity, nor could they come to terms with this shapeless entity. Therefore people have needed images of God, or of the gods, like children, to make sense of that which is unfathomable.

There is, for example the cosmic tree, *Sima-Kade*, which means "The One who stands for all time, who has been standing for all time, and who will continue standing for all time." When I think of this tree I feel connected to it, and that this tree embraces all things. My brothers and sisters are the fruit of this tree, as are all living creatures. And so when I see any tree, I am reminded of Sima-Kade.[21]

In these times, men have ridiculed God, laughed at the Almighty, denied his existence and then, perhaps in some cases come around full circle — today some of them are accepting that there may be a God in this universe after all. We know so much about the world at large, but so little about ourselves, so little about the storms that rage within our own souls. And we know so little about our past, and even less about our future. We are poor in spirit, because, especially recently, mankind has concentrated too much on the materialistic side of life.

It is only now that people are beginning to explore things such as the thing they wrongly call para-psychology. It is only now that the existence of things such as telepathy and telekinesis and communication between human beings and plants is becoming accepted. What have we been doing all this time? Can we accept the fact that our poorly developed spiritual life is holding us back — even, strange to say, in the area of technological development? We cannot know more, because we do not even know how to use well that which we have.

Take these teachings: that we are all brothers and sisters; the children of one father and mother; that all human beings are interconnected; that we share many thoughts and feelings that we imagine about the world, about the future, about each other; and that the images and dreams we hold in our minds and hearts do matter. Treat children and animals with kindness, and pass this wisdom on to the generations yet to come, and I assure you that there will come a time when our grandchildren, or our great-great grandchildren will live in a world of beauty and harmony. And they will hear a far-off music, a beautiful, cosmic music, that will lift them beyond all fear, all suffering and limitation, into a universal brotherhood, beyond this little world and its fearful dreams. That music will draw closer and yet closer with its message of hope and becoming. That music is the Song of the Stars. Indaba.

Notes

INTRODUCTION

1. There are many classes of holy person, roughly equivalent to "shaman," among the Zulus as defined by Mutwa. In his own words:
    Inyanga is the name for a shaman, a witch doctor, a moon person.
    Sangoma is a drum person, a clairvoyant, one who uses the drum to arouse the spirits.
    Sanusi is higher than both of them — the one who causes things to ascend, the uplifter, or the pilot of that which ascends.
2. John Neihardt, *Black Elk Speaks* (Lincoln, NA: University of Nebraska Press, 1961).
3. Marcel Griaule, *Conversations with Ogotemelli: An Introduction to Dogon Religious Ideas* (Oxford: Oxford University Press, 1975).
4. Campbell's vision of the "boundaryless planet" of this coming age, awake to the universality of the human mythic imagination, is remarkably close to that of Credo Mutwa, who never read any of his books or knew of Campbell — until I gave him Campbell's last book, *The Inner Reaches of Outer Space*, in 1990. When I spoke to him a few months later, he told me he had read it —not an easy book — many times. "This book leads you into unknown dimensions and fields of thought," he said. "I think this Professor Campbell must be a wise man for your culture."
5. I am indebted to Dr. Stanley Krippner for his sharing with me his biographical sketch of Mutwa in a paper entitled "Vusamazulu Credo Mutwa: A Zulu Sangoma," as well as Credo Mutwa's own biographical comments on tape and via telephone interview.
6. Credo Mutwa, *Let Not My Country Die* (Pretoria, South Africa: Sigma Press, United Publishers, 1986) p. 53.
7. Op. Cit.
8. Though he formally renounced Christianity, Mutwa retained an understanding of, and sympathy for some of the core aspects of Christianity. He also studied Islam, and some of the Eastern religions, believing such knowledge to be indispensable to a complete knowledge of humanity.
9. In the way that shamans often become transmitters as well as originators of their culture's creative traditions of myth, music or legend, Mutwa felt the two roles of his life to be intertwined. In 1954, Mutwa obtained employment in Johannesburg in a shop which specialized in African tribal art. He was so inspired by the creative energy he felt in the traditional objects that he became an avid student of art history, as well as an artist.

10. Conversation with the editor, July, 1990.
11. Krippner, op cit. p. 3.
12. Stephen Larsen, *The Shaman's Doorway* (New York: Harper and Row, 1976, and Barrytown, N.Y.: Station Hill Press, 1988.)
13. *Let Not My Country Die*
14. Ibid. p. 44.
15. Ibid. p. 2.
16. From chapter 2, "In the Days of the Colour Bar," p. 19.
17. Ibid. p. 132.
18. Ibid. p. 134.
19. Ibid.

CHAPTER 1

1. Compare these symptoms to the classically recognized signs of the "shaman-sickness." See Stephen Larsen, *The Shaman's Doorway*, also Douglas Sharon, *The Wizard of the Four Winds*, (New York: The Free Press, 1978), also John Neihardt's *Black Elk Speaks* (Lincoln, NA University of Nebraska Press, 1961). In most instances this specific, atypical type of illness may only be cured by shamans, and by beginning to shamanize. Eliade, in his masterwork *Shamanism: Archaic Techniques of Ecstasy*, (Princeton: Princeton University Press, Bollingen series No. LXXVI, 1970) says this sickness is often recognized as the genesis of a "greater" shaman; the hereditary role, or the voluntary seeking of the profession create usually a "lesser" shaman. It is the call by the spirits through the shaman sickness that makes the difference.

2. Mutwa does not use the Theosophical term "aura," and seems unacquainted with much that is current in Western esoteric lore, which renders his insights and knowledge fresh and original. The "light" of Mutwa's visions seems analagous to that which the Eskimo shamans call *angakoq*, the x-ray vision that allows one to see the interiors of men and beasts, or even future events.

3. This distressing experience is called "dismemberment" in the shamanic literature and seems to be a universal precursor to rebirth. See my discussion of this in *The Shaman's Doorway*, especially chapter 4, which describes the experience of a contemporary person, J.B., who undergoes this immemorial ritual in visionary form.

4. The "ghostly bride" not infrequently appears to visionaries. See my discussion of this in "Swedenborg and the Visionary Tradition," in *Emanuel Swedenborg: A Continuing Vision* (New York: The Swedenborg Foundation, 1988). The spirit woman, literally "anima," (Lat.: "soul") is described by Jung throughout his collected works as a factor especially active in masculine psychology, where it functions as *psychopompos*: a guide to the soul. In this case, "Amarava" was a mythological ancestress of the Zulu people, from the kindgom of *Amarire*, see chapters 4 and 5. At the time she appeared to the Mutwa in vision, he knew nothing of this traditional Zulu lore.

5. Nananana is described in the following chapter as one of the manifestations of the Goddess, and an important, world-saving figure in Zulu mythology.

6. These instructions are not unlike the preparatory meditations that are employed in Chinese Qi Gong, an ancient art of generating and using subtle energy (qi or chi).

7. This phenomenon obviously seems parallel to the Hindu *Kundalini* system, the "serpent power," and also to the "Num," of the Kalahari bushmen — see Richard Katz's *Boiling Energy*.

8. These two "pathways to transcendence" are also explored in the relatively late North Indian tradition called "Tantra," in which it is believed there are two paths, a left and right-hand path, one of austerities, the other of over-indulgence leading to *verag*, exhaustion — that prepare the soul for the detachment which leads to enlightenment. The "joyous way" has some resemblance to the *sadhana* of *Bhakti*, the yogas which rely upon the joyous outpouring of the heart.

9. An African version of the Sweat Bath, used in initiatory ritual by the Amerindians, among others.

10. Self is the exact equivalent of the Bantu "Ena," "myself" being rendered "miena." Self (*Atman*) is also the term used in Hindu metaphysics for the indwelling soul-spark; and this is the same term, (Self capitalized) which Jung used to refer to the spiritual or transpersonal center of the personality.

11. This notion shows up in African syncretisms, such as the Carribean Voudon. The sacrifices of the living sustain the ancestral dead, who come to act as intermediaries between the human and the divine.

12. Of Western psychiatric approaches, this is perhaps closest to that of British Psychiatrist R.D. Laing, who felt that the therapist must indwell the reality of the client.

13. In effect this is a more drastic form of what Behavior Therapists call "systematic desensitization": placing the phobic person in the presence of the feared stimulus and extinguishing the response to it.

14. This prescription would meet with agreement among modern nutritionists for the condition called "essential hypertension," and also for hyperactivity or "hyperkinesis," treated in modern settings by such regimens as Feingold diet — free of refined sugars and starches and food dyes and additives. In the USA, black males are an extremely high risk group for myocardial emergencies due to hypertension. Women's rates of heart attack have risen with their increased participation in the labor force, particularly, as with men, responsible or executive positions.

15. Credo Mutwa does not seem to be aware of the "poltergeist" (noisy ghost) literature, which is fairly extensive in Western parapsychology. Nonetheless his account agrees substantially with that tradition, including the presence of an inadvertent medium, usually, but not always female, often early adolescent, and with suppressed emotional problems.

16. There are contemporary movements among traditional peoples in America, Australia and elsewhere, to restore sacred objects taken from them by anthropologists and collectors. Some museums and societies with sympathetic values are aiding in the restoration.

CHAPTER 2

1. This is the *flaw in creation* motif, which, in the Judeo-Christian version, enters the world through an historical or proto-historical event in the seduction of Eve by the serpent, and the ejection from the garden into the flawed world.

2. He appears in the figure the Afro-Cuban Haitians refer to as *Obatala*, "He of the White Cloth," who, after a great creation, withdrew beyond the phenomenal world. This figure also resembles the Sankya (Hindu) *Purusha*.

3. This is reminiscent of the myth which Hesiod relates in the *Theogony*, about the great Earth Mother, Rhea, who gives birth to all things but then cannot stop and so gives birth to monsters, grotesque and evil things, such is the irrationality of her generative force and her blind loyalty to her offspring.

4. "Tokoloshe," the word for Zombie, is here used for this strange creation, something like an evil Golem, or a robot.

5. The "deluge motif" is found in mythologies from the Amerindian to the Middle Eastern, the Oriental to the African. Here the waters represent a cathartic force to purge the universe from primordial Evil.

6. The world-creating ability of this evil demiurge echoes the Gnostic mythologies which have evil or self-congratulatory "archons," who bring a corrupted world into being.

Chapter 3

1. This unusual mythogem corresponds to the torture of the Sumero-Babylonian Goddess Innanna, who descends into the underworld to rescue her beloved Dumuzi and encounters her vengeful sister Erishkigal, Queen of the Underworld, who strips her and tortures her. The theme also echoes the disappearance of Persephone and Demeter's blighting of the Earth.

2. Of the many worldwide parallels to the motif of the "forbidden fruit of the Underworld," the legend of Persephone is of course the closest. In her case, it was her mother Demeter who was blighting the Earth because of the abduction of her daughter by Hades, Lord of the Underworld; and it was a pomegranate which she ate. Celtic legends of *Annwyn* and the fruit of the Underworld are comparable. To eat fairy food is to accept the other world.

3. The hammer of Thor is, of course, suggested by this story, but the story seems closer to the legend of Hephaistos, the Hellenic Craftsman of the Gods, who was also very ugly and lame. Hephaistos was depicted as married to Aphrodite, Goddess of Beauty and Love, whereas Ngungi is the sun of Nananana, also Goddess of Beauty and Love. The motif of the sacrifice of the left eye for the sake of wisdom suggests the legend of Odin, who "hung on the windy tree nine days and nights" to acquire the runes of wisdom. It is difficult to be certain whether the African version or the Greco-Nordic versions are prior in this interesting symbolic syncretism.

Chapter 4

1. In Amerindian mythology it is coyote who is the thief of fire.

2. The following fragment was included by Mutwa in the original narrative, but actually seems to break the flow of the story, hence it is appended in this note. (The motif of the four directions and the guardians thereof shows up in many traditional mythologies, among them the Amerindian and Tibetan.)

The Four Brothers:

Long ago there were two suns in the sky, a male sun and a female sun. And there were lots of demons in the Earth. One day, because of hideous things the demons were doing, the female sun got brokenhearted, and she fell down from her high place onto the Earth; and then the Earth was unstable and full of earthquakes and floods and the remaining sun used to rise in the North and set in the South.

Then the Great Earthmother decided to create four brothers. And these brothers she put in the four directions of the earth. The white brother she put in the North where the ice is, the red brother she put where the Sun goes down (West) because that is the direction of the dying of the Sun. The black brother she put in that warm place the South of the world; and the yellow brother she put where the sun rises (East) in all his splendor.

And the Great Earth Mother told all the brothers, "You must all help with your strength and hold up the Earth, and see that it doesn't get unstable again. But when the days of peace come and a new world is created at the end of this one, I the Great Mother will bring you all together into my village of silver and you shall live in that village together for all time."

Our people believe that in the center of the Earth there is a very deep hole, and in that hole there is a sacred mountain made completely of gold or copper. This mountain, we believe, is the mountain from which all the wisdom in the universe flows like a great river, nourishing all places, all lands and all beings. So the four brothers who guard the directions also were the guardians of the sacred mountain.

Now each of these four brothers has got two wives who are also his sisters. It is said they shall all dance together at the beginning of the new world. And when this occurs, the brothers shall bring out the mountain from its great hole, and it will shine for all living beings. Thus all beings shall share in the great knowledge of the gods, and become as gods.

3. The fire-theft appears in many world mythologies, and there is usually a penalty for it; for it is the one thing which in primordial times truly separated the human world from the animal world. Among the Greeks it was Prometheus who dared the wrath of the Olympian Gods and was punished for his sympathy to men. Among the Maori, it was Maui who went to his grandmother, Mahuika, to obtain it. She emitted fire star; and the trees began to burn. The rain put it out, but the fire inheres in the wood of the trees and may be coaxed out of it by rubbing. The Tembe of Brazil tell how an old man stole fire from the vultures and put it in the trees. Among the North American tribes it is also stolen by animals, but passed from one animal to another in a relay that finally outraces the original (divine) owner of the fire.

4. In the Odyssey, it is the breaking of the taboo in regard to the Cattle of the Sun that kills most of Odyyseus' men and initiates the latter sequences of the adventure.

5. The relation of crystals to magical flight is known to the Australian Aborigines and even nudges at the gates of modern science-fiction. In this case it seems to be diamonds — that which is immortal and indestructible — which the star-being eats.

6. European fairy tales have many versions of the clever little man, "Jack," the "little tailor" or whomever, who fools the large stupid giant and ultimately bests him. One hears also echoes in some of the "Uncle Remus" stories, so beloved in Black American Folklore.

CHAPTER 5

1. The Star Sirius, the "Dog Star," visible in the night sky in parts of the Northern and parts of the Southern hemisphere. At eight light years, it is the second closest star system to the Solar System.

2. Somnganise suggests the Greek Hermes or Roman Mercury in his analagous role of "messenger of the gods." Like his counterparts, he is characterized by quickness, intelligence, and a certain deceptiveness.
3. This is the story which we have chosen for the title for the entire book, here only a condensed version is given.
4. Hopi mythology echoes this awareness among traditional peoples that there are many races of mankind, usually designated: White, Black, Yellow and Red.
5. This would seem to be Sirius, approximately eight light years away from the solar system. Mutwa said, "We don't see this star from the part of Africa in which we live (Southern Africa). We know it is far away to the North. This star is of crucial importance in the Dogon mythology, see above, and also in the mythology of the Incas of Peru.
6. See Marcel Griaulle, *Conversations with Ogotomelli*, which documents the Dogon fascination with the Star Sirius, of which they knew that it had an invisible (until modern telescopes) "white dwarf" companion star; and the role that the beings called *Nummo* play in the origins of mankind (bringers of culture, benefactors to humankind).
7. The irresistible comparison here is with the Prometheus myth, but there are, of course, inconsistencies with tantalizing symbolic echo: egg-theft=fire-theft. Zeus=firebird. Both figures are saviors of mankind and are subjected to the same (liver-gnawing) torture.
8. The same belief, based on the actual behavior of dolphins, seems to be almost worldwide. The contemporary fascination with dolphins echoes their legendary intelligence and ability to communicate, as if they were long lost kin of humankind.
9. As Marcel Griaulle notes, it was not known until recent times and powerful astronomical instruments that there is a "white dwarf" companion of the star Sirius. The latter is detectable through small movements of Sirius as it is orbited by its phenomenally dense but hitherto invisible companion. The uncanny knowledge of African peoples, the Dogon and the Zulus especially, about the density of the star, is mirrored in the myth of its being a "pit" of a star devoured by a gigantic being that roams the cosmos snuffing stars — an image which appears in other mythologies, the Hindu, notably, in regard to the moon; and also in the eclipsed sun, in fact, in the periodic eclipses of either body.
10. These stories are not unlike the one told by New York resident Whitley Strieber in his book, *Communion*, or by investigators Bud Hopkins or John Mack. In the literature, people who have had these experiences are called "abductees." Many things in their personal psychology change. Credo's own abduction story is told later in this chapter.
11. The smell usually associated with methane and ammonia, which astronomers identify as the dominant chemistry found on certain planets, for example Jupiter in our solar system.
12. The symptoms seem not unlike those from exposure to radioactivity.
13. These creatures, as described by the Mutwa seem startlingly close to the creatures seen by Strieber and others, both in appearance, and in their activity — which seems to be a scientific research of some kind, conducted on both ani-

mals and humans, and whether the latter like it or not. These days, increasing numbers of people seem to be coming forward with abduction stories, as John Mack of Harvard has noted.

14. This part of the interview occurred in 1990, before the collapse of the Soviet Union.

CHAPTER 6

1. This seems remarkably close to the dream sequence reported among the Malaysian *Temiar* or *Senoi* during the 1930s in a much-referenced monograph by Kilton Stewart, "Dream Theory in Malaysia," in which children learn to fly by falling. See also my discussion of this in *The Shaman's Doorway*, ch.2.

2. Such serpents, called *brimures*, play a very active role in Australian shamanism and may be introduced into the body or extracted, and are important in initiations.

CHAPTER 7

1. The American Iroquois had a similar belief, as did the Malaysian Senoi. (See editor's discussion of this in *The Shaman's Doorway*, under the subject of "The Enactment of Vision.") Fortunately the Iroquois were able to transfer the idea of literal enactment to a more metaphoric level. Though the dream was believed to reflect the "wishes of the soul" that must be carried out, psychodrama or symbol would suffice wherever the dream's message would infringe on another's rights or be destructive or grandiose out of all proportion. The community helped the dreamer with the symbolic enactment.

2. This prophecy was made in 1990, while this book was was in the early stages of being prepared.

3. During the years 1989 and 1990, while we were working on this manuscript, I sensed anxiety coming from Credo Mutwa, that the book would not be done before 1991. When I inquired, he voiced where his fear was coming from — that there was to be a great war in the Middle East at the beginning of 1991. "Can I ask one last question?" he asked. "What is this thing that I and other seers keep on seeing regarding the year 1991? Do other seers overseas also see the remarkable thing that will happen on earth during that year? It's a very very funny thing. I don't know whether it will be a satellite or what, but it will crash upon the world and cause an accident with a great city. This is what worries all of us but then we are a crazy people, we sangomas." He could not foretell the size of it; but that many thousands would die, and it would affect the whole area, if not the world. He thought that chemicals would play a part in it. I must say that I heard Mutwa voice this anxiety long before any media signs, or other signs of the Gulf War were apparent.

4. Could this be referring to the "Boat People," of the recent years, both in South Asia, and in Cuba?

5. Credo Mutwa, at the time of this editing, had just passed his 70th birthday (July 21, 1991). At last report, his health was not so good, and a recurrent cancer was afflicting him, which he claimed was caused by stress. At the time of this publishing, Feb., 1996, he has had several bouts, but is holding his own.

6. Interestingly, this prophecy was made before the huge flow of books on the topic of "soul" into the American Publications market in the 1990s.

7. This is not unlike the message delivered from the mysterious Kogi people of the Andes to the world through a film by Alan Erera, *The Elder Brother's Warning: The Kogi of Columbia*, who was admitted to their community in order to communicate this message. The film was originally made for the BBC, now available through Mystic Fire Video, New York, N.Y.

8. When I first heard these prophecies, I wondered what Credo could possibly mean. Then I learned of "sex on the internet" and the pornography controversy, and began to reconsider my skepticism. Ed.

9. Recently a T.V. broadcast bemused this editor by talking of new plastics, including clothes made from recycled compost — hence food. This is not totally removed from Credo's vision.

10. Bel, "the Babyonian form of the title, Baal, 'Lord or Master,' at first generally applicable to the gods of places..." also related to Enlil or Marduk, the chief of the Gods. Bel was the god of the Earth and also believed to bring on the flood. From *Funk and Wagnalls Standard Dictionary of Folklore, Mythology and Legend*, Harper & Row, Paperback edition, 1984.

11. The association of the Bull with the Sun and with the Moon occurs in Mithraism. The usual association of the Bull is with the Moon, as the horns represent the crescent moon, and the bull dies and is resurrected, as is the moon. The sun is often represented as a lion or leopard because of its golden color, and is shown pouncing on the moon (bull). In these traditions, which extend throughout the middle East to India, the Moon is masculine, the Sun feminine. According to Campbell, the two leopards appear often as guardians of the goddess. See also the Tarot deck, in some versions of which the chariot of the High Priestess is drawn by lions. The wrathful Indian goddess Durga rides upon a lion.

12. Among the !Kung Bushmen of the Kalahari desert, the power is called *num*, and it is believed to rise out of the Earth, travelling like the Indian *kundalini* up the healer's spine. The healer then becomes able to heal through the touch of power. See Richard Katz's *Boiling Energy*.

13. The use of crystals as devices for magical communication is extremely widespread, especially among specifically shamanistic societies, such as the Australian Aborigines. In the comparison of science to magic, it is a curious coincidence that the first radios, only invented at the end of the nineteenth century, used crystals.

14. This is the symbol of the *Ouroboros*, the serpent with the tail in its mouth, which occurs in many creation mythologies, in the Hermetic and the Orphic mysteries, and which, according to Eliade, symbolizes "the eternal return." For Jung and Eric Neumann it also refers to the recursive nature of consciousness, that it turns back upon itself, and also to the instinctual life in that it returns to its origins.

15. The last three paragraphs are quoted verbatim from *Let Not My Country Die*, p. 148. They fit well into the current discussion.

16. The sentiments here uttered by Mutwa are not different from those of the American Indians and the Australian Aborigines, who have always felt that the Euro-white civilization was lacking in some truly fundamental insights, and that for all our technological prowess and scientific wisdom, these character flaws of the whole race would eventually constitute our undoing.

17. Mutwa here seems to be speaking of international arms sales and the kind of high level intrigues that not only strain the ethical sensibilities of all who inquire into them, but place highly dangerous weapons in the hands of precisely those people least well equipped psychologically to deal with them.

18. At the International Transpersonal Conference in Kyoto, many of the presenters and participants visited the sobering shrine at Hiroshima, among them, Elisabeth Kübler-Ross, Stanislav and Christina Grof, Credo Mutwa, the author and his wife, Robin. Mutwa was so moved he laid some of his ceremonial paraphernalia on the shrine, and left it there.

19. Anthony Burgess, *Clockwork Orange*, New York, Norton, 1987.

20. Trinities are very common in mythology. Besides the one's mentioned, there is the Christian Trinity, and the Soma Skanda (Shiva, Parvati, and Ganesha) in Hindu-related cultures.

21. The "World-Ash," *Yggdrasil,* has an equivalent role in the old Norse religion where the tree is seen as the central, unifying symbol of creation. In the dreams of modern people, this archaic imagery still shows up. See C.G. Jung, *Archetypes and the Collective Unconscious,* p. 317, and 370. (New York: Bollingen Foundation, Pantheon Books, 1959)

Index